OUT & ABOUT 47

Walking Tours 47
Excursions 51
Organised Tours 54

SHOPPING 56

Shopping Areas 56
Department Stores 57
Markets 58
Arts & Antiques 61
Clothing & Jewellery 62
Food & Drink 64
Music 65
Books 66
Specialist Shops 68
Shopping for Children 68

PLACES TO EAT 69

Bloomsbury 70
Brixton 70
Camden 71
Chelsea & South Kensington 71
The City 72
Clerkenwell 73
Covent Garden & The Strand 74
East End 74
Greenwich 75
Hammersmith & Fulham 75
Hampstead 75
Islington 76
Knightsbridge & Kensington 76
Mayfair 76
Notting Hill & Bayswater 77
South of the Thames 78
Stoke Newington 79
Trafalgar Square 79
The West End 80
Westminster & Pimlico 82
Internet Cafes 82
High Tea 83

ENTERTAINMENT 84

What's On 85
Theatre 86
Classical Music & Opera 87
Ballet & Dance 88
Comedy 88

Rock & Pop 89
Jazz 90
Folk, Traditional &
    World Music 90
Cinemas 91
Dance Clubs 92
Pubs & Bars 94
Open All Hours 97
Gay & Lesbian London 98
Spectator Sports 100

PLACES TO STAY 102

Deluxe 103
Top End 104
Mid-Range 105
Budget 105
Specialist Hotels 106

FACTS FOR THE VISITOR 107

Pre-Departure 108
Arrival & Departure 109
Getting Around 112
Practical Information 115

INDEX 124

SIGHTS INDEX 128

MAP INDEX

Walking Maps
Westminster Wander 47
Docklands Dawdle 48
Fleet Street Footslog 49
East End Amble 50

Front Cover Gatefold
Map 1 – Excursions
Map 2 – Greater London
Map 3 – Greenwich
Map 4 – Camden & Hampstead
Map 5 – Inner London

Back Cover Gatefold
Map 6 – Central London
Map 7 – West End
London Underground

how to use this book

KEY TO SYMBOLS

- ⊠ address
- ☎ telephone number
- ❷ email/web site address
- ⊖ nearest tube station
- 🚇 nearest train station
- 🚌 nearest bus route
- ⛴ nearest ferry wharf
- ⓘ tourist information
- ◷ opening hours
- Ⓢ cost, entry charge
- ♿ wheelchair access
- ⚲ child-friendly
- ✗ on-site or nearby eatery
- **V** vegetarian, or with a good vegetarian selection

COLOUR-CODING

Each chapter has a different colour code which is reflected on the maps for quick reference.

MAPS & GRID REFERENCES

The fold-out maps on the front and back covers are numbered from 1 to 7. All sights and venues in the text have map references which indicate where to find them, eg (6, H4) means Map 6, grid reference H4. When a map reference appears immediately after a name, the sight is labelled on the map; when it appears after an address (eg with most restaurants, hotels etc), only the street is marked.

PRICES

The abbreviations listed next to multiple prices (eg £10/8/7.5/6/30 a/s/st/c/f) indicate adult (a), senior (s), student (st), child (c) and family (f) charges or admission prices. Most family tickets cover 2 adults and 2 children.

WARNING & REQUEST

Things change – prices go up, schedules change, good places go bad and bad places improve or go bankrupt. So, if you find things better or worse, recently opened or long since closed, please tell us and help make the next edition even more accurate and useful. Everyone who writes to us will find their name and possibly excerpts from their correspondence in one of our publications (let us know if you *don't* want your letter published or your name acknowledged). They will also receive the latest issue of *Planet Talk*, our quarterly printed newsletter, or *Comet*, our monthly email newsletter. Subscriptions to both newsletters are free. The very best contributions will be rewarded with a free guidebook.

Send all correspondence to the Lonely Planet office closest to you (see page 123).

Lonely Planet books provide independent advice. Lonely Planet does not accept advertising in guidebooks, nor payment in exchange for listing or endorsing any place or business. Lonely Planet writers do not accept discounts or payments in exchange for positive coverage of any sort.

LONDON

|CONDENSED|

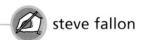 steve fallon

LONELY PLANET PUBLICATIONS
Melbourne • Oakland • London • Paris

contents

Lonely Planet Condensed – London
1st edition – April 2000

Published by
Lonely Planet Publications Pty Ltd
A.C.N. 005 607 983
192 Burwood Rd, Hawthorn,
Victoria 3122, Australia

Lonely Planet Offices
Australia PO Box 617, Hawthorn, VIC 3122
USA 150 Linden St, Oakland, CA 94607
UK 10a Spring Place, London NW5 3BH
France 1 rue du Dahomey, 75011 Paris

Photographs
All of the images in this guide are available
for licensing from Lonely Planet Images.
email: lpi@lonelyplanet.com.au

Front cover photographs
Top: Thames view from London Bridge
   (Juliet Coombe)
Bottom: New tube trains, London Road depot
   (Charlotte Hindle)

ISBN 1 86450 043 3

Text & maps © Lonely Planet 2000
Photos © photographers as indicated 2000

Printed by The Bookmaker International Ltd
Printed in China

FACTS ABOUT LONDON — 5

History — 6
Orientation — 8
Environment — 8
Government & Politics — 9
Economy — 9
Society & Culture — 10
Arts — 11

HIGHLIGHTS — 12

British Museum — 14
Buckingham Palace — 15
Courtauld Gallery — 16
Hampton Court Palace — 17
Houses of Parliament — 18
Imperial War Museum — 19
Kensington Palace — 20
Kew Gardens — 21
Madame Tussaud's — 22
Millennium Dome — 23
Museum of London — 24
National Gallery — 25
Natural History Museum — 26
St Paul's Cathedral — 27
Science Museum — 28
Shakespeare's Globe — 29
Tate Britain — 30
Tower of London — 31
Victoria & Albert Museum — 32
Westminster Abbey — 33

SIGHTS & ACTIVITIES — 34

Museums — 34
Galleries — 36
Notable Buildings — 37
Famous Abodes — 38
Churches & Cathedrals — 39
Parks & Gardens — 40
London for Children — 42
Off the Beaten Track — 44
Quirky London — 45
Keeping Fit — 46

facts about london

What is to be said about London that has not been said so many times before? That the weighty resonance of its very name suggests history and might (and it rhymes with 'ton')? That it is the premier city in Europe in terms of size, population and per-capita wealth (as in 'No 1')? That its opportunities for entertainment by day and by night go on, and on, and on (which means 'fun')?

London is all these things and much, much more. Not only is it home to such familiar landmarks as Big Ben, the Eros statue, Tower Bridge and now the Millennium Dome, it also boasts some of the greatest museums and art galleries anywhere, and more lush parkland than any other world capital.

Along with all that London is the link that unites those who were rocked in the soft cradle of the English language or slept on its comfortable cushions for the first time at a later age. This is both the tongue's birthplace and its epicentre; for many people a visit to London is like a homecoming.

Whether or not London is the 'coolest city in the world' is a moot point; a lot of places do close awfully early (eg most pubs shut at 11pm). But once you've found one of the many clubs with extended licenses, you'll party like you've never partied before. Clubbing is not just a form of entertainment here but a career at which Londoners work very, very hard.

London is an amazingly tolerant place for its size, its people pretty much unshockable. Many first-time visitors are surprised to find how multicultural the British capital is and how individuals and communities from all over the world seem to get along fairly well together.

But this is London – cool, hot or plain lukewarm – and it belongs to its denizens as much as it belongs to you or to me. Having survived the long-anticipated turn into the 3rd millennium, this world-class city belongs to all of us.

Many a bear left with a sore head; the busby-topped Coldstream guards on parade.

HISTORY

London has been continuously inhabited at least since Roman times. As a result, archaeologists have had to wait for redevelopment to make sites available for excavation. The building boom of the 1980s revealed an astonishing number of finds, especially in the City of London. For an easy and highly entertaining run through London's history, visit the Museum of London at the Barbican (p. 24).

Digging for Clues

Early in 1999, Museum of London archaeologists digging near today's Spitalfields Market in east London unearthed a priceless stone and lead coffin. Therein lay the remains of a bejewelled 4th century Roman woman and her personal effects. The tales she will tell us about London's earliest history will be epic.

The Celts & Romans

Although the Celts settled round a ford on the south bank of the river Thames, it was the Romans who first developed the area north of the river, calling it Londinium. They built a bridge and an impressive city wall, and made the city an important port and the hub of their road system.

The Saxons & Danes

The Romans deserted Londinium in about 410AD, and Saxon settlers established farmsteads and small villages in the area. Few clues of Dark Ages London can now be found, but the town survived the 200-year onslaught by the Danes (or Vikings). Less than a decade before the Normans arrived from northern France, Edward the Confessor moved his court to a new palace at Westminster and built an abbey nearby.

The Normans

After his success at the Battle of Hastings in 1066, William the Conqueror found himself in control of a city that was by far the largest, richest and most powerful in the kingdom. The Norman ruler distrusted the 'vast and fierce populace' of London and raised the White Tower, the core of the Tower of London, but he did confirm the city's independence and right to self-government.

Monument to the Great Fire of London

Juliet Coombe

Tudor London

During the reign of Elizabeth I, who succeeded her father Henry VIII in 1558, London began to expand rapidly; in the half-century up to 1600 the population doubled to 200,000. Sadly, medieval, Tudor and Jacobean London was destroyed in a stroke by the Great Fire of 1666. The disaster gave Christopher Wren the opportunity to build his famous churches but did nothing to halt or rein in the city's growth.

Poxy London

In mid-17th century London, the shout 'garde loo' would go up to alert passers-by that a chamber pot was about to be emptied into the street from an upper storey window. Crowded, filthy London suffered from recurrent outbreaks of bubonic plague from the 14th century, but nothing matched the Great Plague of 1665 in which 86,500 people died.

Georgian Period

By 1700 there were approximately 600,000 Londoners and, as the seat of Parliament and focal point for a growing empire, London was becoming ever richer and more important. Georgian architects such as John Nash, the planner of Trafalgar Square, replaced the last of medieval London with imposing symmetrical architecture and residential squares.

Victorian Age

The population exploded in the 19th century, creating a vast expanse of Victorian suburbs to the south and east. Spurred by the Industrial Revolution and the empire's rapidly expanding trade and commerce, the population of London jumped from just under a million in 1801 (the year of the first national census) to 6.5 million a century later.

WWII & Postwar

Much of east London was obliterated by the Blitz, and by the time the war ended in 1945, some 32,000 Londoners had died. After the war, ugly housing and low-cost developments were thrown up on the bomb sites. The docks, once an important mainstay of London's economy, never recovered – shipping moved east to Tilbury, and the Docklands declined to the point of dereliction, until it was redeveloped in the 1980s.

London Today

Riding on a wave of Thatcherite confidence and deregulation, London boomed in the 1980s. The Conservatives were elected for a fourth successive term in 1992, but the economy soon went into a tailspin. The general election of May 1997 returned a Labour government to power for the first time in nearly 19 years, and the capital's booming economy and low unemployment, a feeble and divided opposition and the charismatic leadership of the youthful Prime Minister, Tony Blair, has kept it high in the popularity polls. At the start of the 3rd millennium London is headier and more confident than it has been since the 'swinging 60s'.

ORIENTATION

Greater London is 1580 sq km of south-east England enclosed by the M25 ring road. The Thames is the city's main geographical feature. Running from west to east, it flows in wide bends and creates peninsulas in its wake which can make it unclear what side of the river you're on.

London is technically two traditional 'cities': Westminster and the City of London. 'One square mile' (about 2.7 sq km) of the City of London at the heart of the conurbation is known simply as 'the City'. The East End is traditionally working class and the London of Dickens and Hollywood; to the west lies Covent Garden and the nightlife centre of Soho. In general, areas to the west and north tend to be posher and more affluent than those to the east and south.

North-South Divide

Although the Thames isn't the physical barrier that it was in the Middle Ages, psychologically the gulf is as wide as ever. Most people north (ie most Londoners) don't believe there's anything to see and do down south, and a standard question in Londoner-to-Londoner chat is 'When did you last cross the river?'

ENVIRONMENT

London's horrendous traffic moves at an average 20km/h – about what it did in horse and coach days – and is largely responsible for the city's most serious environmental problem: poor air quality. So bad is the air that many cyclists wear masks to protect themselves from breathing in toxic fumes. Areas of London with the highest levels of nitrogen dioxide pollution include Hyde Park, Mayfair, Knightsbridge and Kensington.

Smog, a word coined by the Victorians to describe the poisonous combination of 'smoke' from coal-fuelled furnaces and London's once ubiquitous 'fog', may be a thing of the past, but anyone with respiratory problems should heed air quality forecasts attached to weather bulletins.

Once considered 'dead' water, the murky and tidal Thames is on the improve.

GOVERNMENT & POLITICS

At the time of writing, London was the only capital city in the world without a self-governing authority and mayor, but in May 2000 Londoners were scheduled to reinstall a city-wide council. Based at the futuristic London Assembly Hall, the new mayor would preside over an assembly of 25 to 30 members governing transport, economic development, strategic planning, the police, fire brigades, civil defence, the environment, and cultural matters.

The City of London is governed from the Guildhall by the Corporation of London, headed by the Lord Mayor and an assortment of oddly named (and even more oddly dressed) aldermen, beadles and sheriffs. These men – and they usually are male – are elected by the freemen and liverymen of the City of London. Greater London is divided into 33 boroughs (13 of them in central London), each run by a local council with significant authority and responsibilities in matters from education to garbage collecting.

London by Numbers

Central London pop.	7 million
Greater London pop.	12 million
Central London GDP/head	£22,214
London's share of UK GDP	15%
Average house price	£132,700
Annual o/s visitors	13.5 million
Av. visitor expenditure/day	£75
Inflation	1.3%
Unemployment	7.8%

ECONOMY

Europe's richest city (central London's GDP per head is twice that of Paris) continues to be the driving force behind the British economy, but you'll see few signs of heavy industry here. It is one of the world's major financial centres, with a flourishing service sector employing 50% of the workforce; tourism is one of the three most successful industries. Economic indicators continue to be upbeat with unemployment and inflation levels low and falling and the city in the midst of a property boom.

Neil Setchfield

Lloyd's of London (1986), Richard Rogers' 'inside-out' architectural masterpiece

SOCIETY & CULTURE

The most common preconceptions about Londoners – reserved, inhibited and stiflingly polite people – are pretty accurate, with passengers travelling in eye-averted silence on the tube and trains. But as London is among the planet's most crowded places, such behaviour is partly a protective veneer, essential for coping with the constant crush of people.

Londoners rise to the fore in a crisis; fall down or have your wallet pinched and the crowds will descend, offering advice, solace and calling the police or an ambulance. In general Londoners are a tolerant bunch, unfazed by outrageous dress or behaviour. Indeed, they seem to take pride in ignoring anyone who appears to be trying to draw attention to themselves.

Ethnic London

London has long attracted (if not always welcomed) immigrants. Today, just under 25% of all Londoners are from 33 sizeable (ie more than 10,000) ethnic communities. These range from the largest groups like the Irish (214,000 Irish-born now resident in London) and Indians (151,000) to smaller ones like those from Mauritius (13,900), Canada (11,600) and Trinidad and Tobago (just over 10,000). Over 300 languages are regularly spoken in the capital.

On the whole, this means relatively low levels of chauvinism, racism, sexism or any other 'ism' you can think of. The Gay Mardi Gras is a vast celebration of homosexual culture that passes off without incident, and London has successfully absorbed wave after wave of immigrants and refugees.

Dos & Don'ts

It's not especially easy to cause offence in London – unless you're trying to. But try starting a general conversation at a bus stop or on a tube platform and you'll find people reacting as if you were mad. Most Londoners would no more speak to a stranger in the street than fly to the moon. However, if you're obviously a tourist in need of directions, there's no problem.

The Banqueting House at Whitehall in the heartland of Her Majesty's Civil Service

Queuing The British have always been notoriously addicted to queuing, and the order of the queue at banks, post offices, newsagents etc is sacrosanct – few things are more calculated to spark an outburst of tongue-clucking than an attempt to 'push in' to a queue.

The Underground The tube has its own etiquette. Where there's an escalator you *must* stand on the right so that people can rush up or down on the left. On platforms move away from the entrance to prevent crowds blocking doorways which could cause someone to fall on to the rails. When a train pulls in, stand aside until everybody inside has left the carriage.

Dress London is very free and easy about what you wear, but it pays to be respectful in places of religion. Hats are best left off in churches, and expect to cover up and remove footwear for mosque or temple visits. A few posh restaurants and many clubs operate strict dress codes. That usually means a jacket and tie for men and no jeans or trainers for anyone; in clubs it means whatever the management and their bouncers choose it to mean on the night.

ARTS

Although London is home to many astounding art collections, British painters have never dominated any particular epoch or style in the way that other European nations have. This is not to discount the works of artists of the calibre of Francis Bacon, Lucien Freud, Richard Hamilton, Henry Moore and more recently Damien Hirst and Helen Chadwick. Rivalled only by New York, London's gallery scene is as vibrant as ever (p. 36).

While the visual arts – and film for that matter– may not be its most enduring gift to the arts, there's no denying the contribution that London and Londoners have made to the written word. English literature is peppered with writers for whom London provided inspiration: Chaucer, Shakespeare, Dickens, Conan Doyle, HG Wells, Iris Murdoch, Doris Lessing, Hanif Kureishi and Will Self to name but a few (see p. 67).

Music of all forms, from highbrow to commercial pop, has had its genesis in London and it has been host to more popular music waves than any other city: from the swinging 60s of the Beatles, Rolling Stones and Kinks to the 90s quintessentially English indie pop bands and the Spice Girls, via 70s glam and prog rock, punk, ska and 80s popsters. Whatever your taste, it's hard not to be spoiled for musical choice (see p. 84).

A long tradition in musical theatre and healthy support – in recent times via National Lottery proceeds – of ballet, opera and classical music continues to provide a fertile, if not always creative, environment. With or without music, London's theatre life is lively and remains top billing for visitors. While plays and performances don't always have the wit of Coward or Wilde, the depth of Pinter or the sheer spectacle of the best of Lloyd-Webber, the West End is full of options and tickets are never impossible to come by (p. 86).

highlights

Even more than most capital cities, London abounds with things to see. Fortunately most of the major sights are clustered together in the centre, either in the City of London, the West End, Bloomsbury or Westminster. You can easily walk between them, bearing in mind the need to conserve enough energy to cope with 'museum fatigue'.

The museums, galleries, palaces, churches, gardens and other attractions listed here are London's top 20 sights; you can't really say you've been to the British capital without having visited – or at least seen – a good portion of them. That's not to say there aren't scores more sights and attractions that are just as interesting, popular or important to see (p. 34-46).

Some sights (eg the Tower of London, British Museum, Madame Tussaud's) can get hopelessly crowded, particularly in summer. Avoid the long queues, by going early in the morning or late in the afternoon and by buying tickets in advance from a tourist information centre or ticket agency.

For keen sightseers the GoSee Card (☎ 7923 0807; www.london-gosee .com) offers admission to 16 museums and galleries including the Imperial War, London, Natural History, Science and Victoria & Albert museums for 3/7 days (£16/26 adults, £32/50 families). Ask at participating venues and tourist and London Regional Transport information centres.

Stopping Over?

Depending on how much time you have in London, there will be some hard choices to make about what to see and do. The following is a suggested itinerary for a first-time visitor with 3 days to spend in this fair city:

One Day Visit Westminster Abbey and view the Houses of Parliament and Big Ben. Walk up Whitehall, passing Downing St, the Cenotaph and Horse Guards Parade. Cross Trafalgar Square to visit the National Gallery. Walk to Piccadilly Circus to see the statue of Eros.

Two Days Visit some of the British Museum and walk west along Oxford St and up Baker St to Madame Tussaud's.

Three Days Visit the one of South Kensington's museums (the Natural History, Science or Victoria & Albert). Kensington Palace is a short distance to the north-west. Alternatively, go up Brompton Rd to Hyde Park Corner and walk along Constitution Hill to view Buckingham Palace.

Simon Bracken

Save on shoe leather – there's plenty of buses, taxis and the tube to get you around.

Opening Times

Museums and other attractions generally observe the Christmas Day and Boxing Day holidays, but stay open for the UK's other 6 public (or bank) holidays. Exceptions are those that normally close on Sunday; they're quite likely to close on bank holidays too. Some smaller museums close on Monday and/or Tuesday, and some venues, including the British Museum, close on Sunday morning.

All hours listed in this chapter are literally the opening and closing times. Last entry to most venues is usually a half-hour or even an hour before closing time.

Free Admission

Some of London's finest museums and galleries – including the British Museum, the National Gallery and the Tate Britain – as well as plenty of the smaller ones, remain free. Others, such as, the Victoria & Albert, Natural History, Science and Imperial War museums as well as the Museum of London offer free admission after 4.30pm. All national museums in the UK were made free for children under 17 in April 1999. It will be seniors' turn in 2000 and the following year they will be made free for everyone.

London Lowlights

Some of the things we could do without (or at least with less of):

- 11pm pub closings
- the Circle line on the Underground
- Buckingham Palace
- Leicester Square
- sealed letter boxes & no rubbish bins in the City
- London Dungeon
- bad signposting on many streets
- poor value in many restaurants
- Heathrow airport

Elliot Daniel

Restored St Pancras station – the pinnacle of Victorian Gothic Revival architecture

BRITISH MUSEUM (6, C6)

This is the UK's largest museum, one of the oldest in the world and the most visited tourist attraction in London (with over 6 million visitors a year). Like so many other sights in London, the museum has been undergoing major renovations. Most importantly, its inner courtyard, hidden from the public for almost 150 years, has been turned into the covered **Great Court**. As a result, some collections may have been moved or closed temporarily.

INFORMATION

- ✉ Great Russell St WC1
- ☎ 7636 1555, 7580 1788 (recording)
- ⊖ Tottenham Court Road or Russell Square
- 🕒 Mon 9.30am-8pm, Tues-Thurs 10am-8pm, Fri-Sun 9.30am-5pm
- $ free (£2 donation requested)
- ⓘ free intro tours Mon-Sat 11am-3pm, Sun 1.30-4.30pm; key collection tours (£3-7)
- [e] www.british-museum.ac.uk
- ♿ good; ☎ 7637 7384; free booklet available
- 🍴 Museum Café

Simon Bracken

The collections inside originated with the curiosities collected by the physician Hans Sloane (of Sloane Square fame), sold to the nation in 1753 and augmented not long afterward with manuscripts and books from the Harleian and Cottonian collections.

The museum is vast, diverse and amazing – so much so that it can seem pretty daunting. To make the most of the museum don't plan on seeing too much in a day; remember, admission is still free so you can come back several times.

The back entrance off Montague Street tends to be less congested than the imposing porticoed main one off Great Russell St. Whether you take a tour or pick up a museum map and go the self-guided route, the most obvious strategy is to home straight in on the highlights, but bear in mind that most people will do the same thing.

Simon Bracken

Join the crowds to view the spoils of empire at the fabulous British Museum.

DON'T MISS

• Benin Bronzes • Elgin Marbles • Egyptian mummies • Rosetta Stone • Oxus, Sutton Hoo & Mildenhall treasures • Lindow Man • Portland vase

BUCKINGHAM PALACE (6, H4)

Buckingham Palace, built in 1803 for the Duke of Buckingham, has been the royal family's London home since 1837 when St James's Palace was judged too old-fashioned and insufficiently impressive. Only 18 out of 661 rooms are open to visitors for a brief period, but don't expect to see the Queen's bedroom. She and the Duke of Edinburgh share a strictly off-limits suite of 12 rooms overlooking Green Park.

The tour of the state apartments begins in the **Guard Room** and includes a peek at the **State Dining Room** (all red damask and Regency furnishings, with a portrait of George III looking rather fetching in fur); **Queen Victoria's Picture Gallery** (a full 76.5m long, with works by Rembrandt, van Dyck, Canaletto, Poussin and Vermeer); the **Blue Drawing Room**, with a gorgeous fluted ceiling by John Nash; and the **White Drawing Room**, where the monarch receives ambassadors accredited to the Court of St James. Visitors get the biggest kick out of seeing the **Throne Room**, with his and her pink chairs with the initials 'ER' and 'P' sitting smugly under what looks like a theatre arch.

The **changing of the guard**, when the old guard comes off duty to be replaced by the new, is one of those quintessential English events. Taking place in the forecourt of Buckingham Palace, tourists have a chance to gape at the guards' bright red uniforms and bearskin hats. If you arrive early, grab a spot by the railings; more likely than not, however, you'll be 10 rows back and hardly see a thing.

INFORMATION

✉ The Mall SW1
☎ 7839 1377, 7799 2331 (recording), 7321 2233 (bookings)
⊖ St James's Park or Victoria
🕐 early Aug-early Oct 9.30am-4.30pm
💲 £10/7.50/5/30 a/s/c/f
ℹ changing of the guard Apr-June 11.30am, July-Mar on alternate odd dates; ☎ 0891 505 452 for exact dates
🌐 www.royal.gov.uk
♿ good
🍴 ICA Café (p. 79)

Queen Victoria Memorial

While you're waiting for the guard to change, take a peek at the Queen Victoria Memorial (1911) in the middle of the roundabout. At almost 25m high, it portrays the seated regina surrounded by a number of allegorical figures representing everything from Charity, Truth and Justice to Progress, Painting and Shipbuilding.

Tourists pop in on Liz and Phil.

COURTAULD GALLERY (6, F8)

Housed in the North Wing (or Strand Block) of Somerset House, the gallery displays some of the Courtauld Institute's marvellous collection of paintings in grand surrounds that are even grander following a £25 million architectural refurbishment. Exhibits include works by Rubens, Velásquez and Botticelli. However, for many visitors the most memorable display is the impressionist and postimpressionist art by van Gogh, Cézanne, Manet, Pissarro, Sisley, Henri Rousseau, Toulouse-Lautrec, Degas, Gauguin, Renoir and Monet shown on the top floor. Rarely have so many celebrated paintings been gathered together in one beautifully lit, undivided room.

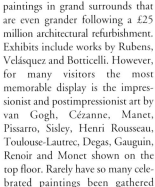

INFORMATION

- ✉ Somerset House, Strand WC2
- ☎ 7848 2526 (Courtauld), 7240 5782 (Gilbert)
- ⊖ Temple
- 🕘 Mon-Sat 10am-6pm, Sun 12-6pm
- $ £4/2/free a/s/c,st; free 10am-2pm Mon; joint Courtauld Gallery/Gilbert Collection ticket £7/5
- ⓘ free talks Tues 1.15pm
- ♿ excellent; ☎ 7873 2531
- 🍴 Gallery Café

Charlotte Hindle

The gallery also has a small exhibition of paintings by the 20th century Bloomsbury artists Duncan Grant, Vanessa Bell and Roger Fry, together with colourful furniture produced by the Omega Workshops (also in Bloomsbury) and influenced by newly discovered African masks and other ethnographical items. A collection of 18th century Huguenot-made silverware is shown in a small room ringed with cartoons by Thomas Rowlandson (1756-1827).

Charlotte Hindle

The stunning façade of Somerset House

Bequeathed to the nation by London-born American businessman Arthur Gilbert, the incredibly rich **Gilbert Collection** contains European silver, gold snuff boxes and Italian mosaics etc. It's housed in the vaults beneath the South Terrace of Somerset House, which boasts one of the finest views of the Thames. Opening hours and fees are the same as those for the Courtauld Gallery.

DON'T MISS

• Manet's *Bar at the Folies Bergères* and *Le Déjeuner sur l'Herbe* • van Gogh's *Self-Portrait with Bandaged Ear* • Rubens' *The Conversion of St Paul* • Cézanne's *Man with a Pipe* • Modigliani's *Female Nude*

HAMPTON COURT PALACE (2, D2)

In 1515 the self-important Cardinal Thomas Wolsey decided to build himself a grand palace, but was later forced to hand it over to Henry VIII. Henry set to work expanding it, adding the Great Hall, the Chapel and the sprawling kitchens. By 1540 this was one of the grandest palaces in Europe. In the late 17th century, William and Mary employed Christopher Wren to build extensions. The result is a beautiful blend of Tudor and 'restrained' baroque architecture.

The interior boasts numerous attractions. Stairs inside Anne Boleyn's Gateway lead up to **Henry VIII's State Apartments** and the **Great Hall**. Off the Great Watching Chamber is the **Haunted Gallery**. Henry's 5th wife Catherine Howard, arrested for adultery in 1542, managed to evade her guards and ran screaming down the corridor in search of the king. Her wretched ghost is said to make the same futile attempt all these centuries later.

The **Tudor Kitchens** have been fitted out to look as they might have done in Tudor days, and the King's Apartments, built for William III towards the end of the 17th century, have been extensively restored.

There are also wonderful gardens, including the award-winning **Privy Gardens**, and the famous half mile-long hornbeam and yew **maze**, planted in 1690. The average visitor takes about 20 minutes to reach its centre.

Rachel Black

INFORMATION

✉ East Molesey, Surrey
☎ 8781 9500
🚆 Hampton Court from Waterloo; 30mns
⛴ Westminster Pier to Hampton Court Pier (3½ hrs) 3 times daily Apr-Oct; ☎ 7930 4721
🕐 Mon 10.15am-6pm, Tues-Sun 9.30am-6pm (mid-Mar-Oct); Mon 10.15am-4.30pm, Tues-Sun 9.30am-4.30pm (Nov-mid-Mar)
$ £10/7.60/6.60/29.90 a/s,st/c/f; Privy Gardens £2.10/1.30 a/c,s,st; maze £2.30/1.50
[i] various free guided tours; garden carriage rides 10am-5.30pm (£14 up to 6 people)
♿ good
🍴 Garden Café, Tiltyard restaurant

Adam McCrow

Glorious riverside Hampton Court Palace

DON'T MISS
• Mantegna Gallery • Clock Court • Queen's State Bedroom
• Fountain Court • Royal Tennis Court • Chapel Royal • Great Wine Cellar

HOUSES OF PARLIAMENT (6, J7)

The Houses of Parliament (ie the House of Commons and the House of Lords) are in what is known as the Palace of Westminster, built by Charles Barry and Augustus Pugin in 1840 when the neogothic style was all the rage. The most famous feature *outside* the palace is the Clock Tower, commonly known as **Big Ben** (the real Ben, a bell named after Benjamin Hall, the Commissioner of Works when the tower was completed in 1858, hangs inside). At the opposite end of the building is Victoria Tower (1860).

Richard I'Anson

London's most famous vista by night

The **House of Commons** is where Parliament meets to propose and discuss new legislation, apart from a 3 month summer recess and Easter and New Year breaks. Expect long queues to visit the Strangers' Gallery where one can see the House at work.

Left of the security area is the stunning hammer beam roof of **Westminster Hall.** Originally built in 1097-99, it is the oldest surviving part of the Palace of Westminster, the seat of English monarchy from the 11th to the early 16th centuries. Added between 1394 and 1401, the roof has been described as 'the greatest surviving achievement of medieval English carpentry'. Westminster Hall served in part as a courthouse until the 19th century and the trials of William Wallace (1305), Sir Thomas More (1535), Guy Fawkes (1606) and Charles I (1649) all took place here. More recently it was used for the lying-in-state of Sir Winston Churchill in 1965.

INFORMATION

- ✉ Parliament Square SW1
- ☎ 7219 3000
- ⊖ Westminster
- 🕐 opening hours vary depending on whether Parliament is sitting; for visit times and permit information ☎ 7219 4272, 7219 5532
- $ free
- ℹ tours for up to 16 people ☎ 7219 2105; handbags and cameras must be left at cloakroom
- [e] www.parliament.uk
- ♿ good
- 🍴 Westminster Arms (p. 47)

Richard I'Anson

House of Commons

Based on St Stephen's Chapel in the original Palace of Westminster, the current chamber, designed by Giles Gilbert Scott, replaced an earlier version destroyed in 1941. Although the Commons is a national assembly of 650 MPs, the chamber only seats 437. Government members sit to the right of the Speaker; the Opposition to the left.

IMPERIAL WAR MUSEUM (6, K9)

The Imperial War Museum is housed in a striking building dating back to 1815 which was crowned with a magnificent copper dome in 1845. Originally this was the site of the Bethlehem Royal Hospital, commonly known as Bedlam, an infirmary for the insane.

Although there's still plenty of military hardware on show and the core of the museum is a chronological exhibition on the 2 world wars, these days the Imperial War Museum places more emphasis on the social cost of war: the Blitz, the food shortages and the propaganda. Especially distressing is a small room where film footage of the discovery of the Bergen Belsen concentration camp is shown. The top floor is devoted to war paintings by the likes of Henry Moore, Paul Nash and John Singer Sargent.

A particularly popular exhibit is the **Trench Experience**, which depicts the grim day-to-day existence of a WWI foot soldier in a frontline trench on the Somme. The **Blitz Experience**, lets visitors sit inside a mock bomb shelter during an air raid and then stroll a set of the ravaged streets of the East End. Another popular one is the **Secret War Gallery**, which takes a look at the work of the secret services, with video footage of the siege of the 1980 Iranian Embassy in Knightsbridge brought to a dramatic end by balaclava-clad SAS commandos. New exhibits are **Conflicts since 1945** – including the campaigns in Korea, Vietnam, the Gulf and the Balkans – as well those covering the Cold War and National Service.

Charlotte Hindle

INFORMATION

✉ Lambeth Rd SE1
☎ 7416 5320, 0891 600140 (recording)
⊖ Lambeth North
🕘 Mon-Sun 10am-6pm
$ £5.20/4.20 a/s,st, free for children and for all after 4.30pm
ⓘ visit early morning or late afternoon to avoid school groups
[e] www.iwm.org.uk
♿ excellent
🍴 The Café

Charlotte Hindle

Above: The Imperial War Museum
Top: A fragment of the Berlin Wall

DON'T MISS
• art galleries • Enigma encrypting machine • V2 Rocket
• Liberation of Bergen Belsen exhibit

KENSINGTON PALACE (5, F3)

Sometime home of Princess Margaret and the residence of the late Princess Diana after her divorce from Prince Charles in 1986, Kensington Palace dates from 1605.

In 1688, William and Mary of Orange bought the house and had it adapted by Wren and Hawksmoor. When George I arrived from Hanover to succeed Queen Anne, he recruited William Kent to modernise the palace. Much of the existing decor is a mix of the small, wood-panelled Stuart State Apartments and Kent's grander, although sometimes clumsy, renovation. A room is preserved as a memorial to Queen Victoria, born here in 1819, and features a painting of her marriage to Prince Albert.

INFORMATION

- ✉ Kensington Gardens W8
- ☎ 7937 9561
- ⊖ High Street Kensington
- 🕘 Mon-Sun 10am-5pm (palace); 5am-half-hour before dusk (gardens)
- $ £8/6.70/6.10/26.10 a/s,st/c/f
- ⓘ 30mn tours of the Stuart and Georgian apartments
- ♿ good
- 🍴 The Orangery café

Simon Bracken

Displayed under low lights are costumes from the **Royal Ceremonial Dress Collection**, including dresses with skirts so ludicrously wide they made it impossible for their wearers to sit down and ensuring that rooms were sparsely furnished, lest tables and chairs be knocked over.

Most striking of all is the **Cupola Room** where the ceremony of initiating men into the exclusive Order of the Garter took place. The order is painted in all its finery on the trompe l'oeil domed ceiling. and the room is ringed with marbled columns and niches in which gilded Roman statues stand.

The **Sunken Garden** near the palace is at its prettiest in summer. Nearby is **The Orangery**, designed by Hawksmoor and Vanbrugh with carvings by Gibbons.

Simon Bracken

A serene haven in central London – beautiful Kensington Palace

DON'T MISS

• van Dyck's *Cupid and Pysche* • Queen Victoria Memorial Room • King's Drawing Room • Round Pond • King's Staircase

KEW GARDENS (2, C2)

One of the most visited sights on the tourist itinerary, Kew can be very crowded during summer. Spring is probably the best time to visit, but at any time of year this expansive array of lawns, formal gardens and botanical greenhouses has delights to offer. As well as being a park, Kew maintains the most exhaustive botanical collection in the world.

Wonderful plants and trees aside, there are several specific sights within the gardens such as the metal and glass **Palm House**, designed by Decimus Burton and Richard Turner between 1844 and 1848, which houses all sorts of exotic tropical greenery. Just north-west of here is the tiny but irresistible **Water Lily House** (open March-December) and the **Princess of Wales Conservatory** housing plants from 10 different computer-controlled climate zones. Beyond that is the **Kew Gardens Gallery**, with exhibitions of paintings and photos on a broadly botanical theme.

Elliot Daniel

INFORMATION

✉ Kew Rd, Kew, Surrey
☎ 8332 5000, 8940 1171 (recording)
⊖ Kew Gardens
⛴ from Westminster Pier (1¾ hrs) up to 8 times a day Mar-Oct; ☎ 7930 4721
🕘 from 9.30am till dusk; hothouses close 5.30pm in summer, earlier in winter
$ £5/3.50/2.50/13 a/s,st/c/f
ℹ free tours 11am & 2pm
[e] www.kew.org
♿ good
🍴 The Orangery restaurant

Set in especially pretty gardens and currently closed for renovations is the early 1600s red-brick **Kew Palace**, once a royal residence and very popular with George III whose wife Charlotte died here in 1818. Among other highlights is the **Marianne North Gallery** featuring the botanical paintings of the indomitable North who rejected the Victorian stay-at-home option in favour of roaming the globe, from 1871 to 1885, documenting its flora.

Elliot Daniel

Flower powerhouse – Kew is an unmatched botanical treasure chest.

MADAME TUSSAUD'S   (6, C1)

Madame Tussaud's is the 3rd most popular sight in London (after the British Museum and National Gallery), with some 2.7 million visitors yearly.

Much of the modern Madame Tussaud's is made up of the **Garden Party** exhibition where you can have your picture taken alongside comedi-

ans like Lenny Henry, actors like Pierce Brosnan and singers like Kylie Minogue. The **Grand Hall** is where you'll find models of world leaders past and present, of the Royal Family (now minus Sarah 'Fergie' Ferguson, the disgraced Duchess of York, and with Diana, the late Princess of Wales, on the sidelines) and of pop stars like the Beatles. And what happens to those whose 15 minutes of fame has ticked by? Their heads are removed as surely as Marie-Antoinette's was and stored in a cupboard – just in case they get another stab at those 15 minutes. In the **Spirit of London time taxi**, you sit in a mock-up of a London black cab and are whipped through a 5 minute summary of London's history.

The revamped **Chamber of Horrors** has models of contemporary prisoners sitting uneasily alongside representations of historic horrors like the mutilated corpse of one of Jack the Ripper's victims. It all seems somewhat tame after the London Dungeon's blood-fest though (p. 45).

Attached to Madame Tussaud's, the **London Planetarium** presents 30 minute spectaculars on the stars and planets livened up with special effects.

Madame Wax

Madame Tussaud's dates back to 1835 when the eponymous Frenchwoman set up her waxworks with 35 figures, many of them those of people guillotined during the French Revolution. The 200 Years exhibition shows Madame T herself working on a death mask from the head of Marie Antoinette in her original studio.

Immortal, immortalised – Alfred Hitchcock

MILLENNIUM DOME   (3, B5)

The all singing, all dancing Millennium Dome, which opened on the 1st day of the new millennium, is the most ambitious building erected in London since St Paul's Cathedral was completed in 1710. The dome's design (not to mention the £750 million price tag, making it the most expensive yet built in the city), was controversial from the outset, but many people believe it is everything modern architecture should and can be: innovative, complementary and startlingly beautiful.

In fact with its enormous cupola of white fibreglass and 12 supporting masts of yellow steel, the Millennium Dome is vaguely reminiscent of the dome and spires of St Paul's. But this dome celebrates things spiritual in only one 'zone'; the rest deals with the temporal world of progress, development and, of course, money.

It's divided into 14 themed (and commercially sponsored) sections – from **Body**, in which visitors explore the world of human biology and medical science, and **Faith** (looking at the spiritual and moral dimensions of the human experience) to the multimedia and digital **Play Zone** and **Living Island**, complete with a mock-up of a British seaside town. There is a also a show, playing up to 3 times daily, based on the theme of creation involving some 200 performers and state-of-the-art visual effects. Performances also take place in the Piazza.

The futuristic **Skyscape** building next to the dome contains two 2500-seat cinemas as well as the largest live performance theatre in the UK. Separate tickets are required for events staged here.

INFORMATION

- ✉ North Greenwich SE10
- ☎ 8305 3456, 0870 606 2000 (booking office)
- ⊖ North Greenwich
- 🚢 Festival Pier (45mns) every 15-30mns; ☎ 7237 5134
- ⏱ Mon-Sun 10am-5.30pm, 6-11pm
- 💲 £20/18/16.50/57 a/s/st,c/f
- ℹ free audioguides; under 16s must be accompanied by an adult
- 🖥 www.dome2000.co.uk
- ♿ excellent
- ✕ some 20 eateries at the dome site and plenty in Greenwich (p.73)

Elliot Daniel

Well, I'll be Domed

- it is the largest dome in the world
- could contain 18,000 double-decker buses, 2 Wembley Stadiums, 13 Albert Halls or the Eiffel Tower lying on its side
- would cover the whole of Trafalgar Square and all the surrounding buildings
- if turned upside down like a bowl, it could hold 3.8 billion pints of beer or if stuck under Niagara Falls it would take 10 minutes to fill

Elliot Daniel

Birthday cake for the 3rd millennium

MUSEUM OF LONDON　　　　　(6, D11)

Despite its unprepossessing setting amid the concrete walkways of the Barbican (look for gate 7), the Museum of London is one of the city's finest museums, showing how the city has evolved from the Ice Age to the Internet. It is also the world's largest urban history museum, with more than 1 million objects on display and in its archives.

INFORMATION

- ✉ London Wall EC2
- ☎ 7600 3699, 7600 0807 (recording)
- ⊖ Barbican
- ⊘ Mon-Sat 10am-5.50pm, Sun 12-5.50pm
- $ £5/3/12 a/s,st/f; free for children and for all after 4.30pm; tickets can be used over 1yr period
- ✺ www.museumoflondon.org.uk
- ♿ excellent
- ✗ Museum Café

Simon Bracken

The museum is divided into 2 sections: the **Department of Early London History** (prehistoric period to 1700), including the Archaeological Archive housing material from archaeological excavations in London; and the **Department of Later London History**, with material relating to London from the start of the 18th century to the present day.

The sections on Roman Britain and Roman Londinium make use of the nearby ruins of a Roman fort discovered during road construction. Otherwise, the displays work steadily through the centuries, using audiovisuals to show such events as the Great Fire of London.

Featured are items like one of the two shirts Charles I wore on the morning of his execution in 1649 – 'lest *my* shivering be taken as a sign of fear'. But the focus is on the experience of ordinary people as much as on royalty, buildings and streets; Dickens' London – a city of mass prostitution, sweatshop labour, hunger and poverty – make particularly poignant stories. The **London Now Gallery** brings the story up to date.

DON'T MISS
- Mithraic finds • Great Fire Experience • 18th century Spitalfields silk dress • reconstructed Newgate Prison cells • Victorian shopfronts

Simon Bracken

The Museum of London's collection illustrates the city's long, fascinating history.

NATIONAL GALLERY (6, F6)

The porticoed facade of the National Gallery extends along the north side of the square. Founded in 1824 and counting some 2100 western paintings on display at any one time, it's one of the world's largest – and richest – art galleries. The lovely **Sainsbury Wing** on the west side was only added after considerable controversy; Prince Charles, not known for his cutting-edge sense of architectural design, dismissed one proposal as 'a carbuncle on the face of a much loved friend'. Outside the gallery – rather incongruously in this, the heart of London – is a **statue of George Washington**, the man who 'robbed' England of its colonies in the New World. The statue was donated by the Commonwealth of Virginia in 1921.

Charlotte Hindle

INFORMATION

✉ Trafalgar Square WC2
☎ 7839 3321, 7747 2885 (recording)
⊖ Charing Cross
🕘 10am-6pm (till 9pm Wed)
$ free (charge for special exhibitions)
ℹ free audioguides; 2 to 3 free 1hr guided highlights tours daily
[e] www.nationalgallery.org.uk
♿ good
🍴 Pret a Manger, Brasserie restaurant

The paintings in the National Gallery are hung in a continuous time line; by starting in the Sainsbury Wing and progressing west you can take in a collection of pictures painted between the mid-13th century and late 19th/early 20th centuries in chronological order. If you're keen on the real oldies (1260-1510), head for the Sainsbury Wing; for the Renaissance (1510-1600), go to the West Wing. The Rubens, Rembrandts and Murillos are in the North Wing (1600-1700); if you're after Gainsborough, Constable, Turner, Hogarth and the impressionists visit the East Wing (1700-1900). For paintings dating beyond that time, you'll have to visit the **Tate Britain** at Millbank (p. 30).

A visit to the National Gallery is a must.

DON'T MISS

- van Eyck's *Arnolfini Wedding* • Velásquez's *Rokeby Venus*
- Botticelli's *Venus & Mars* • da Vinci's *Virgin of the Rocks*
- van Dyck's *Charles I* • van Gogh's *Sunflowers*

NATURAL HISTORY MUSEUM (5, G3)

The Natural History Museum now incorporates the old Geological Museum; the 2 collections are divided between the adjoining Life and Earth Galleries. Where once there were dusty glass cases of butterflies and stick insects, you'll now find wonderful interactive displays on themes like Human Biology and Creepy Crawlies, alongside the crowd-attracting exhibition on mammals and dinosaurs, some of them animatronic creations like the new 4m-tall **Tyrannosaurus rex**.

The **Life Galleries** tend to be overrun with schoolchildren, who flock to see the dinosaurs. Luckily that leaves more space, at the **Blue Whale exhibit** and in the replica rainforest in the **Ecology Gallery**. But in some ways it's the **Earth Galleries** that are most staggering with an escalator that slithers up and into a hollowed-out globe. Around its base fine samples of different rocks and gems are beautifully displayed.

Upstairs there are 2 main exhibits: **Earthquake** and the **Restless Surface**, which explains how wind, water, ice, gravity and life itself impact on the earth. Earthquake is an extraordinary moving and shaking mock-up of what happened to a small grocery shop during the 1995 Kobe trembler in Japan that killed 6000 people. Excellent exhibitions on lower floors include **Earth Today & Tomorrow**, which focuses on ecology and **From the Beginning**, which explores how planets are formed.

Nature's wonders explained

The museum is housed in one of London's finest Gothic Revival buildings. Designed by Alfred Waterhouse between 1873 and 1880 it has a grand cathedral-like main entrance, a gleaming blue and sand-coloured brick and terracotta frontage, thin columns and articulated arches, and carvings of plants and animals crawling all over it.

DON'T MISS
- Creepy Crawlies display
- Diplodocus skeleton
- Wildlife Garden

ST PAUL'S CATHEDRAL (6, E11)

St Paul's Cathedral was built by Wren between 1675 and 1710 after the Great Fire of London destroyed the medieval cathedral standing on the site. A niche in the Crypt exhibits Wren's plans and his 'great' model.

Despite being surrounded by some less-than-pleasant architecture in Paternoster Square (now being demolished and rebuilt), the dome still dominates the City and is only exceeded in size by St Peter's in Rome.

Above the dome are the Whispering, Stone and Golden galleries; all reached by a 627-step staircase. It's worth climbing at least as far as the **Stone Gallery** (370 steps) for a fantastic view of London.

In the cathedral itself are ornately carved **choir stalls** by Grinling Gibbons and **iron gates** by Jean Tijou. Walk around the altar, with its massive gilded oak canopy, to the **American Chapel**, a memorial to the 28,000 Britain-based Americans who lost their lives during WWII.

In the south transept lies the **Crypt,** the **Treasury** and **OBE Chapel**. The Crypt has memorials to military greats including Wellington, Kitchener and Nelson. The memorial to Wren in the OBE Chapel is adorned with his son's famous epitaph: *Lector, si monumentum requiris, circumspice* (Reader, if you seek his monument, look around you). But the most poignant memorial is a new one outside in the churchyard dedicated to the 32,000 Londoners killed during WWII. The inscription reads: 'Remember before God, the people of London 1939-1945'.

Doug McKinlay

INFORMATION

- ✉ Ludgate Hill EC4
- ☎ 7236 4128
- ⊖ St Paul's
- 🕘 Mon-Sat 8.30am-4pm, evensong most weekdays at 5pm, Sun 3.15pm
- $ £3.50/3/1.50/9 a/s,st/c/f; £6.50/5.50/4/16.50 with dome galleries
- ⓘ 45mn audioguide (£3/2.50/7 a/c/f); 90mn guided tours (£2.50/2 a/c) 4 times a day
- [e] www.stpauls.london.anglican.org
- ♿ good
- ✖ St Paul's Café

Dennis Johnson

Wren's masterpiece and resting place – St Paul's Cathedral

DON'T MISS

- Holman Hunt's *The Light of the World* • The Dome
- John Donne Memorial • Jubilee Cope & Mitre
- Memorial to the People of London

SCIENCE MUSEUM (5, G3)

The Science Museum has had a complete makeover since the days when it was a rather dreary place for eggheads and reluctant school children. The ground floor looks back at the history of the Industrial Revolution via examples of its machinery and then looks forward to the exploration of space. There are enough old trains (including **Puffing Billy**, the steam locomotive from 1813) and vintage cars to keep the kids well and truly happy.

INFORMATION

- ✉ Exhibition Rd SW7
- ☎ 7938 8008
- ⊖ South Kensington
- 🕐 10am-6pm
- $ £6.50/3.50 a/s,st, free children and for all after 4.30pm
- [e] www.nmsi.ac.uk
- ♿ excellent; ☎ 7938 9788
- 🍴 The Café

Simon Bracken

Up a floor and you can find out about the impact of science on food, up another one and you're into the world of computers and nuclear power. The 3rd floor is the place to come for the old aeroplanes, among them the **Vickers Vimy** in which Alcock and Brown first flew the Atlantic in 1919 and Amy Johnson's **Gipsy Moth** in which she flew to Australia in 1930. On the 4th and 5th floors you'll find exhibits relating to the history of medicine.

Look out for a modern version of **Foucault's Pendulum** hanging in the hall. As the day wears on the pendulum seems to change direction. In fact, because the earth is moving beneath it, it really stays in the same place all the time. This is how Foucault illustrated how the earth rotates on its own axis.

The basement has imaginative **hands-on galleries for children**: the Garden is for 3 to 6-year-olds, Things is for 7 to 11-year-olds. The Secret Life of the Home, a collection of labour-saving appliances that householders have either embraced or shunned, is for everyone. The new **Wellcome Wing**, due to open in June 2000, will focus on contemporary science, medicine and technology and include a 450-seat IMAX cinema.

Charlotte Hindle

No need to be blinded by science here.

DON'T MISS

- Boulton & Watt Steam Engine • Foucault's Pendulum
- Apollo 10 Command Module • Robert Stephenson's *Rocket*
- Gas Drilling Rig • Watson & Crick's DNA Model
- Amy Johnson's *Gipsy Moth* • Alcock & Brown's *Vickers Vimy*
- Well's Cathedral Clock (1392) • Pasteur's Microscope

SHAKESPEARE'S GLOBE (6, F12)

Shakespeare's Globe consists of the reconstructed Globe Theatre and an exhibition focusing on Elizabethan London and the struggle to get the theatre rebuilt. The original Globe, dubbed the 'Wooden O' for its circular shape and roofless centre, was erected in 1599, burned down in 1613 and immediately rebuilt. In 1642 it was finally closed by the Puritans, who regarded theatres as dreadful dens of iniquity, and it was later dismantled.

Today's Globe was painstakingly restored with 600 oak pegs (there's not a nail or a screw in the house), specially fired Tudor bricks and Norfolk thatching reeds (which, for some odd reason, pigeons don't like); even the plaster contains goat hair, lime and sand as it did in the 1600s. Unlike other venues for Shakespearean plays, this theatre has been designed to resemble the original as closely as possible – even if that means leaving the arena open to the skies and obstructing much of the view from the seats closest to the stage with 2 enormous 'original' Corinthian pillars.

Although there are wooden bench seats in tiers around the stage, many people emulate the 17th century 'groundlings' who stood in front of the stage, shouting, cajoling and moving around as the mood took them. Though plays are staged only in the warmer months, standees should wrap themselves up warmly and bring a flask; umbrellas are not allowed.

Charlotte Hindle

INFORMATION

- ✉ 21 New Globe Walk SE1
- ☎ 7902 1400 (info), 7401 9919 (box office)
- ⊖ London Bridge
- 🕘 Mon-Sun 10am-5pm (exhibition); May-Sept 7.30pm (performances)
- $ £6/5/4/14 a/s,st/c/f; theatre seats £10-12, standing room £5
- ⓘ entry to exhibition includes guided tour of the Globe
- [e] www.shakespeares-globe.org
- ♿ good
- 🍴 The Globe Café, Globe Restaurant

Wanamaker's Dream

The Globe was just a historical footnote when American actor (later director) Sam Wanamaker came searching for it in 1949. Though the theatre's original foundations had vanished beneath a row of listed Georgian houses, Wanamaker set up the Globe Playhouse Trust in 1970 and began fundraising for a memorial theatre. Work started in 1987, but Wanamaker died 4 years before it opened in 1997.

Charlotte Hindle

The 'Wooden O'

TATE BRITAIN (5, G7)

The Tate Britain is part of the Tate Gallery that serves as the historical archive of British art from the early 16th century to the present, and is housed exclusively at the original Millbank site. In its role as custodian of the UK's international collection of contemporary art, the gallery has moved to the new **Tate Modern** (6, F11) across the river to the old Bankside Power Station (1963) at Queen's Walk SE1 (☎ 7401 7302; ⊖ Blackfriars or London Bridge). The new gallery will showcase works by Picasso, Matisse, Cezanne, Rothko, Pollock and promises to carry on the Tate tradition for holding very avant-garde exhibitions.

INFORMATION

- ✉ Millbank SW1
- ☎ 7887 8000, 7887 8008 (recording)
- ⊖ Pimlico
- 🕒 Mon-Sat 10am-5.50pm, Sun 2-5.50pm
- $ free (charges for special exhibitions)
- ⓘ audioguide £3/2 a/c; free guided tours weekdays at 11.30am, 2.30 & 3.30pm; Sat 3pm
- [e] www.tate.org.uk
- ♿ excellent
- 🍴 Whistler restaurant, The Café

Juliet Coombe

The Tate Britain, built in 1897 and with a new entrance on Atterbury St, is expanding and there will soon be 6 new **Sainsbury Galleries** for temporary exhibitions and 9 new or refurbished ones for the permanent collection. With all the moving about it is impossible to say what will be on display (and where), but likely highlights include the mystical paintings by William Blake in Room 7, the Hogarths in Room 3 and the Constables in Room 5, alongside the works of Reynolds and Gainsborough (Room 4), Rossetti, Whistler, Bacon, Spencer and those stuffy paintings of thoroughbred racehorses by the pre-Victorian artist George Stubbs.

Charlotte Hindle

Go to Pimlico – it's got a lovely gallery

Adjoining the main building here is the **Clore Gallery**, James Stirling's quirky stab at acceptable, postmodern architecture, where the bulk of JMW Turner's paintings can be found.

DON'T MISS

• Turner's *The Shipwreck* • Stubbs' *Mares & Foals* • Constable's *The Hay-Wain* • Hogarth's *The Roast Beef of Old England* • Rossetti's *Girlhood of Mary the Virgin*

TOWER OF LONDON (6, F15)

One of London's three World Heritage Sites (the others are Westminster Abbey and surrounding buildings and Maritime Greenwich), the Tower has dominated the south-eastern corner of the City of London since 1078 at which time William the Conqueror laid the first stone of the recently refurbished **White Tower**. Over the next couple of centuries more towers, a moat, a riverside wharf and a palace were added.

INFORMATION

- ✉ Tower Hill EC3
- ☎ 7709 0765
- ⊖ Tower Hill
- ⌚ Mon-Sat 9am-6pm, Sun 10am-6pm (Mar-Oct); closes 1hr earlier (Nov-Feb)
- $ £10.50/7.90/6.90/31 a/s/c/f
- ⓘ audioguide (£1.50); free 1hr Beefeater tours every 30mns 9am-3.30pm
- e www.hrp.org.uk
- ♿ fair
- ✗ Pret a Manger

After Henry VIII relocated to Whitehall Palace in 1529, the Tower's role as a prison became increasingly important. Sir Thomas More, Henry VIII's wives (Anne Boleyn and Catherine Howard), Lady Jane Grey and Princess (later Queen) Elizabeth, were just some of the more celebrated Tudor prisoners. You can see the **Queen's House** where Boleyn is believed to have been imprisoned, and nearby the infamous **Bloody Tower** where Edward V and his younger brother were allegedly murdered by uncle, Richard III.

A neogothic barracks, now housing the **Crown Jewels**, replaced the Grand Storehouse when it burned down in 1841. Since Prince Albert oversaw the repair of the medieval towers the Tower's gruesome history became little more than the tourist attraction it is today. However, prisoners were occasionally kept here up to WWII, most notably Rudolf Hess in 1941.

Ravens & Beefeaters

Legend has it that should the ravens fly away, the White Tower will crumble and a great disaster will befall England. So the Tudor-costumed Yeoman Warders (Beefeaters) guarding the Tower take the safe option and clip the birds' wings. Why Beefeaters? In the 17th century the guards received a daily ration of beef and beer, a luxury beyond the reach of the poor, and thus the envious nickname was born.

Dusk over the former chamber of horrors

DON'T MISS
- Chapel of St John • Traitors' Gate • Scaffold Site on Tower Green
- Chapel Royal of St Peter ad Vincula • Beauchamp Tower

VICTORIA & ALBERT MUSEUM (5, G4)

This vast, rambling, wonderful museum of decorative art and design was created after the Great Exhibition of 1851. Amazingly, most of the V&A's 4 million piece collection is actually on display, so as soon as you're through the turnstile look at the floor plan and decide what you're most interested in – and stick to it.

INFORMATION

- ✉ Cromwell Rd SW7
- ☎ 7938 8500, 7938 8441 (recording)
- ⊖ South Kensington
- 🕘 10am-5.45pm, plus Wed 6.30-9.30pm, Sun from 11am
- $ £6/3 a/s; free for students, children and for all after 4.30pm; Wed late session £3
- [i] free 1½hr tours 10.30am-4.30pm
- [e] www.vam.ac.uk
- ♿ excellent
- 🍴 Millburn's restaurant

Charlotte Hindle

The ground floor is mostly devoted to art and design from Asia and European art. There's a room devoted to costume – everything from absurd 18th century wigs and whalebones to the platform shoes that brought Naomi Campbell crashing to the catwalk.

Another room is devoted to Raphael's sketches that formed the designs for tapestries that now hang in the Vatican Museum. Also on the ground floor are three 1860s refreshment rooms, including the gorgeous **Green Dining Room** designed by William Morris and his friend Edward Burne-Jones.

On level B are collections of ironwork, stained glass and jewellery, and an impressive exhibition of musical instruments. In the **British Galleries** – some of which will be closed for redesign until late 2001 – you may get to see the late 16th century **Great Bed of Ware**, big enough to sleep 5 and designed as an early advertising gimmick for a Hertfordshire inn. The highlights of this floor, though, are the **Silver Galleries**. Up on levels C and D are displays of British art and design, along with ceramics and porcelain from Europe and Asia. The **Henry Cole Wing** contains the largest collection of Constables gathered under one roof.

Charlotte Hindle

Christopher Wren stands proud on the V&A

DON'T MISS

• Norfolk House music room • Tippoo's Tiger • Maharaja Ranjit Singh's throne • Becket casket • Henry VIII's writing desk • Ardabil carpet

WESTMINSTER ABBEY (6, J6)

So rich in history is the abbey that you'll need half a day to do it justice. It's celebrated as the resting place of monarchs and the venue for other great pageants, most notably in recent years as the setting for the funeral of Diana, Princess of Wales, in 1997. The **coronation chair**, where all monarchs except Edward V and Edward VIII have been supposedly crowned since 1066, is behind the altar. Also within its walls is the nation's largest collection of tombs of politicians, poets, scientists and musicians.

The abbey is a spectacular example of various styles of Gothic architecture. The original church was built by Edward the Confessor, later St Edward, who is buried at the east end. Henry III began work on the new building in the 13th century but didn't complete it. Only an expert would be able to tell that the French Gothic nave was finished off as 'late' as 1375. **Henry VII's Chapel** was added in 1503. Above the exit (west door) are two towers built by Sir Christopher Wren and his pupil Nicholas Hawksmoor. Just above this door stand 10 stone statues of 20th century martyrs, which were unveiled in 1998, that count Martin Luther King Jr among them. Separate museums around the Cloister are the **Chapter House**, **the Undercroft (or Abbey) Museum** and the **Pyx Chamber**, once the Royal Treasury. These are open similar hours to the abbey.

One of the best ways to visit the abbey is to attend a service; the atmosphere and acoustics at **evensong** will send shivers down your spine.

Juliet Coombe

INFORMATION

✉ Dean's Yard SW1
☎ 7222 5152
⊖ Westminster
🕘 Mon-Fri 9am-4.45pm, late session Wed 6-7.45pm (photography allowed), Sat 9am-2.45pm; Sun for services only; evensong Mon-Fri 5pm, Sat-Sun 3pm, Eucharist Sun 11am
$ £5/3/2/10 a/s,st/c/f (half-price Wed evening)
ℹ audioguide (£2); 1½hr tours (£3) Mon-Sat 3-6 times a day
[e] www.westminster-abbey.org
♿ good
🍴 Coffee Club (in the Cloister)

Juliet Coombe

St Margaret's church, beside the Abbey

DON'T MISS
• Poet's Corner • Queen Elizabeth Chapel • St Edward's Chapel
• Cloister • Tomb of the Unknown Warrior

sights & activities

MUSEUMS

London boasts smaller, more accessible museums catering to every taste and individual – from train-spotters and thespians to caffeine-freaks, sea dogs and even fan fans. They're spread out across town but well worth an easy tube or bus ride – even to non-aficionados.

Bramah Tea & Coffee Museum (6, H15)
An insight into the story of tea and coffee drinking in the UK; nearby Butler's Wharf once handled 6000 chests of tea a day.
✉ **1 Maguire St, cnr Gainsford St SE1**
☎ **7378 0222**
⊖ **Tower Bridge**
🕘 **10am-6pm** $ **£4/3/10 a/s,st/f** ♿ **good**

Cabinet War Rooms
(6, H6) The British government took refuge here during WWII, conducting its business from beneath 3m of solid concrete. It was from here that Winston Churchill made some of his most stirring speeches.
✉ **Clive Steps, King Charles St SW1**
☎ **7930 6961**
⊖ **Westminster**
🕘 **9.30am-5.15pm** $ **£4.80/3.50 a/s,st (children free)** ♿ **excellent**

Design Museum
(6, H15) The sparkling white Design Museum shows how product design has evolved and how it can make the difference between success and failure for items intended for mass production.
✉ **28 Shad Thames SE1** ☎ **7403 6933**
⊖ **Tower Bridge**
🕘 **11.30am-6pm**
$ **£5.25/4/12 a/st,c/f**
♿ **good**

Fan Museum (3, J3)
Fans dating back to the 17th century from around the world are exhibited and their historical role and importance examined.
✉ **12 Croom's Hill SE10** ☎ **8305 1441**
🚆 **DLR Cutty Sark**
🕘 **Tues-Sat 11am-5pm, Sun 12-5pm**
$ **£3.50/2.50** ♿ **good**

Geffrye Museum
(5, C10) What were once 14 almshouses are now devoted to domestic interiors, with each room furnished to show how wealthier homes would have looked from Elizabethan times right through to today.
✉ **136 Kingsland Rd E2** ☎ **7739 9893**
[e] **www.geffrye-museum.org.uk**
🚆 **Dalston Kingsland**
🕘 **Tues-Sat 10am-5pm, Sun 2-5pm** $ **free**
♿ **excellent**

Horniman Museum
(2, C3) This extraordinary little museum includes a display of instruments and their recordings; the Living Waters Aquarium; and new African Worlds, the UK's first permanent gallery of African, Afro-Caribbean and Brazilian art and culture.
✉ **100 London Rd SE23** ☎ **8699 1872, 8699 2339 (recording)**
🚆 **Forest Hill** 🕘 **Mon-Sat 10.30am-5.30pm, Sun 2-5.30pm**
$ **free** ♿ **excellent**

Jewish Museum
(4, K4) Judaism is examined in the Ceremonial Art Gallery and the UK Jewish community's story is told in the History Gallery.
✉ **129-131 Albert St NW1** ☎ **7284 1997** [e] **www.ort.org/jewmusm/**
⊖ **Camden Town**
🕘 **Sun-Thurs 10am-4pm** $ **£3/2/1.50/7.50 a/s/st,c/f** ♿ **excellent**

Kenwood House
(4, C4) Housed in a neoclassical mansion, this museum contains what is arguably London's finest small collection of European art.
✉ **Hampstead Lane NW3** ☎ **8348 1286**
⊖ **Archway or Golders Green, then bus 210**
🕘 **Apr-Sept 10am-6pm; closes earlier Oct-Mar** ♿ **good**

London Canal Museum (5, C7)
This Victorian warehouse on Regent's Canal near King's Cross contains a small museum about life on the canals. See p. 55 for canal tour information.
✉ **12-13 New Wharf Rd N1** ☎ **7713 0836**
[e] **www.charitynet.org/~LCanalMus**
⊖ **King's Cross** 🕘 **Tues-Sun 10am-4.30pm**
$ **£2.50/1.25 a/s,st,c**

London Transport Museum (7, C8)
LTM shows how London made the transition from streets choked with horse-drawn carriages to the

arrival of the Docklands Light Rail – a more interesting story than you might suspect.
✉ The Piazza WC2 ☎ 7379 6344 🖳 www.ltmuseum.co.uk ⊖ Covent Garden 🕘 Sat-Thurs 10am-5.15pm, Fri from 11am $ £4.95/2.95/12.85 a/s,st,c/f ♿ good

National Maritime Museum (3, J3)
A massive collection of boats, maps, charts, uniforms and marine art is designed to tell the long and convoluted history of Britain as a seafaring nation. Some 16 flash new galleries make the journey that much more pleasant.
✉ Romney Rd SE10 ☎ 8312 6565 🖳 www.nmm.ac.uk 🚆 DLR Cutty Sark 🕘 10am-5pm $ £7.50/6 a/s,st (children free) with Royal Observatory £9.50/7.60 ♿ excellent

Old Operating Theatre & Herb Garret (6, G13)
The garret at the top of St Thomas Church tower was once used by the apothecary of St Thomas's Hospital to store medicinal herbs. It now houses an atmospheric medical museum, delightfully hung with bunches of herbs, that explores 19th century hospital treatment.
✉ 9A St Thomas St SE1 ☎ 7955 4791 ⊖ London Bridge 🕘 10am-4pm $ £2.90/2/1.50/7.25 a/s,st/c/f

St John's Gate & Museum (6, C10)
What looks like a toy-town medieval gate turns out to be the real thing, albeit restored in the 19th century. Inside there's a museum about the Knights of St John of Jerusalem, soldiers who took on a nursing role during the Crusades.
✉ St John's Square EC1 ☎ 7253 6644 ⊖ Farringdon 🕘 Mon-Fri 9am-5pm, Sat 10am-4pm; guided tour (£4) 11am & 2.30pm Tues, Fri & Sat $ free

Sherlock Holmes Museum (6, C1)
Fans of Arthur Conan Doyle's books will enjoy these 3 floors of reconstructed Victoriana though Holmes actually 'lived' in the Abbey National building farther south on the corner with Melcombe St.
✉ 221b Baker St NW1 ☎ 7935 8866 ⊖ Baker Street 🕘 9.30am-6pm $ £5/3 a/c

Sir John Soane's Museum (6, D8)
Partly a beautiful, if quirky, house; partly a small museum representing the personal taste of the highly regarded architect John Soane (1753-1837).
✉ 13 Lincoln's Inn Fields WC2 ☎ 7405 2107 ⊖ Holborn 🕘 Tues-Sat 10am-5pm, 1st Tues/month 6-9pm; 1hr guided tour (£3) Sat 2.30pm $ free

Sutton House (5, A10) A red-brick Tudor structure (1535) in Hackney, this is the oldest house in London and has Tudor, Stuart and Georgian interiors and gardens.
✉ 2 & 4 Homerton High St E9 ☎ 8986 2264 🚆 Hackney Central 🕘 Wed-Sun 11.30am-5.30pm (Sat 2-5pm Feb-Nov only) $ £3/50p/4.50 a/c/f (NT members free)

Theatre Museum (6, E7) A branch of the V&A, this colourful and lively museum displays costumes and artefacts relating to the history of the theatre, including memorabilia of great thespians.
✉ 7 Russell St WC2 ☎ 7836 7891 ⊖ Covent Garden 🕘 Tues-Sun 11am-7pm $ 4.50/2.50 a/c,s,st ♿ excellent

Wimbledon Lawn Tennis Museum (2, D3) The history of tennis-playing from the crucial invention of the lawnmower (in 1830) and of the India rubber ball (in the 1850s) is displayed. A state-of-the-art presentation lets fans relive their favourite moments.
✉ Gate 4, Church Rd SW19 ☎ 8946 6131 ⊖ Southfields or Wimbledon Park 🕘 Tues-Sat 10.30am-5pm, Sun 2-5pm (restricted hrs during games) $ £4/3 a/c,s,st ♿ excellent

Juliet Coombe

Prime meridian views – National Maritime Museum as seen from the Old Royal Observatory

GALLERIES

Important fine art groupings can be found in London's museums, galleries or collections. But what's in a name? There are also scores of smaller, often commercial galleries that host changing exhibitions throughout the year.

Bankside Gallery
(6, F10) Home to the Royal Watercolour Society and the Royal Society of Painter-Printmakers, the gallery has no permanent collection. It hosts frequently changing exhibitions of watercolours, prints and engravings.
✉ 48 Hopton St SE1 ☎ 7928 7521 ⊖ Blackfriars or Waterloo 🕘 Tues 10am-8pm, Wed-Fri till 5pm, Sat-Sun 1-5pm $ £3.50/2 a/s,st ♿ excellent

What's On?

Grab the free monthly publication *Galleries* (☎ 8740 7020; www.artefact.co.uk), available at many art spaces, to find out what's hanging and where.

Dulwich Picture Gallery (2, C3)
The UK's oldest public art gallery (1811) was designed by Soane for paintings collected by dealer Noel Desenfans and painter Francis Bourgeois. See Rembrandt, Rubens, Reynolds, Gainsborough and Lely masterpieces.
✉ College Rd SE21 ☎ 8693 5254 🚆 North Dulwich 🕘 Tues-Fri 10am-5pm, Sat-Sun 11am-5pm $ £3/1.50 a/c (Fri free) ♿ good

Hayward Gallery
(6, G8) Arguably London's greatest eyesore from the outside, the Hayward is also its premier exhibition space for major international art shows and has excellent hanging spaces for contemporary and 20th century art.
✉ Belvedere Rd SE1 ☎ 7928 3144, 7261 0127 (recording) [e] www.hayward-gallery.org.uk ⊖ Waterloo 🕘 Mon & Thurs-Sun 10am-6pm, Tues-Wed 10am-8pm $ prices vary according to exhibit ♿ good

National Portrait Gallery (6, F6)
Put faces to the famous and infamous names in British history. You'll find oil paintings, watercolours, drawings, miniatures, sculptures, caricatures, silhouettes, photographs and even electronic art.
✉ 2 St Martin's Place WC2 ☎ 7306 0055, 7312 2463 (recording) [e] www.npg.org.uk ⊖ Charing Cross 🕘 Mon-Sat 10am-6pm, Sun 12-6pm $ free ♿ good

Royal Academy of Arts (6, F4) Traditionally the Hayward's poor relation, the academy has staged record-breaking exhibitions here in recent years. The Summer Exhibition, a show open to all entrants, is hugely popular.
✉ Burlington House, Piccadilly W1 ☎ 7300 8000 ⊖ Green Park 🕘 10am-6pm (sometimes to 8.30pm Fri) $ prices vary according to exhibit ♿ excellent

Saatchi Gallery
(5, C3) Not the place to come if your tastes run to Constable or Turner; you're likely to find giant pools of oil reflecting the ceiling or scarily likelife models of human figures. The space is light, airy and large.
✉ 98a Boundary Rd NW8 ☎ 7624 8299 ⊖ Kilburn Park 🕘 Thurs-Sun 12-6pm $ £4/2 (free Thurs)

Serpentine Gallery
(5, F3) Beautifully sited, this renovated gallery specialises in contemporary art displaying the work of such artists as William Kentridge, Bridget Riley and Andreas Gursky.
✉ Kensington Gardens W2 ☎ 7402 6075 ⊖ Hyde Park Corner or Lancaster Gate 🕘 10am-6pm $ free ♿ excellent

Wallace Collection
(6, D2) London's finest small gallery is a treasure-trove of paintings from the 17th and 18th centuries. There's works by Rubens, Titian, Poussin, Frans Hals and Rembrandt.
✉ Hertford House, Manchester Square W1 ☎ 7935 0687 [e] www.demon.co.uk/heritage/wallace ⊖ Bond Street 🕘 Mon-Sat 10am-5pm, Sun 2-5pm $ free ♿ excellent

NOTABLE BUILDINGS

Albert Memorial
(5, F3) This over-the-top monument to Queen Victoria's German husband Albert (1819-61) was taken out of wraps in 1998 after an 8 year renovation.
✉ Hyde Park, Kensington Gore SW7
☎ 7495 0916
⊖ South Kensington or Gloucester Road
🕒 guided tours at 10am & 11am Fri-Sat
$ £3/2/50p a/s,st/c

British Library (6, A6)
The newly renovated copyright library stocks every British publication as well as historical manuscripts, books and maps. It has the Magna Carta, a Gutenberg Bible and Shakespeare's First Folio.
✉ 96 Euston Rd NW1
☎ 7412 7000
🌐 www.bl.uk ⊖ King's Cross 🕒 Mon-Fri 9.30am-6pm (Tues till 8pm, Sat till 5pm), Sun 11am-5pm $ free
♿ excellent

Chelsea Royal Hospital (5, H5)
The site of Chelsea's annual Flower Show, the Royal Hospital is a superb Wren building. Stroll in the grounds to the Chapel with its altar painting, the *Resurrection* by Sebastiano Ricci, and to the Great Hall, an ornate refectory bedecked with flags.
✉ Royal Hospital Rd SW3 ☎ 7730 5282
⊖ Sloane Square 🕒 Mon-Sat 10am-noon & 2-4pm, Sun 2-4pm
$ free ♿ fair

Guildhall (6, D12)
Visitors to the City's 800 year old seat of Government can see the Great Hall where the mayor and sheriffs are elected. It also has an art gallery and clock museum.
✉ Gresham St EC2
☎ 7606 3030 ⊖ Bank
🕒 Mon-Sat 9am-5pm, Sun till 4pm $ free; art gallery only: £2.50/1 a/c ♿ excellent

Richard I'Anson

Royal Courts of Justice

The Monument
(6, F13) This 60.6m stone column topped with a gilded bronze urn vase of flames was designed by Wren to commemorate the Great Fire started in a bakery nearby. Tight steps (all 311 of them) lead to a balcony view.
✉ Monument St EC3
☎ 7626 2717 ⊖ Monument 🕒 10am-6pm $ £1.50/50p a/c

Old Naval College
(3, H3) This Wren masterpiece is now used by the University of Greenwich. However, you can still view the fabulous Painted Hall and the Chapel.
✉ King William Walk SE10 ☎ 8858 2154
🚆 DLR Cutty Sark 🕒 2-5pm $ free ♿ fair

Prince Henry's Room
(6, E10) This small museum has a 1611 overhanging half-timbered façade. The 1st floor room, with items related to the life and writings of Samuel Pepys, boasts the best Jacobean plaster ceiling extant in London.
✉ 17 Fleet St EC4
☎ 7294 1158
⊖ Temple 🕒 Mon-Sat 11am-2pm $ free

Royal Courts of Justice (6, E9)
Designed by GE Street in 1874, this is where civil cases (eg libel cases) are tried. Visitors are welcome to watch cases in progress.
✉ Strand WC2
☎ 7936 6000
⊖ Temple 🕒 Mon-Fri 9.30am-4.30pm $ free
♿ excellent

Old Royal Observatory (3, K4)
Since 1884 Greenwich Mean Time (GMT) has been accepted as the universal measurement of standard time. It is here that the globe divides between east and west, and you can place 1 foot either side of the meridian line and straddle the 2 hemispheres.
✉ Romney Rd, Greenwich Park SE10
☎ 8858 4422 🚆 DLR Cutty Sark 🕒 10am-5pm $ £5/4 a/s,st (children free)

St Pancras Station
(6, A6) This architectural gem (see picture p. 13) has a dramatic Brunel glass-and-iron train shed at rear.
✉ Euston Rd NW1
⊖ King's Cross $ free
♿ good

FAMOUS ABODES

Apsley House (Wellington Museum) (6, H2) This striking 18th century mansion overlooking Hyde Park Corner was home to the Duke of Wellington and retains most of its furnishings and collections.
✉ 149 Piccadilly W1 ☎ 7499 5676 ⊖ Hyde Park Corner 🕘 Tues-Sun 11am-5pm $ £4.50/3 a/c

Carlyle's House The great essayist and historian Thomas Carlyle wrote his famous history of the French Revolution in this Queen Anne residence.
✉ 24 Cheyne Row SW3 (5,H4) ☎ 7352 7087 ⊖ Sloane Square 🕘 late Mar-Oct: Wed-Sun 11am-5pm $ £3.30/1.65 a/c

Dickens' House (6, B8) This is the only surviving residence of the many lived in by the great Victorian novelist. He wrote *The Pickwick Papers*, *Nicholas Nickleby* and *Oliver Twist* here.
✉ 49 Doughty St WC1 ☎ 7405 2127 ⊖ Russell Square 🕘 Mon-Fri 9.45am-5.30pm, Sat 10am-5pm $ £3.50/2.50/1.50/7 a/st/c/f

Freud Museum (4, F1) Sigmund Freud spent the last 18 months of his life here after fleeing Nazi-occupied Vienna. The house contains the psychiatrist's original couch, his books and his Greek and Asian artefacts.
✉ 20 Maresfield Gardens NW3 ☎ 7435 2002 [e] www.freud.org.uk ⊖ Finchley Road 🕘 Wed-Sun 12-5pm $ £4/2 ♿ fair

Hogarth's House (2, C2) William Hogarth lived here from 1749-64 and although little original furniture remains, his engravings of Georgian London Life are displayed.
✉ Hogarth Lane, Great West Rd W4 ☎ 8994 6757 ⊖ Turnham Green 🕘 Tues-Fri 1-5pm, Sat-Sun 1-6pm; closes 1hr earlier Nov-Mar $ free ♿ fair

Dr Johnson's House (6, E9) This well-preserved Georgian town house is full pictures of the lexicographer Samuel's friends and intimates.
✉ 17 Gough Square EC4 ☎ 7353 3745 ⊖ Blackfriars 🕘 11am-5.30pm; Oct-Apr: till 5pm $ £3/2/1 a/s,st/c

Blue Plaques

Placing 'Blue Plaques' on the houses of distinguished Londoners began in 1867. The original criteria for the placing of a plaque were that the candidate must been dead for at least 20 years, born more than 100 years prior and be known to the 'well informed passer-by'.

Keats' House (4, E2) Sitting under a plum tree in the garden inspired the Romantic poets' golden boy to write his most celebrated poem, *Ode to a Nightingale*. View original manuscripts and letters, mementoes and Keats' collection of works by Chaucer and Shakespeare.
✉ Wentworth Place, Keats Grove NW3 ☎ 7435 2062 ⊖ Hampstead 🚆 Hampstead Heath 🕘 Mon-Fri 10am-1pm & 2-6pm, till 5pm Sat, Sun 2-5pm; Nov-Mar: reduced hrs $ free

Leighton House (5, G2) This gem of a house was the home of Lord Leighton (1830-96), a pre-Raphaelite painter who decorated parts of it in Middle Eastern style. The house contains notable pre-Raphaelite paintings by Burne-Jones, Watts, Millais and Lord Leighton himself.
✉ 12 Holland Park Rd W14 ☎ 7602 3316 ⊖ High Street Kensington 🕘 Mon-Sat 11am-5.30pm $ free

No 2 Willow Rd (4, E2) Fans of modern architecture will appreciate this house, designed by Erno Goldfinger in 1939 as his family home. The interior features artworks by Henry Moore, Max Ernst and Bridget Riley.
✉ 2 Willow Rd NW3 ☎ 7435 6166 ⊖ Hampstead 🚆 Hampstead Heath 🕘 Apr-Oct: Thurs-Sat 12-5pm $ £4.10/2.05 a/c

CHURCHES & CATHEDRALS

All Souls (6, D3)
This unusual church (1824), with its circular columned porch and distinctive needle-like spire, was John Nash's solution for the curving, northern sweep of Regent St.
✉ Langham Place W1 ☎ 7580 3522 ⊖ Oxford Circus 🕘 Mon-Fri 9.30am-6pm, Sun 9am-9pm ♿ good

St Bartholomew-the-Great (6, D11)
One of London's oldest churches, it has Norman arches and details that lend this holy space an ancient calm; approaching from Smithfield Market through a 13th century archway is like walking back in time.
✉ West Smithfield EC1 ☎ 7606 5171 ⊖ Barbican 🕘 Mon-Fri 8.30am-5pm, Sat 10.30am-1.30pm, Sun 8am-8pm ♿ good

St Bartholomew-the-Great

St Bride's, Fleet St (6, E10) A small but perfect church by Wren, St Bride's is still referred to as 'the journalists' church' or 'the printers' cathedral' due to its Fleet St location.
✉ Fleet St EC4 ☎ 7353 1301 ⊖ Blackfriars 🕘 Mon-Fri 8am-4.45pm, Sat from 9am, Sun 9am-12.30pm & 5.30-7.30pm ♿ good

St Martin-in-the-Fields (7, E7) An early 18th century masterpiece by James Gibbs, this celebrated church occupies a prime site on Trafalgar Square and helps form one of London's greatest vistas.
✉ Trafalgar Square WC2 ☎ 7930 0089 ⊖ Charing Cross 🕘 8am-6.30pm ♿ good

St-Mary-le-Bow (6, E12) Built in 1673, it's famous as the church whose bells dictate who is – and who is not – a cockney; if you were born within their peal, you're the genuine article. The delicate steeple is one of Wren's finest works.
✉ Cheapside EC2 ☎ 7248 5139 ⊖ Bank or St Paul's 🕘 Mon-Thurs 6.30am-6pm, Fri 6.30am-4pm ♿ good

Southwark Cathedral (6, G13) This medieval cathedral is largely a Victorian repair job. It contains, among other things, a memorial to Shakespeare and the tomb of the Bard's brother, Edmond.
✉ Montague Close SE1 ☎ 7407 3708 ⊖ London Bridge 🕘 8am-6pm; evensong: Tues & Fri 5.30pm, Sat 4pm, Sun 3pm $ £2.50 donation requested ♿ fair

Doug McKinlay

St Martin-in-the-Fields graces Trafalgar Square.

Temple Church (6, E9) Originally built by the secretive Knights Templar between 1161 and 1185 the core of the building is 1 of only 4 round churches in the UK.
✉ King's Bench Walk, Inner Temple EC4 ☎ 7353 1736 ⊖ Temple or Blackfriars 🕘 Wed-Sat 10am-4pm ♿ good

Westminster Cathedral (6, K4)
The British headquarters of the Roman Catholic Church is the only good example of neo-Byzantine architecture in London. The interior is part splendid marble and mosaic, part bare brick.
✉ Victoria St SW1 ☎ 7798 9064 ⊖ Victoria 🕘 7am-7pm ♿ good

PARKS & GARDENS

London boasts more parks, gardens and open spaces than any city of its size in the world.

Flora

Plant-lovers won't want to miss Kew Gardens (p. 21), but if you're more interested in less exotic plants, London's parks boast a wide range of common garden variety trees, shrubs and flowers. Many Londoners also take pride in their private gardens, some of which open to the public for a few days each year (generally May-Sept) through the National Gardens Scheme. Call ☎ 01483-211535 to receive a *London Gardens* pamphlet.

Swans

Cygnus olor have always had royal associations, featuring in mythologies as far back as ancient Greece. In the 17th century 2 city livery companies, the Dyers and the Vintners, were given the concession to keep swans and today, along with the monarch, they are the only ones allowed to keep swans on the Thames 'from the towne of Graveshende to Chicester'.

Fauna

The mammal you're most likely to spot in London is the grey squirrel, a North American import that has decimated the indigenous red squirrel population and colonised every park.

Birdwatchers, will have a, well, field day in London. There are ducks, pelicans and the Queen's swans in St James's Park and beautiful, chestnut-headed great crested grebes in Hyde Park's Serpentine. Herons can often be seen feeding in the Thames, and cormorants are attracted to the Docklands. Garden birds, like blue and great tits, robins and blackbirds, roost in all the parks and Kestrels nest around the Tower of London.

London has more than 50 nature reserves maintained by the London Wildlife Trust (☎ 7278 6612). Battersea Park Nature Reserve has several organised nature trails, while the Trent Country Park (2, B3; 🚇 Cockfosters) has a Braille trail through the woodlands. Parts of Hampstead Heath are designated Sites of Special Scientific Interest for their wealth of natural history.

Open air theatre at Regent's Park

Regal swan, St James's Park

Battersea Park

(5, J5) Stretching out between Battersea Bridge and Chelsea Bridge this 50-hectare space of greenery is filled with attractions and distractions, most prominently the Japanese Peace Pagoda. Hire boats can be rowed on the lake.
✉ Albert Bridge Rd SW11 ☎ 8871 7530 ⊖ Sloane Square then bus 137 ⊙ dawn-dusk

Green Park (6, H3)

Just across the Mall from St James' Park though less fussy (and less crowded), with more naturally rolling park – trees and open space, sunshine and shade.
✉ Green Park SW1 ☎ 7930 1793 ⊖ Green Park or Hyde Park Corner ⊙ 5am-midnight

Hampstead Heath (4)

The heath covers 320 hectares, most of it woods, hills and meadows. Some sections of the heath are laid out for sports like football and cricket and there are several bathing ponds (recommended for strong swimmers only, see p. 46).
✉ Hampstead Heath NW3 ☎ 7485 3873 ⊖ Hampstead ⊞ Gospel Oak or Hampstead Heath ⊙ 24hrs

Hyde Park (5, F4)

The park is central London's largest open space. Expropriated from the church by Henry VIII, it became a hunting ground for kings and aristocrats, and then a venue for duels, executions, horse racing, the 1851 Great Exhibition, an enormous wartime potato field and, more recently, huge music concerts. It's a riot of colour in spring, and full of lazy sunbathers and boats on the Serpentine in summer.
✉ Hyde Park W2 ☎ 7298 2100 ⊖ Hyde Park Corner, Knightsbridge, Lancaster Gate or Marble Arch ⊙ 5am-midnight

Regent's Park (5, C5)

Like London's other parks, this park was subsequently farmed and then revived as a place for fun and leisure during the 18th century. It contains the London Zoo (p. 42), the Grand Union Canal, an open-air theatre and, around the perimeter, John Nash's immaculate, stuccoed terraces.
✉ Regent's Park NW1 ☎ 7486 7905 ⊖ Baker Street or Regent's Park ⊙ May-Sept: 8am-dusk (from 9am Oct-Apr)

Speak your Mind

Every Sunday at Speaker's Corner, just south of Marble Arch in Hyde Park, anyone with a soapbox can hold forth on whatever subject takes their fancy. Unless you expect the silver-throated oratory of a modern-day Churchill, you shouldn't be disappointed with your day in the park.

Preaching to the sceptical – a Speaker's Corner orator has his day in the sun.

Richmond Park

(2, C2) One of London's finest and wildest parks, it is home to all sorts of wildlife: herds of red and fallow deer; elusive foxes and badgers. It's a great place for birdwatchers too.
✉ Richmond, Surrey ☎ 8948 3209 ⊖ Richmond ⊙ dawn-30mns before dusk

St James's Park

(6, H5) The neatest and most regal of London's parks, it has the best vistas across Westminster, Buckingham Palace and St James's Palace.
✉ The Mall SW1 ☎ 7930 1793 ⊖ St James's Park or Charing Cross ⊙ 5am-midnight

No tiptoeing through these St James's Park tulips

LONDON FOR CHILDREN

The London Tourist Board's Visitorcall service operates a 24hr 'What's on for Children' line (☎ 09064-123404), while *Time Out* issues a bimonthly supplement, *Kids Out* (£2), with all sorts of information for parents in search of something to entertain their kids.

BBC Experience
Features video clips of popular BBC programs and the Marconi Collection of early wireless equipment. Through interactive displays, kids can try their hands at presenting a weather report, a sporting event, handling a TV camera or directing an episode of the evergreen BBC1 soap opera *EastEnders*.
✉ Broadcasting House, Portland Place W1 (6, D3) ☎ 0870-603 0304 ⊖ Oxford Circus 🕘 Tues-Sun 10am-5.30pm (from 11am Mon) $ £6.95/5.95/4.95/19.95 a/s,st/c/f

Babysitting

Need a break from the anklebiters? Contact Babysitters Childminders at 6 Nottingham St W1 (6, C2; ☎ 7487 5040; www.babydirectory.com/babysit) or Pippa's Pop-Ins, a hotel and childcare centre (p. 106).

Bethnal Green Museum of Childhood (6, B15)
Guaranteed to entertain the kids and to bring dear memories of your own childhood flooding back, it's packed with dolls, dolls' houses, train sets, model cars, children's clothes, old board games, books, toy theatres and puppets.
✉ Cambridge Heath Rd & Old Ford Rd E2 ☎ 8983 5200 ⊖ Bethnal Green 🕘 Mon-Thurs & Sat-Sun 10am-5.50pm $ free ♿ good

Cutty Sark (3, H2)
Stroll the decks and peep inside the refitted cabins of the beautiful *Cutty Sark* clipper (1869), the fastest ship that had ever sailed the seven seas at that time.
✉ King William Walk SE10 ☎ 8858 3445 🚆 DLR Cutty Sark 🕘 10am-6pm $ £3.50/2.50/8.50 ♿ fair

FA Premier League Hall of Fame (6, H8)
This temple to English football traces the history of the sport. It has life-sized wax figures of the first 12 inductees, shows clips of some of the greatest football moments, and allows visitors to test their skills by computer.
✉ County Hall, Members Carriageway, Westminster Bridge Rd SE1 ☎ 7928 3636 [e] www.hall-of-fame.co.uk ⊖ Westminster 🕘 10am-6pm $ £9.95/7.50/6.50 a/s,st/c ♿ good

HMS Belfast (6, G14)
This large cruiser saw a lot of action during WWII and was decommissioned in the 1960s. Kids will love exploring the 8 zones on 9 decks and scrambling up and down steep ladders.
✉ Morgan's Lane, Tooley St SE1 ☎ 7407 6434 [e] www.hmsbelfast.org.uk ⊖ London Bridge 🕘 10am-6pm (till 5pm Nov-Feb) $ £4.70/3.60/11.80 a/s,st/f (children free) ♿ fair to good

London Aquarium (6, H8)
This state-of-the-art 'zoo' for fish lacks the colour and airiness of more purpose-built structures, but the coral reef display is quite impressive.
✉ County Hall, Riverside Building, Westminster Bridge Rd SE1 ☎ 7967 8000 [e] www.londonaquarium.co.uk ⊖ Westminster 🕘 10am-6.30pm (till 6.00pm Sept-May) $ £8/6.50/5/22 a/s,st/c/f

London Zoo (4, K2)
One of the world's oldest zoos, which now focuses on conservation and education and keeps far fewer species than previously. Web of Life, a glass breeding pavilion containing 65 animal exhibits (from termites and jellyfish to the birds and the bees), is alone worth the visit.
✉ Regent's Park NW1 ☎ 7722 3333 ⊖ Camden 🕘 10am-5.30pm (till 4pm Nov-Feb) $ £9/8/7/28 a/s,st/c/f ♿ good

Pepsi Trocadero & Segaworld (6, F5)
This indoor entertainment complex on 6 levels has many high-tech attractions, anchored by the Segaworld indoor theme park. Great for youngsters not into more cultural attractions; just don't expect a peaceful – or cheap – outing.
✉ Piccadilly Circus W1 ☎ 7434 0030 (Pepsi T.); 7734 2777 (Segaworld) ⊖ Piccadilly Circus 🕘 Mon-Thurs & Sun 10am-midnight, Fri-Sat till 1am $ £3 per ride; IMAX Theatre £6.75/5.50/19.98 a/c,s,st/f

Pollock's Toy Museum (6, C5)
This little find is full of antique toys – some of them dating back to 2000 BC. The collection of old model theatres is lovely.
✉ 1 Scala St W1 ☎ 7636 3452 ⊖ Goodge Street 🕘 Mon-Sat 10am-5pm $ £3/1.50 a/c

City Farms

To demonstrate to urban Londoners young and old that cows' udders are not shaped like milk bottles, farms have been set up all over the city. They're more popular with local people than visitors, so they offer a good way of getting off the beaten track.

Coram's Fields (6, B7) ✉ 93 Guildford St WC1 ☎ 7837 6138 ⊖ Russell Square 🕘 9am-7pm (till 4.30pm in winter)
Hackney City Farm (5, C10) ✉ 1A Goldsmith's Row E2 ☎ 7729 6381 ⊖ Bethnal Green 🕘 Tues-Sun 10am-4.30pm
Kentish Town City Farm (4, G4) ✉ Cressfield Close, Grafton Rd NW5 ☎ 7916 5420 ⊖ Kentish Town 🕘 Tues-Sun 9.30am-5.30pm
Spitalfields Farm (5, D10) ✉ Weaver St, off Pedley St E1 ☎ 7247 8762 ⊖ Shoreditch 🕘 Tues-Sun 10am-5.30pm

Thames Flood Barrier (2, C4) Kids love the barrier. Built between Greenwich and Woolwich from 1972-82 to protect London from flooding, it consists of 10 surreal-looking movable gates supported between 7 concrete piers. The mechanisms are checked once a month; ring for details.
✉ 1 Unity Way SE18 ☎ 8305 4188 🚆 Charlton 🚌 177 or 180 from Greenwich ⛴ to/from Greenwich Pier 4 times a day Mar-Oct 🕘 Mon-Sat 10am-5pm, Sun 10.30am-5.30pm $ £3.40/2/7.50 ♿ good

Charlotte Hindle

Giant sea snail about to eat London? No, it's the otherworldly Thames Flood Barrier.

OFF THE BEATEN TRACK

If you want to escape the masses, consider visiting one of the lesser known sights or ones that attract Londoners rather than visitors.

Abney Park Cemetery (5, A9)
This overgrown and vaguely spooky cemetery was laid out in 1840. Among the permanent residents is General William Booth (1829-1912), founder of the Salvation Army.
✉ Stoke Newington Church St N16 ☎ 7275 7557 🚆 Stoke Newington 🚌 73 🕒 Apr-Sept: 8am-dusk $ free ♿ good

Baker St Underground Station (6, C1) Has part of one of the original stations of the first underground train line (the Metropolitan Railway) that opened in 1863. It's on platform Nos 5 & 6 and was restored to its dimly lit former self in 1983.
✉ Baker St W1 ⊖ Baker Street 🕒 Mon-Sat 5.30am-midnight (from 7am Sun) $ £1.40/90p or Travelcard

Chelsea Physic Garden (5, H4)
This peaceful oasis, created by the Society of Apothecaries in 1673 to study the relationship of botany to medicine, is one of Europe's oldest botanical gardens.
✉ Swan Walk SW3 ☎ 7352 5646 ⊖ Sloane Square 🕒 Apr-Oct: Wed noon-5pm, Sun 2-6pm (Mon-Fri 12-5pm during Chelsea Flower Show) $ £4/2

Ham House (2, C2)
On the west side of Richmond Park, this 'Hampton Court in miniature' (and minus the crowds) was built in 1610. It's furnished with all the grandeur you might expect; the Great Staircase is a magnificent piece of Stuart woodworking. On display are Constable, Reynolds and Kneller paintings.
✉ Ham, Richmond, Surrey ☎ 8940 1950 ⊖ Richmond, then bus 371 🕒 Apr-Oct: Sat-Wed 1-5pm (house), 10.30am-6pm (garden) $ house: £5/2.50/12.50 a/c/f; garden: £1.50/75p/3.75 ♿ good

Museum of Gardening History (6, K8) This lovely place was inspired by the work of the 'Tradescants'. A father and son team and gardeners to the king, they roamed the globe, bringing back exotic plants including the pineapple. There's a 17th century replica knot garden – a formal garden of intricate design – in the small churchyard.
✉ St Mary-at-Lambeth Church, Lambeth Palace Rd SE1 ☎ 7401 8865 [e] www.museumgardenhistory.org ⊖ Lambeth North 🕒 Mon-Fri 10.30am-4pm, Sun 10.30am-5pm $ free ♿ good

Royal Geographical Society
The Queen Anne-style red-brick edifice (1874) is easily identified by the statues of explorers David Livingstone and Ernest Shackleton outside. Some exploring greats have used the reading room for map research.
✉ 1 Kensington Gore SW7 (5, F3) ☎ 7591 3040 ⊖ South Kensington 🕒 Mon-Fri 11am-5pm $ free ♿ good

Young's Ram Brewery (5, K3)
The place to head when you're 'museumed out' and want to digest history with a cup (or several) of good cheer.
✉ cnr Wandsworth High & Ram Sts SW18 ☎ 8875 7005 🚆 Wandsworth Town 🕒 Mon-Sat 10am-6pm; tours 10am, 12, 2 & 4pm $ £3.50/2/9 a/c/f

Londoners bask in the park at the first hint of sun.

QUIRKY LONDON

Beckton Alps Ski Centre (2, C4)
It's a *very* loose use of the term 'skiing', but you can slalom down a 200m slope made out of a substance that looks like the bottom of a bathmat here.
✉ **Alpine Way E6 ☎ 511 0351 ⊖ East Ham then bus 101 🚆 DLR Beckton 🕐 Sept-Apr: 10am-10pm, May-Aug: Fri-Tues 12-10pm $ £8.50 (2hrs)**

Castle Climbing Centre (2, B3)
It ain't Everest or even the Matterhorn but this is the UK's foremost climbing centre. For everyone from beginners to experienced climbers, it's uniquely located in an enormous neogothic castle.
✉ **Green Lanes N14 ☎ 8211 7000 ⊖ Manor House 🚌 171A or 141 🕐 Mon-Fri 2-10pm, Sat-Sun 10am-7pm $ £6/3.50 a/c**

London Dungeon (6, G13) Watch people hanging on the Tyburn gallows, listen to Anne Boleyn pleading her case before her head was so deftly separated from her soft narrow shoulders and observe St Thomas à Becket's murder. It's still all pretty scary stuff – especially the mock-ups of the Whitechapel back streets as Jack the Ripper knew them.
✉ **28-34 Tooley St SE1 ☎ 7403 0606 ⊖ London Bridge 🕐 10am-5.30pm (till 6.30pm Apr-June & 9pm July-Aug) $ £9.50/7.95/6.50 a/s,st/c ♿ good**

Eye in the Sky

Since its March 2000 opening, the 135m high **London Eye** observation wheel in the Jubilee Gardens (6, G8; ⊖ Waterloo or Embankment) has become one of the city's most popular attractions. Passengers enjoy fabulous views from capsules carrying up to 25 people. Book tickets for the 30min rides on ☎ 870 5000 600 (£7.95/6.45/5.45 a/s/c) or try the ticket office in the adjacent County Hall. The wheel turns from 9am to 10pm (Apr-Oct); 10am to 6pm (Nov-Mar). Check out [e] www.ba-londoneye.com for a preview of the view.

Museum of... (6, F10)
A new concept for a museum: quirky, changing exhibits that, among other things, focus on what everyday people amass. The Museum of Collectors exhibit featured different collections with items as varied as drinks cans and Dolly Parton memorabilia.
✉ **Bargehouse, Oxo Tower Wharf, Bargehouse St SE1 ☎ 7928 1255 ⊖ Waterloo or Blackfriars 🕐 Wed-Sun 12-6pm $ free ♿ good**

Shri Swaminarayan Mandir (2, C2)
For a quick trip to the Subcontinent without flying, go to this enormous *mandir*, or temple, an astonishing sight with its icing-sugar towers and pinnacles. Visit 9am-noon or 4-6pm when the *murtis*, the representations of gods and saints, are on view. Leave your shoes near the door and women should cover up.
✉ **105-115 Brentfield Rd NW10 ☎ 8965 2651 ⊖ Neasden or Stonebridge Park 🚆 Wembley Park and then bus PR2 🕐 9am-6pm $ free; exhibition centre £2/1.50 a/c ♿ good**

Vinopolis (6, G12)
A bizarre attraction in a country with little in the way of wine-making history and negligible amounts produced from its own vines. Located in a hectare of Victorian wine vaults in Bankside, it's an entertaining tour (literally) through the world of wine.
✉ **1 Bank End, Park Street SE1 ☎ 0870-444 4777 ⊖ London Bridge 🕐 10am-5.30pm $ £10 (£9 pre-booked); under 18s must be with an adult**

KEEPING FIT

Golf

Visitors can have a hit at **Brent Valley Golf Course** (2, C2), Church Rd, Cuckoo Lane W7 (☎ 8567 1287 ▣ Hanwell) or **Richmond Park Golf Course**, Roehampton Gate SW15 (2, C2; ☎ 8876 3205 ▣ Barnes).

Gyms

London is short on for places to work up a sweat. If your hotel doesn't have gym facilities (and most don't) try **Oasis Sports Centre** (6, E6), 32 Endell St WC2 (☎ 7831 1804 ⊖ Covent Garden), a popular and central sports centre with heated indoor and outdoor 25m pools, gymnasium facilities and squash courts for casual hire. A dip will cost you £2.80 and court hire is £3-5.50/30mns. Use of gym facilities requires a compulsory gym induction (£8.50 with use of fitness studio and pools; thereafter £5.20 per visit).

Horse Riding

Horses can be hired for £27/hr (riding lessons: £30/260 1hr/10hrs) from **Hyde Park Stables**, 63 Bathurst Mews W2 (5, E4; ☎ 7723 2813; ⊖ Lancaster Gate). **Mudchute Park Farm** (3, E2), Pier St E14 (☎ 7515 0749 ▣ DLR Mudchute) is another option and costs £18/16 a/c per/hr.

Pool, Spas & Baths

London once had many 'stews' or public baths (today's spas). Few survive today, but the ones that do are worth a visit. Try the Art Deco **Porchester Spa**, Queensway W2 (5, E3; ☎ 7792 3980 ⊖ Bayswater; £18.20 or £26 per couple). **Ironmonger Row Baths** (6, B12), Ironmonger Row EC1 (☎ 7253 4011 ⊖ Old St; £9.60/£5.70 mornings) is the closest London gets to a Turkish bath. Both have separate sessions for men, women and mixed; call for details.

Are you a Sport?
Sportsline (☎ 7222 8000) provides information on London's many sporting facilities.

Ooops

The city is full of places to swim; see the telephone directory for public pools or try Oasis (above). Hardy souls head for Hampstead Heath's ponds (☎ 7485 4491 ⊖ Hampstead Heath ▣ Gospel Oak). The east side **Highgate Ponds** (4, D4), open all year 7am-7pm, have one for men, one for women only and a summer only mixed pool. One of the **Hampstead Ponds** (4, E3), on west side of the heath, is open to all.

Tennis

Most London parks have courts; book in advance to secure a game. For a free *Where to Play Tennis in London* pamphlet, send stamped addressed envelope to: Lawn Tennis Association, Queen's Club, Palliser Rd W14 (☎ 7381 7000).

out & about

WALKING TOURS
Westminster Wander

Start at Prince Charles' residence, St James's Palace **(1)**. Skirt around its east side down Marlborough Rd and emerge in The Mall **(2)**, with Buckingham Palace **(3)** to the west (right). Cross into St James's Park **(4)** and follow the lake to its east end. Turn south (right) onto Horse Guards Rd, past the Cabinet War Rooms **(5)**.

Continue south and left into Great George St to Parliament Square and Westminster Abbey **(6)**. Across St Margaret St are the Houses of Parliament **(7)** with Clock Tower (AKA Big Ben) **(8)**. Refuel at the *Westminster Arms* **(9)** (☎ 7222 8520), west across the square at 9 Storey's Gate SW1.

SIGHTS & HIGHLIGHTS

Buckingham Palace (p. 15)
St James's Park (p. 41)
Cabinet War Rooms (p. 34)
Westminster Abbey (p. 33)
Houses of Parliament (p. 18)
Big Ben (p. 18)
Trafalgar Square
National Gallery (p. 25)
National Portrait Gallery (p. 36)
St Martin-in-the-Fields (p. 39)

From Parliament Square, walk north towards Whitehall (lined with the grand buildings of government departments). The ordinary-looking house to the left at No 10 Downing St **(10)** has accommodated UK prime ministers since 1732. Farther along on the east (right) is the Banqueting House **(11)**, the last remnant of the Tudor Whitehall Palace. Charles I, accused of treason by Cromwell, was executed outside the house on 30 Jan 1649.

Finally, you arrive in Trafalgar Square **(12)** with Nelson's Column **(13)** in the centre, the National Gallery **(14)** and National Portrait Gallery **(15)** to the north, St Martin-in-the-Fields **(16)** to the east and, to the south-west, Admiralty Arch **(17)**, erected for Queen Victoria in 1910.

distance 3.4km **duration** 3hrs
start ⊖ Green Park or Piccadilly Circus **end** ⊖ Charing Cross

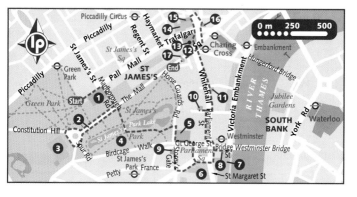

Docklands Dawdle

Begin at the Tower of London **(1)** and walk east under Tower Bridge **(2)** to St Katherine's Dock **(3)**, the first of London's docks to be renovated (in 1968). East along the river from the dock is Wapping **(4)**. Quiet

SIGHTS & HIGHLIGHTS

Tower of London (p. 31)
Tower Bridge
One Canada Square/Canary Wharf

St Katherine's Dock

cobbled Wapping High St leads south-east past Execution Dock **(5)** at Wapping New Stairs, where convicted pirates (including Captain William Kidd) were hanged and their bodies chained to a post at low tide.

Head north along Wapping Lane and across the Highway to St George-in-the-East **(6)**, designed by Hawksmoor in 1726. Cannon St Rd leads to Cable St, where ropes were once manufactured. Head east along Cable St to the town hall building **(7)**, which bears a mural marking the 1936 confrontation when British Fascist Blackshirts tried to intimidate the local Jewish population.

Enter the Limehouse **(8)** district by following Cable St east and north to Commercial Rd and Limehouse Rd. Current reminders of London's first Chinatown are limited to street names like Ming and Mandarin but take a noodle stop at *Old Friends* **(9)** (☎ 7790 5027), 659 Commercial Rd E14.

Follow Limehouse Rd east to West India Dock Rd, leading south to the Isle of Dogs **(10)**, which is dominated by Cesar Pelli's 500m steel and glass colossus One Canada Square **(11)** commonly known as Canary Wharf Tower.

Norman Foster's new Jubilee Line Canary Wharf Underground station **(12)** is another interesting example of modern design.

distance 6km **duration** 3½hrs
start ⊖ Tower Hill
end Ⓡ DLR Canary Wharf

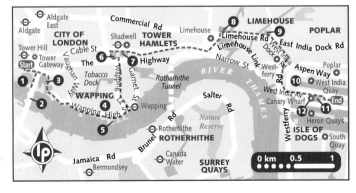

Fleet Street Footslog

Begin at Ludgate Circus and walk west along Fleet St; on the south side (left) is St Bride's **(1)**. Farther along on the north (right) side is an alleyway called the Wine Office Court leading to *Ye Olde Cheshire Cheese* pub **(2)**. Goldsmith wrote parts of *The Vicar of Wakefield* in house No. 6.

Continue west and turn north (right) into Johnson's Court, which leads to Dr Johnson's House **(3)**. A bit farther along Fleet St on the south side is *Ye Olde Cock Tavern* **(4)** at No 22, the oldest pub on Fleet St and a favourite of the good doctor, Pepys, Goldsmith, Dickens and TS Eliot. Opposite stands the octagonal St Dunstan-in-the-West **(5)** where the figures of Gog and Magog chime bells on the hour.

Prince Henry's Room **(6)** is at No 17 and beyond that an archway leads to Temple Church **(7)**. The griffin statue **(8)** in the centre of the street marks the site of the original Temple Bar, where the City of Westminster becomes the City of London and the Strand begins.

SIGHTS & HIGHLIGHTS

St Bride's (p. 39)
Ye Olde Cheshire Cheese pub (p. 72)
Dr Johnson's House (p. 38)
Prince Henry's Room (p. 37)
Temple Church (p. 39)
Royal Courts of Justice (p. 37)
Somerset House & Courtauld Gallery (p. 16)

There's some lovely architecture along the south side of the Strand, including the *Wig & Pen Club* **(9)** at No 229-230, the Law Courts branch of Lloyd's Bank a few doors west and, at No 216, Thomas Twinings **(10)**, operating since 1706. To the north is the extraordinary Royal Courts of Justice **(11)**. In middle of the road is St Clement Danes **(12)** where at 9am, noon, 3 and 6pm the bells chime 'Oranges and Lemons'. Farther west, again in the centre of the road, is St Mary-le-Strand **(13)**; the elegant building to the south-west is Somerset House **(14)** which houses the Courtauld Gallery and the Gilbert Collection.

distance 2.2km **duration** 2½hrs
start ⊖ Blackfriars
end ⊖ Temple

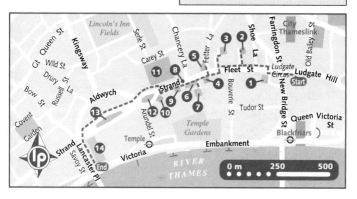

East End Amble

Emerging from the tube, have a look at the restored Liverpool St Station **(1)** and the modern Broadgate Centre **(2)**. Cross the road and walk north, turning east (right) on Brushfield St to covered Spitalfields Market **(3)**. On

SIGHTS & HIGHLIGHTS

Spitalfields Market (p. 60)
Brick Lane (p. 58)

Neil Setchfield

Commercial St farther east, opposite the market, is Christ Church, Spitalfields **(4)**, a magnificent baroque structure built for French Huguenot weavers in 1729 by Nicholas Hawksmoor; open Monday to Friday 12-2.30pm.

Continue east along Fournier St, admiring the fine wooden-shuttered Georgian houses. At the Brick Lane end is the New French Church **(5)**, also built for the Huguenots in 1743; in 1899 the church became a synagogue and later, in 1975, a mosque.

Brick Lane **(6)** is a wonderful mix of small curry houses and shops selling bright fabrics, spices and Islamic religious items. For a bite to eat and a drink, it's worth walking south along Brick Lane and turning west (right) onto Whitechapel High St. At No 80-82 the Whitechapel Art Gallery **(7)** (☎ 7522 7888) often shows daring contemporary exhibitions. A pleasant upstairs cafe opens Tues-Sun 11am-5pm. Walk eastward to Whitechapel Rd and to the Whitechapel Bell Foundry **(8)** (☎ 7247 2599) at No 32-34, where Big Ben and the Liberty Bell were cast (tour Saturday 10am).

Farther along at the corner of Cambridge Heath Rd is the famous *Blind Beggar* **(9)**, the pub where Ronnie Kray shot George Cornell in 1966 in a gang war over control of the East End's organised crime.

distance 2.6km **duration** 2hrs
start ⊖ Liverpool St
end ⊖ Whitechapel

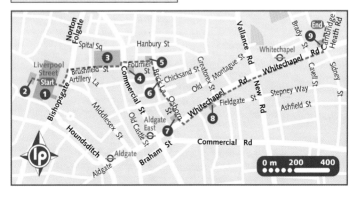

EXCURSIONS

Brighton (1, E2)

Brighton, with its heady mix of seediness and sophistication, is every Londoner's favourite seaside resort. The town's character essentially dates from the 1780s when the dissolute Prince Regent (later King George IV) built his outrageous summer palace, the Royal Pavilion, here for lavish parties by the sea. Brighton still has some of the hottest clubs and venues outside London, a vibrant student population, excellent shopping, a thriving arts scene, and great restaurants, pubs and cafes.

The **Royal Pavilion** is an extraordinary fantasy – all Indian palace on the outside and Chinese temple on the inside. Visit the Long Gallery, Banqueting Room, South Galleries, the superb Great Kitchen and Rex Whistler's humorous painting *HRH The Prince Regent Awakening the Spirit of Brighton* (1944).

INFORMATION

82km south of London

🚆 Victoria (40 fast trains a day), King's Cross, Blackfriars & London Bridge (slower Thameslink trains)

🚌 National Express

ℹ TIC, 10 Bartholomew Square ☎ 01273-292599; **Royal Pavilion** ☎ 01273-290900 🕒 Mon-Sun 10am-6pm (till 5pm Oct-May) £4.50/3.25/2.75/11.75 a/s,st/c/f ♿ good

🍴 *The Dorset Street Bar* 28 North Rd ☎ 01273-605423

Canterbury Cathedral (1, C5)

This magnificent cathedral (above right), is the successor to the church St Augustine built after he began converting the English to Christianity in 597. After the martyrdom of Archbishop Thomas à Becket in 1170, the cathedral became the focus for one of Europe's most important medieval pilgrimages, later immortalised by Chaucer in *The Canterbury Tales.* Today Canterbury is one of Britain's most impressive and evocative cathedrals and one of the country's World Heritage sites. The bustling city centre is atmospheric and alive.

INFORMATION

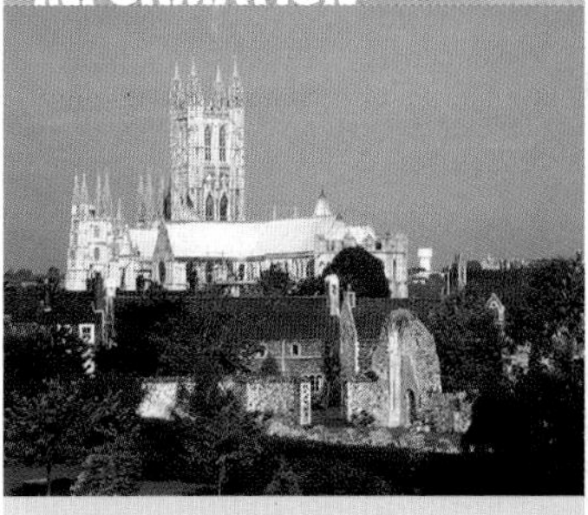

Dennis Johnson

90km east of London

🚆 90mn from Charing Cross, Victoria & Waterloo

🚌 National Express

[e] www.canterbury.co.uk

ℹ TIC, 34 St Margaret's St ☎ 01227-766567; guided 90mn town walks Mon-Sun 2pm Apr-Oct also at 11.30am Mon-Sat July-Aug; £3.50/3/8.50 a/s,st,c/f

🕒 Mon-Sat 9am-7pm (till 5pm Oct-Mar); Sun 12.30-2.30pm & 4.30-5.30pm; choral evensong Mon-Fri 5.30pm, Sat-Sun 3.15pm

$ £3/2/1 a/s,st/c; 1hr tours at 10.30am, noon & 2.30pm; £3/2/1.20 a/s,st/c; 30mn audioguide £2.95/1.95 a/c

🍴 *Il Vaticano* 33-35 St Margaret's St ☎ 01227-765333; *Flap Jacques* 71 Castle St ☎ 01227-781000

Cambridge   (1, A3)

The university at Cambridge was founded in the 13th century, several decades after Oxford. There is fierce rivalry between the 2 cities and universities, and an ongoing debate over which is best and most beautiful. If you have the time, you should visit both. If you've only time for one and the major colleges (St John's, Trinity, King's etc) are open, choose Cambridge. Oxford draws more tourists and can seem more like a provincial city. Cambridge's architectural treasure house makes it the foremost English university town. The 3 eight-week academic terms are Michaelmas (Oct-Dec), Lent (Jan-Mar) and Easter (Apr-June).

The **Fitzwilliam Museum** has an important collection of ancient Egyptian sarcophagi and Greek and Roman art in its lower galleries and a wide range of paintings upstairs.

INFORMATION

87km north of London
- 🚆 1hr; every 30mns from King's Cross; 1/hr from Liverpool St
- 🚌 National Express 2hrs
- 🌐 www.cambridge.gov.uk/leisure
- ℹ TIC, Wheeler St near Market Square ☎ 01223-322640, 2hr tours Mon-Sun 1.30pm, £6.50/4 a/c; **Fitzwilliam Museum** ☎ 01223-332923 Tues-Sat 10am-5pm, Sun 2.15-5pm, free, ♿ good
- ✗ Browns (☎ 01223-461655), 23 Trumpington St

TAKING A PUNT

Be sure to try your hand at that favourite of Cambridge pastimes: punting along the gentle River Cam. Hire boats are available from Trinity Punts (☎ 01223-338483) Garret Hostel, Lane Bridge (£7/hr, £25 deposit), or from Scudamore's (☎ 01223-359750) at Mill Lane (£10/hr, £50 deposit).

Punting along the 'Backs' – a fun, but we way to see college views and lush scenery

King's College and chapel (from 1446) – one of Europe's most sublime buildings

Jon Davison

Windsor Castle (1, C1)

Standing on chalk bluffs overlooking the Thames, Windsor Castle has been home to British royalty for over 900 years and is one of the greatest surviving medieval castles. Prime attractions are **St George's Chapel**, a fine example of late Gothic architecture and packed with the tombs of royalty (including those of George III and Henry

INFORMATION

37km west of London

🚆 Waterloo to Riverside Station, Paddington to Windsor Central Station

🚌 Green Line bus 700 or 702

☎ 01753-868286, 01753-831118

🌐 www.royal.gov.uk

ⓘ TIC 24 High St ☎ 01753-743900; Changing of the guard: Mon-Fri 11am May-June, even dates only in July; Guide Friday (☎ 01789-294466; www.guidefriday.com) town bus tours £6.50/5.50/2.50 a/s,st/c; French Brothers (☎ 01753-851900) 30mn boat trips £3.60/1.80 between Windsor and Runnymede. **Eton** (☎ 01753-671177) 2-4.30pm term hrs, 10.30am-4.30pm holiday hrs; guided tours: 2.15 & 3.15pm £3.80/3 a/c

🕐 10am-5.30pm; till 4pm Nov-Feb

💲 Mon-Sat £10/7.50/5/22.50 a/s/c/f, reduced prices when parts of the castle closed

✗ *Francesco's* (☎ 01753-863773), 53 Peascod St

♿ good; ☎ 01753-868286 extension 2235

VIII), and the **State Apartments**, now restored after having been partially destroyed by fire in 1992. Windsor Castle is the weekend residence of the royal family and parts of the castle may be closed off at that time, including St George's Chapel on Sunday.

A bonus to visiting Windsor is that just across the River Thames and within easy walking distance is **Eton College**, the celebrated public (meaning private) school that has educated no fewer than 18 prime ministers and now counts the princes William and Harry among its 1250-odd pupils.

Top: Windsor Castle
Below: 21st century Eton scholars

ORGANISED TOURS

TOUR GUIDES

Association of Professional Tourist Guides (Blue Guides)

La crème de la crème of British guides are the 900 knowledgeable members of the APTG who study for 2 years and sit both written and practical examinations before being awarded their coveted 'blue badge'. You can decide where you want to go and for how long or take advice from them. They're not cheap but it can be affordable if there's a number of you.
✉ **50 Southwark St SE1 (6, G12) ⊖ London Bridge ☎ 7171 4064 [e] www.touristguides.org.uk $ £81/121 half/full day**

BICYCLE TOURS

London Bicycle Tour Company

Cycle tours of the East End (Globe Theatre, Tower Bridge, Tobacco Dock, the East End proper, the City and St Paul's Cathedral) Sat 2pm; West End (Houses of Parliament, Lambeth Palace, Kensington and Chelsea, the Royal Albert Hall, Buckingham Palace, St James's, Trafalgar Square and Covent Garden) Sun 2pm; often the group elects a different routing altogether in consultation with the leader.
✉ **1a Gabriel's Wharf, 56 Upper Ground SE1 (6, F9) ⊖ Blackfriars ☎ 7928 6838 $ £11.95 (inc bike)**

BUS TOURS

Original London Sightseeing Tour

The best known of many London sightseeing bus companies, this one hits the main sights in double-decker buses, allowing you to hop on and off along the way and reboard the next bus. Convenient starting points are in Trafalgar Square, in front of Baker St Station next to Madame Tussaud's, on Haymarket south-east of Piccadilly Circus, and in Grosvenor Gardens opposite Victoria Station.
☎ 8877 1722 [e] www.TheOriginalTour.com $ £12/6 a/c

ON THE WATER

City Cruises

Operates a Pool of London jump-on, jump-off ferry service Apr-Oct (weekend only Nov-Mar) Tower Pier to London Bridge City Pier, *HMS Belfast*, Butlers Wharf and St Katherine's Pier in a continuous loop every 30mns from 11am-5pm. Also runs services between Tower and Westminster piers from 10.20am-5pm (to as late as 8.30pm June-Aug).
✉ **Tower Pier E1 (6, F14) ☎ 7237 5134 $ Pool of London: £2/1 a/s,c (valid all day); Tower-Westminster service: £4.60/2.30 one-way, £5.80/2.90 return**

Westminster Passenger Services Association

Cruise boats run east along the Thames from Westminster Pier to Greenwich, and west to Kew Gardens and Hampton Court Palace. They generally operate from between Mar/Apr to Sept/Oct – phone for exact schedules.
✉ **Westminster Pier SW1 (6, H7) ☎ 7930 4097 (eastward services); 7930 4721 (westward services) $ to/from Greenwich: £6/4.80/3.20/16.20 one-way a/s/c/f, return costs**

Guided Walks

These companies offer guided walks:

Capital Walks (☎ 8650 7640)
Historical Tours (☎ 8668 4019)
Original London Walks (☎ 7624 3978)
Mystery Walks of London (☎ 8558 9446)
Ripping Yarns (☎ 7488 2414)

Time Out's Around Town/Visitors section lists what's on offer. Some popular themes are Jack the Ripper tours and, inevitably, Princess Diana's London. Walks take about 2hrs and cost around £4.50/3.50 a/s,st.

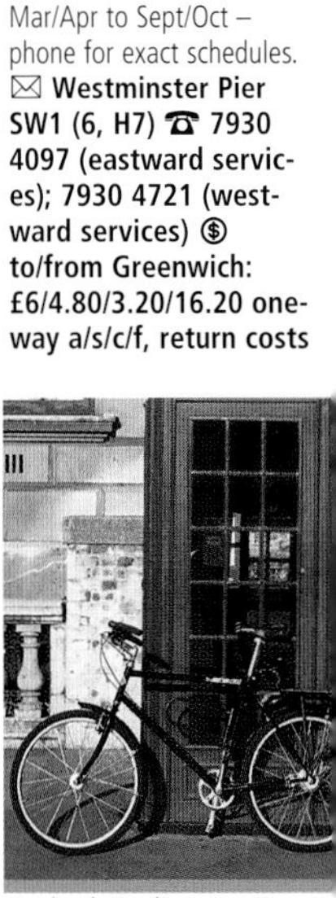

Parked, Parliament Square

£7.30/6/3.70/19.20; Kew: £6/5/3 one-way, £10/8/5 return; Hampton Court Palace £8/7/4 one-way, £12/10/7 return

Jenny Wren
Dinner (Tues-Sat 8pm-11pm) and Sunday lunch (1-3.30pm) canal cruises available aboard the *My Fair Lady.*
✉ **Waterside Café, 250 Camden High St NW1 (4, K4) ⊖ Camden Town ☎ 7485 4433 $ dinner cruise: £29.95; Sunday lunch cruise: £16.95**

London Waterbus Company
Boat trips lasting 80mns on Regent's Canal between Camden Lock and Little Venice, passing through London Zoo and Regent's Park on the way.
✉ **Middle Yard, Camden Lock NW1 (4, J4) & Warwick Crescent W2 (5, D3) ⊖ Camden Town & Warwick Ave ☎ 7482 2550 $ £3.80/2.40 one-way a/c, £5/3 return**

DAY TRIPS
Adventure Travel Centre
Organises Sunday coach trips specifically aimed at the Australasian market with trips usually taking in 2 destinations (eg Oxford and Blenheim Palace or Leeds Castle and Canterbury).
✉ **131 Earl's Court Rd SW5 (5, G2) ⊖ Earl's Court ☎ 7370 4555 $ £12**

Astral Tours
Mini-coach Magical Tours cover one or several of the following: Bath, the Cotswolds, Oxford, Brighton, Salisbury, Stonehenge, Avebury and Glastonbury. There's also a half-day tour to Windsor, Runnymede, Eton and Henley.
☎ 0700-078 1016 [e] www.astraltravels.co.uk $ day trip: £30-£42, includes all entry fees; half-day tour £20

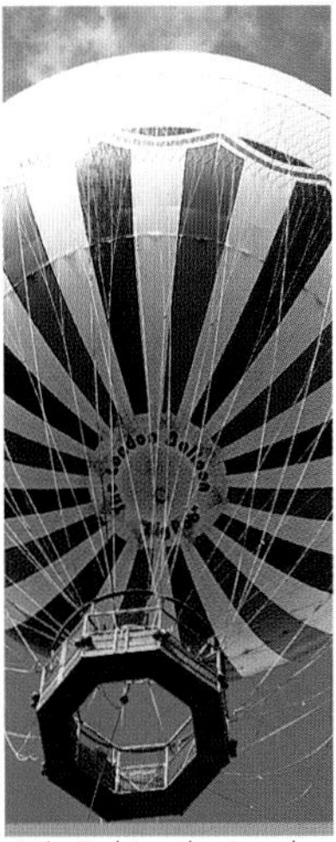
Charlotte Hindle

'Big Bob' – the London Balloon

Evan Evans Tours
Offers coach excursions with pick-ups from most large London hotels to a great number of destinations (eg Windsor, Windsor with Hampton Court Gardens, Oxford, Stratford, Bath and Stonehenge etc).
☎ 7950 1777 [e] www.evanevans.co.uk $ half-day trip to Windsor and Runnymede £25/22.50 a/c (includes admission to castle); to Leeds Castle £31.50/29

Not Quite Venice
London's 65km of inner-city canals, constructed in the early 19th century, are being given a new lease of life. Regent's Canal, looping around north London from Little Venice in Maida Vale to Camden Lock passing near London Zoo and Regent's Park, is a popular route for boating tour groups. British Waterways (☎ 7286 6101; www.british-waterways.co.uk) has a free *Explore London's Canals* pamphlet that lists 6 towpath walks.

UP, UP & AWAY
London Balloon (5, H7)
Takes you 170m off the ground and offers fabulous views of London and the Thames, but don't expect to get very far; the helium-filled balloon remains firmly tethered to the ground. Rides from 10am to dusk (to midnight Fri-Sun).
✉ **Spring Gardens, Kennington Lane SE11 ⊖ Vauxhall ☎ 0345-023842 $ £12/7.50/35 a/c/f**

Transport Information

National Express Bus Services	☎ 0990-808080
Green Line Bus Station	☎ 8668 7261
National Rail Enquiries	☎ 0345-484950

shopping

London is a mecca for shopaholics, and if you can't find it here, it probably doesn't exist. If you're looking for something with a British 'brand' on it, eschew the Union Jack-emblazoned kitsch of Carnaby and Oxford Sts – areas resting on past laurels rather than what they have to offer today – and go for what the Brits know are of good quality, sometimes stylish and always well-made: Dr Marten boots and shoes, Burberry raincoats and umbrellas, tailor-made shirts from Jermyn St and costume jewellery (be it for the finger, wrist, nose, eyebrow or navel). London's music stores and, especially, bookshops are celebrated on the street and in literature; many cater for the most obscure of tastes. And the world 'antique' does not always have to be prefaced by 'priceless'; you'll find any number of affordable curios and baubles at London's 350 markets.

Shopping Areas

Although most things can be bought throughout London, a trip to the **West End** makes for particularly good shopping. **Covent Garden**, the vegetable market of the West End for 150 years, was redeveloped in the 1980s; the twee shops and stalls inside the old market building tend to be pricey and tourist-oriented. Luckily the nearby streets, Neal Street and Neal's Yard in particular, remain a happy hunting ground for seekers of designer and/or street clothing and footwear, funky gifts and homewares and natural therapy products.

Oxford St can be a great disappointment. Selfridges is up there

> ### West End Buys
> Some streets have particular specialities:
>
> **Tottenham Court Rd** – electronics and computer shops
> **Charing Cross Rd** – a book worm's delight
> **Cecil Court** – antiquarian bookshops
> **Denmark St** – musical instruments, sheet music, books about music
> **Hanway St** – used records

with Harrods as a place to visit; Peter Jones' sister store, John Lewis, makes the same claim to unbeatable prices; and the flagship Marks & Spencer at the Marble Arch end has its fans. But the farther east you go, the tackier and less interesting it gets. Regent St, with Liberty and Hamleys, is much more upmarket. For streetwear **High St Kensington** and the **King's Road** are a good alternatives to Oxford St. Any international designer – from the Italians and French to the Japanese – worth his or her threads has at least one outlet in London, usually in Sloane or Bond Sts or in **Knightsbridge**. In **the City** check out the lovely boutiques in Bow Lane, between Cheapside and Cannon St.

Juliet Coombe

Portobello Market wares tickle many a fancy.

DEPARTMENT STORES

Some London department stores are tourist attractions in their own right; few visitors leave without popping into Harrods and Fortnum & Mason, even if only to browse. And the cult TV series *Absolutely Fabulous* has made Harvey Nichols (or 'Harvey Nicks') another must-see attraction.

Fortnum & Mason
(6, G4) Noted for its exotic, old-world food hall on the ground floor, it also has plenty of fashion on the next 4 floors. All kinds of unusual foodstuffs can be purchased here along with the famous food hampers. This is where Scott stocked up before heading off for the Antarctic.
✉ **181 Piccadilly W1**
☎ **7734 8040**
✪ **Piccadilly Circus** ⊙ **Mon-Sat 9.30am-6pm**

Harrods (5, G4)
This celebrated store is truly unique: it can even lay claim to having installed the world's first escalator in 1898. There are the down sides – it's always crowded, there are more rules than an army boot camp and it's hard to find what you're after. But the toilets are fab, the food halls will make you swoon,

and if they haven't got it, it ain't worth having.
✉ **87-135 Brompton Rd SW1** ☎ **7730 1234**
✪ **Knightsbridge**
⊙ **Mon-Sat 10am-6pm (Wed-Fri till 7pm)**

Harvey Nichols
(6, H1) The city's heart of high fashion has a great 5th floor food hall and an extravagant perfume department and jewellery to save up for. All the big names are here, from Miyake to Lauren, Hamnett to Calvin Klein and there's a whole floor of up-to-the-minute menswear.
✉ **109-125 Knightsbridge SW1**
☎ **7235 5000**
✪ **Knightsbridge**
⊙ **Mon-Sat 10am-7pm (Wed-Thurs till 8pm), Sun 12pm-6pm**

John Lewis (6, E3)
This London institution, part of the same group as Peter Jones, is the place to know about if you're planning the sort of extended stay that requires stocking up on household goods. John Lewis' motto – 'Never knowingly under-sold' – is not just hype; buy something and find it cheaper elsewhere and they'll make up the difference.
✉ **278-306 Oxford St W1** ☎ **7629 7711**
✪ **Oxford Circus** ⊙ **Mon-Wed & Fri 9.30am-6pm, Thurs 10am-8pm, Sat 9am-6pm**

Liberty (6, E4)
Almost as unique and with as much history as Harrods, Liberty was born out of the Arts and Crafts Movement, and in Italy Art Nouveau is still called *Stile Liberty*. It has high fashion, fab modern furniture, super luxury fabrics and those inimitable Liberty silk scarves.
✉ **214-220 Regent St W1** ☎ **7734 1234**
✪ **Oxford Circus**
⊙ **Mon-Sat 10am-6.30pm (Thurs till 7.30pm), Sun 12-6pm**

Sales

The biannual sales at London's department stores, when every tourist, London resident *and* their grandmothers seem to be queuing up outside Harrods or some other big shop, take place in January and July.

Marks & Spencer
M&S is almost as British as fish & chips and warm beer. It has the full range of fashion goods, but most people shop here for underwear, well-made affordable clothes and ready-made meals.
✉ **458 Oxford St W1 (6, E2)** ☎ **7935 7954**
✪ **Bond St or Marble Arch** ⊙ **Mon-Fri 9am-8pm, Sat 9am-7pm, Sun 12-6pm**

rrods' hallowed retail halls

VAT

Value-added tax (VAT) is a 17.5% sales tax levied on most goods and services in Britain. If you're not an EU citizen, it's sometimes possible to get a VAT refund on goods you take home with you. Not all shops participate in the refund scheme, and minimum-purchase conditions vary (normally around £75). Ask for details when making a purchase.

Peter Jones (5, G5)
Due to its posh locale and more well-heeled clientele than sister-store John Lewis, it's been described as the 'best corner shop in Chelsea' (a term unbefitting the huge range of goods on sale). The store label Jonelle is great value.

✉ **Sloane Square SW1**
☎ **7730 3434**
⊖ **Sloane Square**
◷ **Mon-Sat 9.30am-6pm (Wed till 7pm)**

Selfridges (6, E2)
Arguably the grandest shop on Oxford St, it's undergone a major renovation.

Come here for food halls much less confusing, cramped and crowded than those at Harrods.
✉ **400 Oxford St W1**
☎ **7629 1234** ⊖ **Bond St** ◷ **Mon-Fri 10am-7pm (Thurs-Fri till 8pm), Sat 9.30am-7pm, Sun 12-6pm**

Harrods' horse & cart

MARKETS

Bermondsey Market
This is the place to come if you're after old opera glasses, bowling balls, hat pins, costume jewellery, porcelain or any other 'antique'. The main market on Friday takes place outdoors on the square although adjacent warehouses shelter the more vulnerable furnishings and bric-a-brac and are open throughout the week. Tower Bridge Rd is another good street to check out; the **Old Cinema Antique Warehouse** (☎ 7407 5371) at No 157 specialises in Victoriana.
✉ **Bermondsey Square, junction of Long Lane and Bermondsey St SE1** (6, H14) ☎ **7351 5353** ⊖ **Borough** ◷ **Fri 4am-2pm**

Brick Lane Market
A few streets east of Petticoat Lane and Spitalfields markets (p. 60),

is Brick Lane, home to the East End's Bangladeshi community. On Sundays, activity spreads out along Bethnal Green Rd to the north and there's a mix of stalls selling clothes, fruit and vegetables, household goods, paintings, bric-a-brac and junk.
✉ **Brick Lane E1 (6, C15)** ⊖ **Shoreditch or Aldgate East** ◷ **Sun 8am-2pm**

Brixton Market (5, K8)
Brixton Market is a cosmopolitan treat that mixes everything from the Body Shop and reggae music to slick Muslim preachers, South American butcher shops and exotic fruits. In Electric Ave and the covered Granville Arcade you can buy wigs, unusual foods like tilapia fish and Ghanaian eggs (really a type of vegetable), unusual spices and homeopathic root cures.
✉ **Brixton Market SW9**

⊖ **Brixton** ◷ **Mon-Sat 8am-5.30pm (Wed till 1pm)**

Camden Market
(4, J4) To see Camden Market at its most lively, visit on a weekend, although most days there'll be some stalls open. This massive market comprises several markets, including the Electric Market housed in an old ballroom; the Camden Canal Market selling bric-a-brac from around the world; Camden Market itself, which houses stalls for fashion, clothing and jewellery; and the Stables, the northernmost part of the market, where it is possible to snap up antiques, Asiania, rugs and carpets, pine furniture and all manner of retro clothing.
✉ **Camden High St & Chalk Farm Rd NW1** ⊖ **Camden Town** ◷ **Sat-Sun 8am-6pm**

Camden Passage

This cavern of almost 3 dozen antique shops and stalls in Islington has nothing to do with Camden Market. The stalls sell pretty much everything to which the moniker 'antique' or 'curio' could reasonably be applied, and the stall holders know their stuff, so real bargains are few and far between. (Psssst! Camden Passage is *the* place to come to spot British and American stars of stage and screen; Sophia Loren and Sylvester Stallone have been seen haggling with stallholders over gewgaws.)
✉ **Upper St & Essex Rd N1 (5, C8)** ☎ **7359 9969** ⊖ **Angel** ⊘ **Wed 7.30am-2pm, Sat 7.30am-5pm; secondhand books Thurs 7am-4pm**

Columbia Rd Flower Market

A stroll along Columbia Rd is a fun way to spend a Sunday morning and, along with the flower and plant

Camden Market: a great place to bag some boots

To market, to market. . .

Other interesting markets close to central London are:

Berwick St (6, E5) – fruit and vegetables

Billingsgate (2, C4) – wholesale fish market (🚈 DLR West India Quay)

Borough (6, G13) – general produce, English farm cheeses, specialist sausages and pastries

Leather Lane (6, D9) – cheap videos, tapes and CDs, household goods and clothing

Ridley Rd (5, A10) – Caribbean/African/Turkish/Jewish fare

Roman Rd Market (2, C4) – famous for discount fashion clothes (⊖ Bow Road)

The London Market Guide (£3.99), by Andrew Kershman has the lowdown on London's markets, including those smaller and hard-to-get-to ones.

---

stalls, a couple of arty shops open their doors.
✉ **Columbia Rd E2 (6, A15)** ⊖ **Bethnal Green** 🚈 **Cambridge Heath** 🚌 **26, 48 or 55** ⊘ **Sun 8am-2pm**

Covent Garden (6,F7)

While the shops in the Covent Garden Piazza are open daily, several markets also take place here. The best is the Apple Market (☎ 7240 7405) in the North Hall with quality crafts Tues-Sun 10.30am-7pm. On Monday there's an antiques and bric-a-brac market here and also on the south side of the Piazza in Jubilee Hall (which is full of schlock for the rest of the week).
✉ **Covent Garden Piazza WC2** ⊖ **Covent Garden** ⊘ **Apple Market: Mon 5am-7pm, Tues-Sun 10.30am-7pm; Jubilee Hall Market: Mon 9am-6pm**

Greenwich Market

(3, H2) This is a great place to look for decorated glass, rugs, prints, wooden

---

toys and other craft items. There's also antiques and curios on Thursday. South of Church St and opposite St Alfege Church , there's the small Village Market Antiques Centre, with the obligatory mix: second-hand clothes, handmade jewellery, plants and household bric-a-brac.
✉ **King William Walk & Greenwich Church St SE10** 🚈 **DLR: Cutty Sark** ⊘ **Thurs-Sun 9.30am-5.30pm**

Leadenhall Market

(6, E14) The Market sells food and drink as well as fresh fish, meat and cheese to busy City folk. The selection is excellent for an urban market, and you're in good company; Robinson Crusoe stocked up here before running away to sea. The Victorian glass-and-iron market hall, designed by Horace Jones in 1881, is an architectural delight.
✉ **Whittington Ave off Gracechurch St EC1** ⊖ **Bank** ⊘ **Mon-Fri 7am-4pm**

Pocket a watch at Portobello Market.

Petticoat Lane Market (6, D15)

Petticoat Lane is east London's long-established market on Middlesex St (the border of the City and Whitechapel). These days, it's full of run-of-the-mill trash, with faintly bemused tourists struggling to get past locals sifting through the stalls of cheap T-shirts and underwear.

✉ **Middlesex St E1** ⊖ **Aldgate, Aldgate East or Liverpool St** ⏱ **Sun 8am-2pm**

Portobello Rd Market (5, E1)

After Camden, this is London's most famous (and crowded) weekend street market. Starting at Notting Hill Gate, it wends its way to the Westway flyover in Ladbroke Grove. Antiques, handmade jewellery, paintings and ethnic stuff are concentrated at the Notting Hill Gate end. West to Elgin Crescent and east to Colville Terrace the stalls dip downmarket, selling fruit and veg, second-hand clothing, cheap household goods and general junk. Beneath the Westway are more stalls selling cheap clothes, shoes and CDs. Portobello Green arcade is home to some cutting-edge clothes and jewellery designers, plus bric-a-brac on Friday and Saturday.

✉ **Portobello Rd W10 & W11** ☎ **7727 7684** ⊖ **Notting Hill Gate, Ladbroke Grove or Westbourne Park** ⏱ **Sat 6am-5pm (antiques), Sun 6am-2pm (Portobello Green flea market)**

Smithfield Market (6, D10)

Smithfield is central London's last surviving meat market and would be a vision of hell itself for vegetarians. The eastern end has been wonderfully

Frames for famous 'four-eyes', Portobello Market

restored to its 1868 original design (by Horace Jones of Leadenhall Market and Tower Bridge fame). But it remains to be seen whether the meat market can hang in here or whether it will be forced out like the original Billingsgate fish and the Covent Garden fruit and vegetable markets.

✉ **West Smithfield EC1** ⊖ **Farringdon** ⏱ **Mon-Fri 3-9am**

Spitalfields Market (6, C15)

More interesting than Brick Lane Market is Spitalfields, a large market housed in a huge covered Victorian warehouse. There's a great mix of arts and crafts, organic fruit and veg, stylish new and retro clothes, and second-hand books. Interesting many-cultured shops ring the central area; a football pitch and children's model railway keep those non-shoppers entertained.

✉ **Between Bishopsgate & Commercial St E1** ☎ **7247 6590** ⊖ **Liverpool St** ⏱ **Sun 9.30am-5.30pm**

Fruit and vegetables from the 'barrow', Brixton Market

ARTS & ANTIQUES

Antique and artisan piece hunters may find something worthwhile at the Saturday antiques market along Portobello Rd, but better pickings are to be had at Camden Passage and Bermondsey Market (p. 58-9).

Antiquarius Antiques Centre

The Antiquarius Antiques Centre is packed with 120 stalls selling everything from top hats and ancient corkscrews to old luggage and jewellery. It's definitely worth a fossick.
✉ **131-141 King's Rd SW3 (5, H4)** ☎ **7351 5353** ⊖ **Sloane Square** ⊘ **Mon-Sat 10am-6pm**

Chelsea Old Town Hall

This solid pile built in 1886 hosts one of the most popular antiques fairs in London. Call or check website for exact dates
✉ **Chelsea Old Town Hall, King's Rd SW3 (5, J3)** ☎ **01225-723 094** ⓔ **www.antiques-web .co.uk\mainwaring's -chelsea-fairs** ⊖ **Sloane Square** ⊘ **one Sun per month 11am-5.30pm**

London Architectural Salvage & Supply Company

LASSCo is a recycler's dream come true, with everything from slate tiles and oak floorboards to enormous marble fireplaces and garden follies – along with much smaller curios – available. Its location, in an old church, is worth the trip alone.
✉ **St Michael's Church, Mark St EC2 (6, B14)** ☎ **7739 0448** ⊖ **Old St** ⊘ **10am-5pm**

London Silver Vaults

The 72 subterranean shops in Chancery House, collectively known as the London Silver Vaults, is the largest collection of silver under 1 roof in the world. The shops sell anything that is precious metal – from jewellery and picture frames to candelabra and tea services. Though everything is on sale, you might just want to ogle at some of the merchandise – much of it seriously over the top – and wonder which stately home it came from. Silver marks posted in the corridors will help; London's has been the uncrowned leopard since 1821.
✉ **Chancery House, 53-63 Chancery Lane WC2 (6, D9)** ☎ **7242 3844** ⊖ **Chancery Lane** ⊘ **Mon-Fri 9am-5.30pm, Sat 9am-1pm**

Sean Arnold Sporting Antiques

This is the place to come for pricey toys for grown-up boys and girls.
✉ **21-22 Chepstow Corner W2 (5, E2)** ☎ **7221 2267** ⊖ **Bayswater** ⊘ **Mon-Sat 10am-6pm**

Ceramic figurine, Village Market Antiques Centre, Greenwich Market

Once, twice, SOLD!

Fancy a spot of upmarket shopping without the predictability of fixed price tags? Pop into one of London's auction houses, those household-name powerhouses where van Goghs routinely change hands for zillions of pounds, but where sales of more affordable ephemera also take place. The best known ones are:

Bonhams Montpelier St SW7 (5, G3) ☎ 7393 3900 ⊖ Knightsbridge
Christie's 8 King St SW1 (5, G4) ☎ 7839 9060 ⊖ Green Park or Piccadilly Circus
Phillips 7 Blenheim St, off New Bond St W1 (6, F3) ☎ 7629 6602 ⊖ Bond St
Sotheby's 34-35 New Bond St W1 (6, F3) ☎ 7493 8080 ⊖ Bond St

CLOTHING & JEWELLERY

Singlets for patriots

DESIGNER FASHION

Nicole Farhi
Smart and classic Farhi knitwear, suits and dresses are snapped up by working women for the beautiful fabrics used and attention given to comfort. Samples, seconds and last season's designs branch at 75-83 Fairfield Rd E3 (2, C4) ☎ 7399 7000 ⊖ Bow Rd.
✉ **158 New Bond St W1 (6, E3) ☎ 7499 8368**

⊖ **Bond St** ⏲ **Mon-Sat 10am-6pm (till 7pm Thurs, 6.30pm Sat)**

Paul Smith
The name might be banal, but the clothes are far from it. Cleverly cut and very wearable men's and women's lines have made Smith one of the most sought after Brit designers.
✉ **40-44 Floral St WC2 (7, C7) ☎ 7379 7133**
⊖ **Covent Garden**
⏲ **Mon-Sat 10.30am-6.30pm (Thurs till 7pm)**

Red or Dead
Check out their flash-trash shoes which can be bought for a fraction of the price of a pair of Manolo Blahniks. Lots of cool clothes for chics and chaps.
33 Neal St WC21 (7, B7) ☎ 7379 7571
⊖ **Covent Garden**
⏲ **Mon-Fri 10.30am-7pm, Sat 10am-6.30pm, Sun 12-5.30pm**

Vivienne Westwood
Longevity has not tamed the unpredictable offerings of punk's grandmother. Branches at 430 King's Rd SW10 (☎ 7352 6551) and 44 Conduit St (☎ 7439 1109).
✉ **6 Davies St W1 (6, E3) ☎ 7629 3757**
⊖ **Bond St** ⏲ **Mon-Sat 10am-6pm (till 7pm Thurs)**

STREET FASHION & RETRO

CM Store
Cutting-edge young designers cram this warehouse. It stocks fetish, leather boots, lace-up tops etc.
✉ **121 King's Rd SW3 (5, H4) ☎ 7351 9361**
⊖ **Sloane Square**
⏲ **Mon-Sat 10am-7pm, Sun 12-6pm**

Hype Designer Forum
This large emporium is crammed with street fashion by struggling young designers who are more than a little keen to sell their imaginative glad rags.
✉ **46-52 Kensington High St W8 (5, G2) ☎ 7938 3801** ⊖ **High Street Kensington**
⏲ **Mon-Sat 10am-6pm (Thurs & Sat till 6.30pm, Fri till 8pm), Sun 12-6pm**

Kensington Market
(5, G2) Three-storeys and something of a dinosaur and a hot, sticky shambles in summer, this place is still a lot of fun. More leather and patchouli oil than high fashion – more 60s than 00s – it's the place to come for second-hand Levis, army jackets, chain-mail bikinis, hand-made jewellery and Gothic gear. Be warned: the market

---

Britpack
Watch out for hip British designers like Alexander McQueen, Tracey Mulligan, Antonio Beradi, Andrew Groves, Bruce Oldfield and Lisa Bruce, who like to mix formal design with hip streetware. The following designer shops are always windowshoppable even if you can't afford their fripperies:

Amanda Wakeley 80 Fulham Rd SW3 (5, H3)
☎ 7584 4009 ⊖ South Kensington
Betty Jackson 311 Brompton Rd SW3 (5, H3)
☎ 7589 7884 ⊖ South Kensington
Katherine Hamnett 20 Sloane St SW1 (5, G5)
☎ 7823 1002 ⊖ Knightsbridge
Paul Costelloe 156 Brompton Rd SW3 (5, G4)
☎ 7589 9480 ⊖ Knightsbridge

New jewellery designs are showcased at Janet Fitch.

faces an uncertain future.
✉ **49-53 Kensington High St W8** ☎ **7938 4343** ⊖ **High Street Kensington** ☼ **Mon-Sat 10am-6pm**

TRADITIONAL APPAREL
Burberry
This is the place to come for that most London of articles of accessories – the raincoat. Burberry also has a factory outlet in the East End at 29-53 Chatham Place E9 (☎ 8985 3344; 🚇 Hackney Central).
✉ **18-22 Haymarket SW1 (6, F5)** ☎ **7930 3343** ⊖ **Piccadilly Circus** ☼ **Mon-Sat 10am-6pm (Thurs till 7pm), Sun 12-6pm**

James Smith & Sons
No one, but no one, makes and stocks umbrellas (along with canes and walking sticks) like James Smith & Sons; the shop's exterior is a museum piece.
✉ **53 New Oxford St WC1 (6, D6)** ☎ **7836 4731** ⊖ **Tottenham Court Road** ☼ **Mon-Fri 9.30am-5.30pm, Sat 10am-5.30pm**

JEWELLERY
Asprey & Garrard
For the kind of trinkets that you'll need to win the lottery to afford, this is the place to come and you'll be in good company; Asprey & Garrard (well, the second half anyway) has been the Crown Jewellers since 1843.
✉ **165-169 New Bond St W1 (6, E3)** ☎ **7734 7020** ⊖ **Green Park** ☼ **Mon-Sat 9.30am-5.30pm**

Janet Fitch
For more up-to-date baubles, try Janet Fitch, a chain of shops showcasing the best of young British jewellery designers. Other branches in Covent Garden and in King's Rd, Chelsea.
✉ **25A Old Compton St W1 (6, E5)** ☎ **01932-**

> ## Crown Jewels
> For common or garden variety jewellery, try any of the markets, or stalls in the main-line stations. If it's classic (read old-fashioned) settings and unmounted stones you want, stroll along Hatton Garden EC1 (6, C9; ⊖ Chancery Lane); it's chock-a-block with gold, diamond and jewellery shops.

866449 ⊖ **Tottenham Court Road** ☼ **Mon-Sat 11am-7pm, Sun 12-6pm**

Into You
If you want to fill in your holes (the man-made ones anyway), Into You can oblige, with lots of interesting body jewellery. They body-pierce and tattoo too.
✉ **144 St John St EC1 (6, C10)** ☎ **7253 5085** ⊖ **Farringdon** ☼ **Tues-Fri 12-7pm, Sat 12-6pm**

Retro kitsch and cool collectibles, Portobello Market

Juliet Coombe

FOOD & DRINK

Run-of-the-mill food shops are 10 a penny all over London, but the food halls at Harrods and Fortnum & Mason (see p. 57) are attractions in themselves. It's also worth tracking down some of the more specialist stores for savoury and sweet treats.

Algerian Coffee Stores

The Algerian Coffee Stores is *the* place to go to buy all sorts of teas and coffees, including Maragogype, the biggest coffee bean in the world.
✉ **52 Old Compton St W1 (6, E5)** ☎ **7437 2480** ✚ **Leicester Square** ☺ **Mon-Sat 9am-7pm**

Rococo

Chocoholics will have a gobble-fest in this Chelsea shop – with everything from lowly British Cadbury to Belgian Godiva and French Valrhona cooking chocolate available.
✉ **321 King's Rd SW3 (5, H4)** ☎ **7352 5857** ✚ **Sloane Square** ☺. **Mon-Sat 10am-6.30pm, Sun 12-5pm**

Oil & Spices Shop

The Oil & Spices Shop has the delightful aroma of a Middle Eastern bazaar and a dazzling array of oils in beautifully shaped bottles. It's part of the Le Pont de la Tour complex, which also incorporates a gourmet food and wine shop.
✉ **Butler's Wharf, Shad Thames SE1 (6, G15)** ☎ **7403 4030** ✚ **Tower Bridge** ☺ **12-6pm**

Simply Sausages

This place in the Berwick St fruit and veg market is a great place to stock up for a barbecue or picnic. Among the many sausages on sale are ones made with duck, black cherry and port, Thai sausages and vegetarian mushroom and tarragon sausages. There's a branch in Smithfield Market at 341 Central Markets (p. 60).
✉ **93 Berwick St W1 (6, E5)** ☎ **7287 3482** ✚ **Oxford Circus** ☺ **Mon-Fri 8am-6pm, Sat 9.30am-1.30pm**

The Tea House

The Tea House has a great range of teas (60 varieties) plus the pots to brew them in and all sorts of associated paraphernalia.
✉ **15 Neal St WC2 (7, B6)** ☎ **7240 7539** ✚ **Covent Garden** ☺ **Mon-Sat 10am-7pm, Sun 12-6pm**

Paxton & Whitfield has the cheese to please.

Lee Foster

Say Cheese

While having nowhere near reputation of the French variety, UK cheese has its moments in the hard varieties like Cheddar and Cheshire and crumbly to soft cheeses like Wensleydale and Stilton. In London cheese nibblers should visit:

Neal's Yard Dairy 17 Shorts Gardens WC2 (7, B6) ☎ 7379 7646) ✚ Covent Garden – has the more esoteric British cheeses and helpful, enthusiastic staff
Paxton & Whitfield 93 Jermyn St SW1 (6, F5) ☎ 7930 0259) ✚ Piccadilly Circus – London's oldest cheesemonger claims to stock 200 different varieties and specialises in English hard cheese
The International Cheese Centre 21 Goodge St W1 (6, D5) ☎ 7631 4191 ✚ Goodge Street – 100s of varieties, including vegetarian and organic selections

MUSIC

The West End has several mega-sized music shops with the largest collections of CDs and tapes in London. There's also a number of smaller shops selling used records in Denmark St (7, 5A) and Hanway St (7, A4).

HMV Records (6, D4)
HMV is great for special orders, classical music and specialist categories, although the store can get very loud and crowded.
✉ 150 Oxford St W1
☎ 7631 3423 ⊖ Oxford Circus ◷ Mon-Fri 9.30am-8pm, Sat 9am-7.30pm, Sun 12-6pm

Tower Records
(6, F5) You can't miss Tower Records on Piccadilly Circus and it stays open later than any of the standard-fare CD and tape shops. Its jazz, world music and soundtrack sections are pretty good, but overall it's hectic and difficult to negotiate.
✉ 1 Piccadilly Circus W1 ☎ 7439 2500
⊖ Piccadilly Circus ◷ Mon-Sat 9am-midnight, Sun 12-6pm

Virgin Megastore
(6, D5) This is by far the most pleasant and relaxed of the giant trio. The layout is a tad bewildering, but it's worth persevering for some excellent bargains.
✉ 14-30 Oxford St W1
☎ 7631 1234
⊖ Tottenham Court Road ◷ Mon-Sat 9am-9pm, Sun 12-6pm

Black Market
This is where DJ wannabes go when looking for club dance music.
✉ 25 D'Arblay St W1 (7, B4) ☎ 7437 0478
⊖ Oxford Circus ◷ Mon-Sat 11am-7pm

Jungle or Jazz? You'll find it all in London's record shops.

Honest Jon's
Honest Jon's is where you'll find reggae, soul and rap and almost any genre of black music.
✉ 278 Portobello Rd W10 (5, E1) ☎ 8969 9822 ⊖ Ladbroke Grove ◷ Mon-Sat 10am-6pm, Sun 11am-5pm

Mole Jazz
Two floors of vinyl, tapes and CDs – all of it jazz in its many variations.
✉ 311 Gray's Inn Rd WC1 (6, A7) ☎ 7278 8623 ⊖ King's Cross ◷ Mon-Thurs & Sat 10am-6pm, Fri 10am-8pm

On the Beat
The place for the serious record collector; all styles and genres are on offer.
✉ 22 Hanway St W1 (7, A5) ☎ 7637 8934
⊖ Tottenham Court Road ◷ Mon-Sat 11am-7pm

Ray's Jazz Shop
Ray's has both rare and recent jazz, and the staff are helpful and knowledgeable.
✉ 180 Shaftesbury

Ave WC2 (6, E6)
☎ 7240 3969
⊖ Tottenham Court Road ◷ Mon-Sat 10am-6.30pm

Rough Trade
This famous punk music stockist has as much indie and obscure music as you'd care to listen to.
✉ 130 Talbot Rd W11 (5, E1) ☎ 7229 8541
⊖ Ladbroke Grove or Notting Hill Gate ◷ Mon-Sat 10am-6.30pm

Reckless Records
These 2 shops are crammed with quality mainstream and used records and CDs.
✉ 26 & 30 Berwick St W1 (7, B4) ☎ 7437 4271 ⊖ Oxford Circus ◷ 10am-7pm

Trax
Serious dance music attracts a switched-on, hip crowd.
✉ 55 Greek St W1 (7, B5) ☎ 7734 0795 ⊖ Tottenham Court Road ◷ Mon-Thurs 12-7pm, Fri 11am-9pm, Sat 11am-7pm

BOOKS

For those who read the book or saw the movie *84 Charing Cross Rd*, the road in question will need no introduction; this is where to go when you want reading material old or new. But it certainly isn't the only place to find general or specialist book shops.

GENERAL

Borders
This big branch of the American chain close to Oxford Circus has 3 floors of books, magazines and newspapers from around the world and a coffee shop/bar in which to read them. There's a smaller branch at 120 Charing Cross Rd WC2 (6, E6; ⊖ Tottenham Court Road).
✉ **203 Oxford St W1 (6, E4)** ☎ **7292 1600** ⊖ **Oxford Circus** ⏲ **Mon-Sat 8am-11pm, Sun 12-6pm**

Foyle's
Foyle's is the biggest and by far the messiest and most confusing bookshop in London, but it often stocks titles you may not find elsewhere.
✉ **113-119 Charing Cross Rd WC2 (6, E6)** ☎ **7437 5660**

⊖ **Tottenham Court Road** ⏲ **Mon-Sat 9am-6pm (Thurs till 7pm)**

Waterstone's
The Waterstone's chain's many stores are well stocked, and the helpful staff are knowledgeable. Also at 82 Gower St WC1 (6, B5; ⊖ Goodge Street) and the mega-branch, Europe's biggest bookstore, at 203-206 Piccadilly (7, E4; ⊖ Piccadilly Circus).
✉ **121-129 Charing Cross Rd WC2 (6, E6)** ☎ **7434 4291** ⊖ **Tottenham Court Road** ⏲ **Mon-Sat 9.30am-8pm, Sun 12-6pm**

SPECIALIST

Books for Cooks
This place has an enormous collection of cookery books; there's even a small cafe attached where you

can sample some of the recipes from the books.
✉ **4 Blenheim Crescent W11 (5, E1)** ☎ **7221 1992** ⊖ **Ladbroke Grove** ⏲ **Mon-Sat 9.30am-6pm**

Compendium
Compendium focuses on left-wing and alternative titles; if you're searching for a very specialised title this is the place to try first.
✉ **234 Camden High St NW1 (4, K4)** ☎ **7485 8944** ⊖ **Camden Town** ⏲ **Mon-Sat 10am-6pm, Sun 12-6pm**

Gay's the Word
Gay's the Word stocks guides and literature for, by and about gay men and lesbians.
✉ **66 Marchmont St WC1 (6, B6)** ☎ **7278 7654** ⊖ **Russell Square** ⏲ **Mon-Sat 10am-6.30pm, Sun 2-6pm**

Silver Moon – one of the hundreds of specialist book shops London has in store.

Grant & Cutler

This is positively the best foreign-language bookshop in London – for books in or about everything from Arabic to Zulu.

✉ **55-57 Great Marlborough St W1 (6, E4)** ☎ **7734 2012** ⊖ **Oxford Circus** ⏱ **Mon-Sat 9am-5.30pm, Thurs 9am-7pm**

Ian Allan

The train-spotter in you won't be able to resist Ian Allan, which specialises in transport and defence: aircraft, motor vehicles and, of course, trains.

✉ **45-46 Lower Marsh SE1 (6, H9)** ☎ **7401 2100** ⊖ **Waterloo** ⏱ **Mon-Fri 9am-5.30pm, Sat 9am-5pm**

Murder One

This is the place for crime fiction in all its guises.

✉ **71-73 Charing Cross Rd WC2 (6, E6)** ☎ **7734 3485** ⊖ **Tottenham Court Road** ⏱ **Mon-Sat 10am-7pm (Thurs-Sat till 8pm)**

Silver Moon

Silver Moon specialises in books for, by and about women.

✉ **64-68 Charing Cross Rd WC2 (6, E6)** ☎ **7836 7906** ⊖ **Leicester Square** ⏱ **Mon-Sat 10am-6.30pm (Thurs till 8pm), Sun 12-6pm**

Sportspages

Magazines, fanzines and books about sport are the offerings at Sportspages.

✉ **94-96 Charing Cross Rd WC2 (6, E6)** ☎ **7240 9604** ⊖ **Leicester Square or Tottenham Court Road** ⏱ **Mon-Sat 9.30am-7pm**

Stanfords

Stanfords has one of the world's largest and best selections of maps, guides and travel literature. Smaller branches at the British Airways Travel Shop (☎ 7434 4744), 156 Regent St W1 (6, F4; Piccadilly Circus) and Campus Travel (☎ 7730 1314), 52 Grosvenor Gardens SW1 (5, G5; ⊖ Victoria).

✉ **12-14 Long Acre WC2 (6, E7)** ☎ **7836 1321** ⊖ **Covent Garden** ⏱ **Mon 10am-6pm, Tues-Sat 9am-7pm**

The Travel Bookshop

The Travel Bookshop, the best 'boutique' travel bookshop in the world and the inspiration for Hugh Grant's shop in *Notting Hill*, has all the new guides, plus a selection of out-of-print and antiquarian gems.

✉ **13 Blenheim Crescent W11 (5, E1)** ☎ **7229 5260** ⊖ **Ladbroke Grove** ⏱ **Mon-Sat 10am-6pm**

Zwemmer

Zwemmer has all kinds of art books – from photography and sculpture to design and architecture

✉ **24 Litchfield St WC2 (7, C6)** ☎ **7379 7886** ⊖ **Tottenham Court Road** ⏱ **Mon-Fri 10am-6.30pm, Sat 10am-6pm**

Simon Bracken

Where's Hugh? Great books too at the Travel Bookshop.

London Tales and True

Ever since Chaucer's pilgrims in *The Canterbury Tales* gathered for their trip at the Tabard Inn in Southwark, London has provided inspiration, or at least the backdrop, for writers. Doris Lessing's collection of short stories *London Observed* contains some of the funniest and most vicious portrayals of 1990s Britain. *London Fields* by Martin Amis is heavy going; read his more acclaimed *Money*, set in Notting Hill, instead. In *Metroland*, Julian Barnes wrote of growing up in the suburbs along the Metropolitan line. Nick Hornby's *High Fidelity* about a fanatical indie music lover in London is a satisfying, easy read. An excellent sampler of contemporary writing on London is *Granta 65: London – The Lives of the City* (Granta Books), edited by Ian Jack.

SPECIALIST SHOPS

Gerry's
Gerry's stocks a frightening array of alcohol garnered from far-flung parts. Come here if you just can't

Gerry's global groggery

manage without a bottle of Peruvian pisco, African peanut liqueur or Polish zubrówka ('bison-grass' flavoured vodka).
✉ **74 Old Compton Rd W1 (6, E5)** ☎ **7734 4215** ⊖ **Leicester Square** ◷ **Mon-Fri 9am-6.45pm, Sat 9am-5.30pm**

Kite Store
This shop stocks at least 100 different models as well as frisbees, boomerangs and other things that 'fly'.
✉ **48 Neal St WC2 (7, B6)** ☎ **7836 1666** ⊖ **Covent Garden** ◷ **Mon-Fri 10am-6pm**

(Thurs till 7pm) Sat 10.30am-6pm

Papier Marché
Papier Marché is a lovely shop selling all manner of jewellery, toys, mirrors, birds and animals made out of papier-mâché. Parents who'd like a little liquid refreshment while admiring the luridly decorated beasties should head across the road to the Three Kings of Clerkenwell pub (p. 96).
✉ **53 Clerkenwell Close EC1 (6, C9)** ☎ **7251 6311** ⊖ **Farringdon** ◷ **Mon-Sat 11am-6pm**

SHOPPING FOR CHILDREN

With that old dictum 'a child should be seen and not heard' a firm belief (though not necessarily a practice) in the UK, there's lots of shops selling toys, board games and books to keep the little tykes busy – and quiet.

Benjamin Pollock's Toy Shop
Pollock's is light years from the all-inclusive Hamleys. It's a quiet, charming, cluttered little shop that specialises in handmade toys, many with a theatrical theme.
✉ **44 The Market, Covent Garden WC2 (6, E7)** ☎ **7379 7866** ⊖ **Covent Garden** ◷ **Mon-Sat 10.30am-6pm, Sun 12-5pm**

Children's Book Centre
This is a wonderful shop for children with standard books as well as the talking variety, videos, CDs and toys.
✉ **237 Kensington High St W8 (5, G1)** ☎ **7937 7497** ⊖ **High**

Street Kensington ◷ **Mon-Sat 9.30am-6.30pm (Tues till 6pm, Thurs till 7pm) Sun 12-6pm**

Compendia
Compendia is piled high with board and other games, including a good selection of travel games.
✉ **10 The Market, Greenwich SE10 (3, H2)** ☎ **8293 6616** 🚇 **DLR: Cutty Sark** ◷ **Mon-Thurs 12-5.30pm, Fri 11am-5.30pm, Sat-Sun 10am-5.30pm**

Hamleys
Hamleys is an enormous Aladdin's cave stocked with every imaginable toy in the universe but prices can be high. The crowds in the weeks leading up to Christmas must be seen to be believed.
✉ **188-196 Regent St W1 (6, E4)** ☎ **7734 3161** ⊖ **Oxford Circus** ◷ **Mon-Wed 10am-7pm, Thurs-Fri 10am-8pm, Sat 9.30am-7pm, Sun 12-6pm**

Shopping Guides
The *Time Out Shopping Guide* (£7) lists many shopping opportunities in the capital. Seekers of the cheap and cheerful should seek out Andrew Kershman's *Bargain Hunters' London* (Metro Publications; £5.99)

places to eat

London is the undisputed culinary capital of the UK, and the growth in the number of restaurants and cafes – some 8500 at last count, representing 70 different cuisines – has made the city much more international. No matter what you fancy eating, there's bound to be a restaurant serving it. Things have improved remarkably since the 1970s and why not? There was only one way but up from 'caffs' serving greasy fried breakfasts and fish & chips boiled in rancid-smelling oil.

Now food in all its guises has become the new sex in London, and everyone wants a piece of the action. Just don't count on value for money. We can't remember the number of times we've eaten over-refined Italian food or the ubiquitous Modern European/British, dropped £35 a head and wondered why we'd bothered. For that kind of money, this would be inconceivable in cities like New York, Paris or Sydney. On the other hand we've had Pakistani in Whitechapel, Turkish in Dalston and Indonesian in Brixton that have made our hearts and taste buds sing and our wallets only a little bit lighter.

What we've done in this chapter is separate the wheat from the chaff. All of the restaurants, pubs and cafes listed have been tried personally by us or by trusted foodie friends. They range from pretty good (convenient location, cheap price, unusual cuisine) to 'fantabulous' (worth a big splurge or lengthy journey). Hopefully this list will lead you in the right direction and you won't walk out wondering why you had bothered. Bon appétit!

Simon Bracken

Meal Costs

The pricing symbols we've used generally include 2 courses and a drink per person:

£	Under £10
££	£10-20
£££	£20-35
££££	Over £35

Two symbols (ie ££/£££) indicate prices for lunch/dinner.

Getting that Table

Note that flavour of the month restaurants in London can be booked up weeks – even months – in advance. Some places may ask for a credit card number to confirm a booking. If you don't show up, a cancellation fee may be charged to your card. As a general rule, it's a good idea to make a reservation for the more expensive places.

Juliet Coombe

Another satisfied diner at Portobello Market foodstalls

BLOOMSBURY

BRITISH
North Sea Fish Restaurant £/££

The North Sea sets out to cook fresh fish and potatoes, a somewhat limited ambition in which it succeeds admirably: cod, haddock and plaice, deep-fried or grilled, served with a huge helping of chips. It's advisable to book for dinner. ✉ **7-8 Leigh St WC1 (6, B6)** ☎ **7387 5892** ⊖ **Russell Square**

⊙ Mon-Sat 12-2.30pm, 5.30-10.30pm

VEGETARIAN
Mandeer £

This is Indian vegetarian food – in fact, *Ayurvedic* dishes, including various thalis, are served. Booking is a good idea. ✉ **8 Bloomsbury Way WC1 (6, D7)** ☎ **7242 6202** ⊖ **Tottenham Court Road** ⊙ **Mon-Sat 12-3pm, 5-10pm** **V**

Spitalfield's Food Village

BRIXTON

ASIAN
Satay Bar £/££

One of our favourite Asian eateries, the Satay Bar serves surprisingly authentic Indonesian food: rendang ayam, laksa, mixed satays and mee goreng as well as rijstaffel. Even more authentic are all the doors that open onto the busy street – you could easily be in a *warung* in Jogjakarta. Book ahead. ✉ **447-450 Coldharbour Lane SW9 (5, K8)** ☎ **7326 5001** ⊖ **Brixton** ⊙ **Mon-Fri 12-3pm, 6pm-midnight,** Sat 1pm-midnight, Sun 2-10.30pm ⏩ yes

ITALIAN
Eco Brixton £/££

This is the sister-restaurant of **Clapham's Eco** at 162 Clapham High St (5, K6; ☎ 7978 1108), which has arguably the best pizza, antipasto and cappuccino in south London. ✉ **4 Market Row, Brixton Market, Electric Lane SW9 (5, K8)** ☎ **7738 3021** ⊖ **Brixton** ⊙ **Mon-Tues & Thurs-Sat 12-5pm** ⏩ yes **V**

VEGETARIAN
Bah Humbug ££

Located in the crypt of a disused church, Bah Humbug is one of the best vegetarian restaurants in London with quite a global range – from Thai vegetable fritters to Cantonese mock duck and masala curry. Booking is a must on the weekend. ✉ **St Mathew's Church, cnr Brixton Hill & St Matthew's Rds (5, K8)** ☎ **7738 3184** ⊖ **Brixton** ⊙ **Mon-Fri 6-11pm, Sun 10.30am-11.30pm, Sun 10.30am-10.30pm** **V**

Fresh fish, Brixton Market

Juliet Coombe

English Eats

The most English of dishes is fish & chips: cod, plaice or haddock dipped in batter, deep-fried and served with chips (french fries) doused in vinegar. But from the middle of the 19th century until just after WWI the staple lunch for many Londoners was a pie filled with spiced eel and served with mashed potatoes and liquor and parsley sauce. Nowadays the pies are usually meat-filled and the eel served smoked or jellied as a side dish. The best places to try these are **Manze's** near Bermondsey Market (p. 78), **Goddards** in Greenwich (p. 75) or **Porters** in Covent Garden (p. 74).

CAMDEN

ASIAN

Asakusa   ££

For affordable Japanese – not necessarily an oxymoron – in Camden Town, head here for inexpensive set menus like prawn tempura with miso soup and rice. Weekends are busy so book ahead.
✉ 265 Eversholt St NW1 (5, C6) ☎ 7388 8533 ⊖ Mornington Crescent ⏰ Mon-Fri 6-11.30pm, Sat 6-11pm V

Lemon Grass   ££

Lemon Grass is one of the better Thai eateries in Camden, with authentic food and charming decor and staff. Book ahead.
✉ 243 Royal College St (4, K5) ☎ 7284 1116 ⊖ Camden Town ⏰ Mon-Sat 7-11pm V

EASTERN EUROPEAN

Trojka Russian Tea Room   ££

Also known as the Primrose Brasserie, Trojka serves good-value Eastern European/Russian dishes like herrings with dill sauce and salt beef, in an attractive, skylit restaurant. They have house wine but it's also BYO. Reserve for dinner on the weekend.
✉ 101 Regents Park Rd NW1 (4, H3) ☎ 7483 3765 ⊖ Chalk Farm ⏰ 9am-11pm ♿ yes

INTERNATIONAL

Sauce barorganicdiner ££/£££

This oddly named basement cafe/restaurant serves dishes prepared only with ingredients certified by the UK and EU as organic. Try the crab cakes with sweet chilli sauce or even the hamburgers. They also do a great all-day breakfast.
✉ 214 Camden High St NW1 (4, K4) ☎ 7482 0777 ⊖ Camden Town ⏰ Mon-Sat 12-11pm, Sun 12-4pm V

WEST INDIAN

Mango Room   ££

An upmarket, refined choice for island food, with delightful starters like fluffy crab and potato balls and unusual mains like a platter of cooked vegetables including ackee, a yellow-skinned Jamaican fruit. Booking is recommended.
✉ 10 Kentish Town Road NW1 (4, J4) ☎ 7482 5065 ⊖ Camden Town ⏰ noon-midnight ♿ yes V

CHELSEA & SOUTH KENSINGTON

ASIAN

New Culture Revolution   £/££

This trendy, good-value bar/cafe has dumplings, noodles and rice dishes. There are other branches at 43 Parkway NW1 (4, K3) ☎ 7267 2700 and at 42 Duncan St N1 (5, C8) ☎ 7833 9083.
✉ 305 King's Rd SW3 (5, H4) ☎ 7352 9281 ⊖ Sloane Square ⏰ Mon-Fri 12-11pm, Sat-Sun 1.30-11pm ♿ yes V

EASTERN EUROPEAN

Daquise   ££

Daquise is a real dinosaur – but a lovable little Tyrannosaurus rex indeed – and close to the museums. It's a rather shabby-looking Polish cafe/diner, with a good range of vodkas and extremely reasonably priced food is rather popular at dinner time.
✉ 20 Thurloe St SW7 (5, G4) ☎ 7589 6117 ⊖ South Kensington ⏰ 10am-11pm ♿ yes V

MODERN BRITISH

Bibendum   ££/££££

This Conran restaurant is in one of London's finest settings for a restaurant, the Art Nouveau Michelin House (1911). The popular **Bibendum Oyster Bar** is on the ground floor, where you really feel at the heart of the architectural finery. Upstairs it's all much lighter and brighter. Book for both.
✉ 81 Fulham Rd SW3 (5, H3) ☎ 7581 5817 ⊖ South Kensington ⏰ lunch 12.30-2.30pm (till 3pm weekends), dinner 7-11pm (till 10.30pm Sun)

Tipping

Many restaurants now include a 'discretionary' service charge (average around 12.5%), which should be clearly indicated on the bill. At places that don't levy a charge you are expected to leave a 10-15% tip unless the service was unsatisfactory.

THE CITY

ASIAN
Dim Sum £

A budget traveller's delight convenient to St Paul's, Dim Sum serves à la carte Peking and Sichuan dishes but the best deal is the all-you-can-eat buffet (minimum 4 people) available in the evening.

✉ 5-6 Deans Court EC4 (6, E11) ☎ 7236 1114 ✜ St Paul's ◷ Mon-Fri 11am-3pm, 6-10.30pm **V**

BRITISH
Ye Olde Cheshire Cheese ££/£££

Rebuilt 6 years after the Great Fire and popular with Dr Johnson, Thackeray, Charles Dickens and the visiting Mark Twain, the Cheshire Cheese is touristy but the traditional Chop Room is a good place to take visitors. Booking can be a good idea.

✉ Wine Office Court from 145 Fleet St EC4 (6, E10) ☎ 7353 6170 ✜ Blackfriars ◷ Mon-Fri 11.30am-11pm, Sat 11.30am-2pm & 5.30-11pm, Sun 12-4pm ♿ yes

INDIAN
Café Spice Namaste ££

One of our favourite Indian restaurants in London, Namaste serves Goan and Keralan cuisine (with South-East Asian hints) in an old courthouse that has been decorated in 'carnival' colours. Try frango piri-piri, a fiery hot chicken tikka marinated in red masala, or the mughlai maas, Kashmiri lamb in a nut-based sauce. Do book.

✉ 16 Prescot St E1 (6, E15) ☎ 7488 9242 ✜ Tower Hill ◷ Mon-Fri 12-3pm, 6.30-10.30pm, Sat 6.30-10pm ♿ yes **V**

Business Munch
Some good places to mix business and dining are:

Novelli (p. 73), **St John** (p. 73), **Moro** (p. 73), **Café Spice Namaste** (at left), **Blue Print Café** (p.78), **Oxo Tower** (p. 78) and **River Café** (p.75)

ITALIAN
Da Vinci ££

Here's a rare bird indeed: a decent, affordable neighbourhood Italian place in the City. Booking for lunch is advisable.

✉ Carter Lane EC4 (6, E10) ☎ 7236 3938 ✜ St Paul's ◷ Mon-Fri 11.30am-3.30pm & 6-11pm

VEGETARIAN
Place Below £

This pleasant vegetarian restaurant in a church crypt has salads, pastas and soups and if you arrive between 11.30am (when lunch begins) and noon, you'll get a £2 discount on most main dishes.

✉ St Mary-le-Bow Church, Cheapside EC2 (6, E12) ☎ 7329 0789 ✜ St Paul's or Mansion House ◷ Mon-Fri 7.30-10.30am, 11.30am-2.30pm **V**

The Cheshire Cheese – purveyor of sustenance to hungry wordsmiths and tourists alike for over 300 years.

Richard l'Anson

CLERKENWELL

ASIAN
East One   **££**

East One is another one of those Asian do-it-yourself places, with all-you-can-eat stir-fry buffets, but it's a cut above.

✉ 175-179 St John St EC1 (6, B10) ☎ 7566 0088 ⊖ Farringdon ⏰ Mon-Fri 12-3pm, 5-11pm, Sat 5-11pm

BRITISH
St John   **£££**

St John is the place to come if you fancy sampling old-fashioned British dishes like tripe and sausage soup, pigeon and Jerusalem artichoke and sweetbreads, peas and broad beans. While there are some fish dishes, this place is all about meat – and offal in particular (after all, it is right next to Smithfield Market). Book ahead to secure a seat.

✉ 26 St John St EC1 (6, C10) ☎ 7251 0848 ⊖ Farringdon ⏰ Mon-Fri 12-3pm, Mon-Sat 6-11.30pm

FRENCH
Novelli   **£££**

This is the less expensive cousin of chef-owner Jean-Christophe Novelli's flagship **Maison Novelli** restaurant next door. It too serves sublime modern French food in a brasserie overlooking Clerkenwell Green. Reservations are essential.

✉ 29-31 Clerkenwell Green EC1 (6, B10) ☎ 7251 6606 ⊖ Farringdon ⏰ Mon-Fri 12-3.30pm & 6-11pm, Sat 6pm-midnight **V**

SPANISH
Moro   **£££**

As its name implies, this place serves 'Moorish' cuisine, a fusion of Spanish, Portuguese and North African flavours. Try the crab brik, a crispy deep-fried packet served with piquant harissa, and the wood-roasted red mullet with sharp Seville orange. Booking's essential.

✉ 34-36 Exmouth Market N1 (6, B9) ☎ 7833 8336 ⊖ Farringdon ⏰ Mon-Fri 12.30-2.30pm & 7-10.30pm, Sat 12.30-2.30pm

Self-Serve Savings

The best way to keep eating prices down is to self-cater. **Tesco Metro** stores have the makings of a good sandwich. There are branches at: Covent Garden, 22-25 Bedford St WC2 (7, C7); opposite Liverpool St Station, 158-164 Bishopsgate EC2 (6, D14); the City, 80B Cheapside EC2 (6, E12); 311 Oxford St W1 (6, E3); Notting Hill , 224-226 Portobello Rd W11 (5, E11); and Canary Wharf, 15 Cabot Place E14 (2, C3). Branches of **Safeway**, **Asda** and **Sainsbury** are also competitively priced while **Waitrose** is more upmarket.

Fortnum & Mason's foodhalls (p. 57) have delicacies from all over the world.

COVENT GARDEN & THE STRAND

AMERICAN
Joe Allen ££/£££

A long-established American-style eatery, this is a star-spotter's paradise. There's a real buzz here and it gets crowded, so book. Starters and main dishes (lamb chops, grilled halibut etc) with some vegetarian choices are varied.

✉ **13 Exeter St WC2 (7,C8)** ☎ **7836 0651** ⊖ **Covent Garden** ◷ **Mon-Fri noon-12.45am, Sat 11.30-12.45am Sun 11.30am-11.30pm** **V**

ASIAN
Mongolian Barbecue £

This place with its all 'All You Khan Eat' stir-fry buffet is a cut above the rest, but we don't think much of their jokes.

✉ **12 Maiden Lane WC2 (7, D8)** ☎ **7379 7722** ⊖ **Leicester Square** ◷ **Mon-Thurs & Sun 12-11pm, Fri-Sat noon-midnight** **yes**

BELGIAN
Belgo Centraal ££

Taking the lift down to the basement and walking through the kitchens is all part of the fun at Belgo, where the waiters dress up as 16th century monks. This being a Belgian restaurant, *moules et frites* (mussels and chips/french fries) and spit roasts are the specialities, and beer (100 different flavoured pilsners, including banana, peach and cherry) is the drink. Book unless you have the patience of a monk.

✉ **50 Earlham St WC2 (7, B7)** ☎ **7813 2233** ⊖ **Covent Garden** ◷ **Mon-Sat 12-11.30pm, Sun 12-10.30pm** **yes**

BRITISH
Porters £/££

Porters specialises in pies, long a staple of British cooking but not regularly found on modern menus. They have the usual ones like steak and kidney pie and pudding and the less common: lamb and apricot or chicken and broccoli.

✉ **17 Henrietta St WC2 (7, C7)** ☎ **7836 6466** ⊖ **Covent Garden** ◷ **Mon-Sat 12-11.30pm, Sun 12-10.30pm** **yes**

Rock & Sole Plaice £/££

This no-nonsense fish and chips shop has basic Formica tables and delicious cod or haddock in batter. They have house wine but you can BYO. Dinner booking advisable.

✉ **47 Endell St WC2 (7, B7)** ☎ **7836 3785** ⊖ **Covent Garden** ◷ **Mon-Sat 11.30am-10pm, Sun 11.30am-9pm** **yes**

VEGETARIAN
Food for Thought £

This tiny, non-smoking vegetarian cafe features dishes like West Indian curry or stir-fried vegetables with brown rice.

✉ **31 Neal St WC2 (7, B7)** ☎ **7836 0239** ⊖ **Covent Garden** ◷ **Mon-Sat 9.30am-9pm, Sun 12-4pm** **yes** **V**

Pickled condiments, Rock & Sole Plaice

EAST END

INDIAN
New Tayyabs £

Do what we do: give the Bangladeshi restaurants of Brick Lane the miss and head south to Whitechapel for authentic Pakistani food at this wonderful place. Choose shish kebabs, lamb chops or one of several *karahi* (wok) dishes, a veg-etable and one of several dahls. BYO only.

✉ **83 Fieldgate St E1 (6, D15)** ☎ **7247 9543** ⊖ **Whitechapel** ◷ **5pm-midnight** **yes** **V**

VEGETARIAN
Whitechapel Art Gallery Café £

This vegetarian place serves dishes such as spinach Florentine and salad and soups.

✉ **80-82 Whitechapel High St E1 (6, D15)** ☎ **7522 7878** ⊖ **Aldgate East** ◷ **Tues-Sun 11am-5pm (Wed till 8pm)** **yes** **V**

GREENWICH

BRITISH
Goddards Ye Olde Pie Shop £

Goddards is truly a step back in time: a real London caff with wooden benches and things like steak and kidney pie with liquor and mash and shepherd's pie with beans and a rich brown gravy. There are also fruit-based sweet pies.
✉ 45 Greenwich Church St SE10 (3, H2)
🚊 DLR: Cutty Sark
🕐 Tues-Fri & Sun 11am-3pm, Sat 10.45am-4.30pm ♿ yes

INTERNATIONAL
North Pole ££/£££

This pleasant place has a bar/pub on the ground floor and an excellent, if somewhat stuffy (chintz drapes etc), restaurant on the 1st floor. There's a decent Sunday brunch from noon to 6.30pm and a 25% discount on dinner on Monday.
✉ 131 Greenwich High Rd SE10 (3, K2)
☎ 8853 3020 🚊 DLR Greenwich 🕐 Mon 5-11pm, Tues-Sat 12-11pm, Sun 12-10.30pm
V

HAMMERSMITH & FULHAM

BRITISH
Chelsea Bun £/££

This London version of an American diner is a great value place in the area known as World's End. Breakfast is served all day, and there's seating on an upstairs veranda.
✉ 9A Lamont Rd SW10 (5, H3) ☎ 7352 3635
⊖ Fulham Broadway or Earl's Court 🕐 Mon-Sat 7am-11.30pm, Sun 9am-6pm

ITALIAN
River Café ££££

The very buzzy, see-and-be-seen River Café owes its fame as much to the cookbooks it has spawned as to the food served here, but it does have the best Modern Italian cuisine in London. Booking is a must.
✉ Thames Wharf, Rainville Rd W6 (5, H1)
☎ 7381 8824
⊖ Hammersmith
🕐 Mon-Sat 12.30-3pm, 7-9.30pm, Sun 12.30-3pm ♿ yes **V**

HAMPSTEAD

CAFE
Café Base £

This bright and clean cafe has unusual ciabatta sandwiches and wraps as well as salads and pastas.
✉ 70-71 Hampstead High St NW3 (4, E2)
☎ 7431 3241
⊖ Hampstead 🕐 8am-10pm **V**

MIDDLE EASTERN
Al Casbah £/££

Al Casbah is a small, friendly Moroccan restaurant with very good couscous and tajines.
✉ 45 Hampstead High St NW3 (4, E1)
☎ 7435 7632
⊖ Hampstead 🕐 5.30-11.30pm **V**

Veggie Victuals

Vegetarianism is now an accepted part of the restaurant scene, and it's rare to find somewhere that does not offer something for non-carnivores. **Cranks** is the best known vegetarian/vegan restaurant chain with an outlet at 8 Marshall St W1 (7, B3) ☎ 7437 9431 ⊖ Oxford Circus and one at 17-19 Great Newport St WC2 (7, C6) ☎ 7836 5226 ⊖ Leicester Square.

Elliot Daniel

Hungry & Confused?

Restaurant Services (☎ 8888 8080; www.restaurant-services.co.uk; 9am-7pm) gives free dining advice. If you specify a certain cuisine or even atmosphere in a certain price range per head and within a postcode, they'll come up with a suitable list for you and even book you a table.

ISLINGTON

BRITISH
Upper St Fish Shop £
This legendary fishmonger's doles out classy fish & chips and seafood such as Irish oysters by the half-dozen.
✉ 324 Upper St N1 (5, C8) ☎ 7359 1401 ⊖ Highbury & Islington ⏱ Tues-Sat 12-2.15pm (till 3.00pm Sat) & 6-10.15pm (from 5.30pm Fri-Sat)

ITALIAN
Casale Franco £/££
This great little find just off Upper St serves some of the best pizza in north London.

✉ 134-137 Upper St N1 (5, B8) ☎ 7226 8994 ⊖ Angel ⏱ Tues-Sat 12-2.30pm & 6-11pm, Sun 12-9pm ⅍ yes **V**

MIDDLE EASTERN
Inter Mezzo £/££
This Turkish mezze bar and restaurant gets our vote as one of the best value and friendliest eateries in town. There are reasonably priced 2 and 3 course set lunches and dinners. TJ's Special Seafood Pot, chock-a-block with things from the sea in a spicy broth, is to die for and enough for 2.
✉ 207 Liverpool Rd N1

(5, B8) ☎ 7607 4112 ⊖ Angel ⏱ Mon-Sat 11.30am-11pm, Sun 10am-11pm ⅍ yes

VEGETARIAN
Ravi Shankar £
This small, very inexpensive restaurant has some of the best Indian vegetarian food in London. A branch called **Chutneys** is near Euston at 124 Drummond St NW1 (6, B4) ☎ 7388 0604.
✉ 422 St John St EC1 (5, D8) ☎ 7833 5849 ⊖ Angel ⏱ Mon-Sat 12-2.45pm & 6-11.30pm, Sun 12-2.45pm ⅍ yes **V**

KNIGHTSBRIDGE & KENSINGTON

INTERNATIONAL
Fifth Floor £££
This restaurant, bar and cafe at Harvey Nichols department store is the perfect place to drop after you've shopped. It's quite expensive, but there's a good value 3 course set lunch when it is a good idea to book; in the evening it's essential.

✉ Harvey Nichols, 109-125 Knightsbridge SW1 (6, H1) ☎ 7493 3320 ⊖ Knightsbridge ⏱ 12-3pm (till 3.30pm weekends), Mon-Sat 6.30-11.30pm **V**

ITALIAN
Bellini's ££
This stylish restaurant with a few pavement tables and

views of a flower-bedecked alley near the Kensington Market serves great 2 and 3 course set lunches as well as a dinner menu.
✉ 47 Kensington Court W8 (5, G2) ☎ 7937 5520 ⊖ High Street Kensington ⏱ Mon-Sat 12-11pm, Sun 12-10.30pm ⅍ yes

MAYFAIR

MIDDLE EASTERN
Sofra Bistro ££
A branch of a chain of decent Turkish eateries, Sofra's offerings include a set array of mezzes. There's a good choice for vegetarians too. There's another Sofra branch at 36 Tavistock St WC2 (7, C7) ☎ 7240 3773.
✉ 10 Shepherd Market W1 (6, G3) ☎ 7493 3320 ⊖ Green Park ⏱ noon-midnight **V**

Stop for a yummy cake at Mildred's, Soho (p. 81)

NOTTING HILL & BAYSWATER

AFRICAN

Mandola ££

Mandola offers something entirely different: vegetarian Sudanese dishes like *tamia* (a kind of felafel) or *fifilia* (a vegetable curry). Meat dishes include chicken *halla* and *shorba fude*, an unusual meat and peanut soup. Booking for dinner is recommended.

✉ **139-141 Westbourne Grove W2** (5, E2) ☎ **7229 4734** ⊖ Bayswater ⏰ 12-11.30pm (Sun till 10.30pm) ♿ yes **V**

BRITISH

Sausage & Mash Café £

Situated under the elevated Westway, this is just the ticket if you're looking for cheap English stodge in relatively upbeat surrounds.

✉ **268 Portobello Rd W10** (5, E1) ☎ **8968 8898** ⊖ Ladbroke Grove ⏰ Tues-Sat 11am-10pm, Sun 11am-8pm ♿ yes

The Portobello Market area has loads of funky eateries.

Veronica's £££

Veronica's is trying to establish that England does have a culinary heritage, with some fascinating dishes going back as early as the 14th century. There are well-priced 2 and 3 course set menus at lunch weekdays and at dinner Monday to Thursday. Booking is advisable.

✉ **3 Hereford Rd W2** (5, F1) ☎ **7229 5079** ⊖ Bayswater ⏰ Mon-Fri 12-3pm & 7-11.15pm, Sat 7-11.15pm

ITALIAN

L'Accento ££/£££

This highly stylish restaurant offers a 2 course set menu, which could include mussel stew in white wine with fresh herbs, followed by roast leg of lamb with balsamic vinegar. Once you step away from this menu, though, L'Accento becomes a lot more expensive. It's a good idea to book.

✉ **16 Garway Rd W2** (5, E2) ☎ **7243 2201** ⊖ Bayswater ⏰ 12.30-2.30pm & 6.30-11.15pm **V**

With a View to Eating

For great views from the comfort of a restaurant you couldn't do much better than the 8th floor of the **Oxo Tower** (p. 78) or even the **People's Palace** (p. 78) in the Royal Festival Hall. A more down-to-earth approach is looking at the city and its bridges from one of the riverside pubs such as the Anchor (p. 94) or **Horniman's** in the Hay's Galleria, a renovated warehouse on Battle Bridge Lane SE1 (6, G14; ⊖ London Bridge). Some people like the views across Hyde Park from the **Windows on the World** bar on the 29th floor of the Hilton Hotel, Park Lane W1 (6, H2; ⊖ Hyde Park Corner). But for our money, we'll take the cheap option and grab some fish & chips and head for Waterloo Bridge at sunset.

SOUTH OF THE THAMES: BERMONDSEY TO BATTERSEA

Doug McKinlay

Tic tac toe for giants; the Oxo Tower

BRITISH
Manze's £
London's oldest pie shop is still going strong after a century of trading. Handy to the Bermondsey Market, they serve masses of jellied eels and pie, mash and liquor in a pleasantly tiled interior.
✉ **87 Tower Bridge Rd SE1 (6, H14)**
☎ **7407 2985**
⊖ **London Bridge**
🕐 Mon 11am-2pm, Tues-Thurs 10.30am-2pm, Fri 10am-2.15pm, Sat 10am-2.45pm ♿ yes

CAFE
Konditor & Cook £
This cafe at the Young Vic serves meals all day, but we come here for the pastries and cake made by arguably the best 'bespoke' bakery in London.
✉ **66 The Cut SE1 (6, H10)** ☎ **7620 2700**
⊖ **Waterloo** 🕐 Mon-Fri 8.30am-11pm, Sat 10.30am-11pm V

INTERNATIONAL
Blue Print Café £££
Modern European cooking is the order of the day at this flagship Conran restaurant. Being right on the river, booking is essential to secure your view.
✉ **Design Museum, Butlers Wharf SE1 (6, H15)** ☎ **7378 7031**
⊖ **Tower Hill** 🕐 Mon-Sat 12-3pm & 6-11pm; Sun 12-3pm V

Oxo Tower (6, F9) ££££
The conversion of the old Oxo Tower into housing with this restaurant on the 8th floor helped spur much of the restaurant renaissance south of the river. The food – a bit Mediterranean, a bit French, some Pacific Rim – is satisfactory in that Fifth Floor sort of way (it's owned by Harvey Nichols). If you can't get in there's always the cheaper **Bistrot 2 Riverside** (☎ 7498 8200) on the 2nd floor of the tower.
✉ **Barge House St SE1**
☎ **7803 3888**
⊖ **Waterloo** 🕐 Mon-Sat 12-3pm & 5.30-11.30pm, Sun 12-3pm & 6-10.30pm V

People's Palace £££
Easy to miss inside the Royal Festival Hall and boasting some enviable fine views of the Thames and the City, this rather deceptively named 3rd floor restaurant serves such delights as beetroot tart tatin and roast rabbit. Reserve a table to be sure.
✉ **Level 3, Royal Festival Hall SE1 (6, G8)**
⊖ **Waterloo** 🕐 12-3pm & 5.30-11pm ♿ yes V

Kosher Restaurants
Searching for a kosher meal in central London is a joyless task, though for simple Ashkenazi favourites there's always **Reubens** at 79 Baker St W1 (6, C1) ☎ 7486 0035 ⊖ Baker St. Middle Eastern/Sephardic dishes can be had at **Solly's**, 148a Golders Green Rd NW11 (4, A1 ☎ 8455 2121 ⊖ Golders Green. The London Beth Din Kashrut Division (☎ 8343 6255; fax 8343 6254; ✉ info@kosher.org.uk) is the place to contact for information on kosher eating in London.

ITALIAN
Gourmet Pizza Company   ££

It may not look like much but there are always queues here, waiting for such unusual toppings as Thai chicken and Cajun chicken with prawns along with the more usual cheese and tomato and Italian sausage.

✉ Gabriel's Wharf, 65 Upper Ground SE1 (6, F9) ☎ 7928 3188 ⊖ Waterloo ⏰ Mon-Sat 12-11pm, Sun 12-10.30pm ♿ yes **V**

MEDITERRANEAN
Cantina del Ponte   £££

This is a more affordable riverside Conran restaurant serving Italian/Mediterranean food. Good deals for set-price weekday lunches and Sunday dinner. Fabulous outside seating in warm weather. Book to secure a seat.

✉ Butlers Wharf Building, 36C Shad Thames SE1 (5, F10) ☎ 7403 5403 ⊖ Tower Hill ⏰ 12-3pm & 6-11pm (closes 1hr earlier Sun) ♿ yes **V**

MODERN BRITISH
Fish!   ££/£££

In a glassed-in Victorian pavilion overlooking Borough Market and Southwark Cathedral, Fish! serves fresher-than-fresh fish and seafood prepared simply: steamed or grilled swordfish, cod, skate, squid (or whatever is ticked off on the placemat) served with one of 5 sauces. Booking is a good idea.

✉ Cathedral St SE1 (6, G13) ☎ 7836 3236 ⊖ London Bridge ⏰ Mon-Sat 11.30am-3pm & 5.30-11pm

STOKE NEWINGTON

MIDDLE EASTERN
Mangal   £

This hole-in-the-wall Turkish eatery is everyone's little secret: the freshest kebabs and other grilled meat cooked over a smoking *ocakbasi* (wood-fired brazier) and served with excellent salads. It's a BYO only affair.

✉ 10 Arcola St E8 (5, A10) ☎ 7275 8981 🚇 Dalston Kingsland 🚌 67, 76, 149 or 243 ⏰ noon-midnight

VEGETARIAN
Rasa   ££

This non-smoking South Indian vegetarian restaurant gets rave reviews (and attracts queues) for dishes not often seen (or tasted) outside private homes. Booking is recommended.

✉ 55 Stoke Newington Church St N16 (5, A9) ☎ 7249 0344 🚇 Stoke Newington 🚌 73 ⏰ Mon-Thurs 6-11pm, Fri 6pm-midnight, Sat 12-2.30pm & 6pm-midnight, Sun 6-11pm **V**

TRAFALGAR SQUARE

INTERNATIONAL
Café in the Crypt   £

Good food, with plenty of vegetarian offerings, can be had in this atmospheric crypt beneath St Martin-in-the-Fields church; though grave-side dining is not for the squeamish. Lunchtimes in the crypt are often hectic and noisy.

✉ St Martin-in-the-Fields, Duncannon St WC2 (6, F6) ☎ 7839 4342 ⊖ Charing Cross ⏰ Mon-Sat 10am-8pm, Sun 10am-6pm **V**

Simon Bracken

Creepy! A cafe in a crypt

ICA Café (6, G6)   £/££

You can lunch at this bohemian cafe at the Institute for Contemporary Arts for less than £10, but you'll pay considerably more in the evening when it's advisable to book. It's non-smoking, there's lots of vegetarian dishes, and it's licensed to serve alcohol until 1am.

✉ The Mall SW1 ☎ 7930 8619 ⊖ Charing Cross ⏰ 12-5.30pm (self-service), 5.30-11pm (restaurant) **V**

THE WEST END: PICCADILLY, SOHO & CHINATOWN

ASIAN

Mr Wu £

Mr Wu offers a 10 course all-you-can-eat Chinese buffet. Don't expect gourmet but it's filling. Branch at 26 Wardour St W1 (6, F5) ☎ 7287 3885.
✉ **6-7 Irving St WC2 (7, D6)** ☎ **7839 6669** ⊖ **Leicester Square** ⏰ **12-11.30pm ♿ yes**

Poons ££

This hole-in-the-wall eatery is where the upmarket Poons empire started. It has OK food at very good prices and specialises in air-dried duck and pork. Be prepared to queue at busy times if you haven't booked and to be hustled out again pretty quickly.
✉ **27 Lisle St WC2 (7, C5)** ☎ **7437 4549** ⊖ **Leicester Square** ⏰ **12-11.30pm** [V]

Soba £

Soba is our first choice for an easy (and cheap) bowl of Japanese noodles.
✉ **38 Poland St W1 (7, B3)** ☎ **7734 6400** ⊖ **Oxford Circus** ⏰ **Mon-Sat 12-3.30pm & 5.30-11pm** [V]

Wagamama woks!

Simon Bracken

Tokyo Diner £

The Tokyo Diner is a good-value place to stop for a quick bowl of noodles or plate of sushi before the cinema or theatre.
✉ **2 Newport Place WC2 (7, C6)** ☎ **7287 8777** ⊖ **Leicester Square** ⏰ **noon-midnight** [V]

Tokyo Diner, in the heart of London's Chinatown

Wagamama £/££

This brash and spartan place does great Japanese food but is hardly the place for a quiet dinner. You have to share long tables and, having queued to get in, may feel pressured to move on quickly. Has several branches including Camden Town 9-11 Jamestown Rd NW1 (4, J4) ☎ 7428 0800.
✉ **10A Lexington St W1 (7, C4)** ☎ **7292 0990** ⊖ **Piccadilly Circus** ⏰ **Mon-Sat 11.30am-11pm, Sun 12.30-10.30pm ♿ yes** [V]

Yo! Sushi £/££

Yo! Sushi is one of London's livelier (!) sushi bars, where diners sit around the bar and the dishes come to them via a 60m long conveyor belt (drinks, on the other hand, arrive on a robotic trolley). Branches at Selfridges (6, E2) ☎ 7318 3885 where you can eat your fill for £18, and on the 5th Floor of Harvey Nichols (6, H1) ☎ 7235 5000.
✉ **52-53 Poland St W1 (7, B3)** ☎ **7287 0443** ⊖ **Oxford Circus** ⏰ **noon-midnight ♿ yes**

BRITISH

Franx Snack Bar £

Franx is as authentic a London 'caff' as you'll find in these parts, with eggs and bacon and other specials served all day.
✉ **192 Shaftesbury Ave WC2 (7, B6)** ☎ **7836 7989** ⊖ **Tottenham Court Road** ⏰ **Mon-Sat 7am-6pm**

French House Dining Room £££

At this restaurant above an old-fashioned Soho pub the short menu changes frequently and offers robust English/Modern British food like roast duck and sweetbreads with shallots and red chard. They have an excellent range of British cheeses. It's very popular so booking

is recommended.
✉ 49 Dean St W1
(6, E5) ☎ 7437 2477
⊖ Tottenham Court
Road ⏰ Mon-Sat 12-
3pm, 6.30-11.15pm V

CAFE
Pâtisserie Valerie   f
You can't beat this Soho
institution for coffee or tea
and something sweet, a
filled croissant or club
sandwich though you'll be
lucky to get a seat.
Branches at 79 Regent St
W1 (6, F4) and 215
Brompton Rd SW5 (6, G4).
✉ 44 Old Compton St
W1 (6, E5)
☎ 7437 3466
⊖ Leicester Square
⏰ Mon-Fri 8am-8pm,
Sat 8am-7pm, Sun
9.30am-6pm V

INTERNATIONAL
New Piccadilly   f
Entering New Piccadilly is
like taking a step back in
time; nothing has changed
since it first opened in the
1950s, except the prices.
Even those haven't
increased by as much as
you'd expect for their
acceptable pastas and piz-
zas, chicken and steaks.
✉ 8 Denman St W1
(7, C4) ☎ 7437 8530
⊖ Piccadilly Circus
⏰ 12-9.30pm

Soup   f
Another one of those up-
market 'soup kitchens' that
are all the rage, *Soup* has a
wide variety of choices – from
pea and mushroom claret to
Indonesia crab laksa. A similar place is *Soup Works*, 9
D'Arblay St W1 (7, B4).
✉ 1 Newburgh St W1
(7, B3) ☎ 7287 9100
⊖ Oxford Circus
⏰ Mon-Sat 8am-5pm
♿ yes V

Stockpot   f/ff
This old standby does a
long list of basic dishes like
fish & chips, spaghetti
bolognese, chicken
provençale and some vege-
tarian options. They have
branches at 273 King's Rd
SW3 (5, J3) ☎ 7823 3175
and 6 Basil St SW3 (5, G4)
☎ 7589 8627.
✉ 18 Old Compton St
W1 (5, E5) ☎ 7287
1066 ⊖ Leicester
Square ⏰ Mon-Sat
11.30am-11.30pm, Sun
12-11pm ♿ yes V

Sugar Club   fff
New Zealand Chef Peter
Gordon concentrates on
Pacific Rim cooking –
dishes like grilled kangaroo
loin with coriander and
mint and roast pigeon
breast on wok-fried black
beans, that cleverly mix
and match traditions of
east and west. Do book.
✉ 21 Warwick St W1
(7, C3) ☎ 7437 7776
⊖ Oxford Circus ⏰ 12-
3pm & 6-11pm V

ITALIAN
Kettners   ff
If you fancy something
with fewer links than the
Pizza Express chain,
Kettners serves up similar
fare but in a wonderful
atmosphere of gently fading
grandeur with a piano
tinkling in the background.
✉ 29 Romilly St W1
(7, B6) ☎ 7734 6112
⊖ Leicester Square
⏰ noon-midnight
♿ yes V

Pollo   f
Pollo attracts a student
crowd with its budget-
friendly pastas, risottos,
pizza and chicken dishes.
✉ 20 Old Compton St
W1 (7, B5) ☎ 7734

5917 ⊖ Leicester
Square ⏰ noon-mid-
night ♿ yes V

Spiga   ff
Head here for great value
authentic pizza, pasta or
Italian main dishes in
sleek, pleasant surrounds.
It has a cheaper branch,
Spighetta at 43 Blandford
St W1 (6, D1) ☎ 7486
7340. Book for both.
✉ 84-86 Wardour St
W1 (7, B4) ☎ 7734
3444 ⊖ Tottenham
Court Road
⏰ Mon-Wed & Sun 12-
3pm & 6-11pm (to mid-
night Thurs-Sat)
♿ yes V

MIDDLE EASTERN
Momo   fff
The kasbah comes to
London at this trendy and
expensive Moroccan
restaurant, with excellent
couscous and tajines. Book
ahead for good value 2
and 3 course set lunches.
✉ 25 Heddon St W1
(7, D3) ☎ 7434 4040
⊖ Piccadilly Circus ⏰
Mon-Fri 12.30-2.15pm
& 7-11.15pm, Sat
11am-4pm & 6.30pm-
midnight; Sun 11am-
4pm & 6-9.30pm V

VEGETARIAN
Mildred's   f/ff
Mildred's is so small (and
popular) that you may have
to share a table. The chaos
is worth it, however,
because the vegetarian
food – stir-fried vegetables,
bean burgers etc – is both
good and well-priced.
✉ 58 Greek St W1
(7, B5) ☎ 7494 1634
⊖ Tottenham Court
Road ⏰ Mon-Sat 12-
11pm, Sun 12.30-
6.30pm ♿ yes V

WESTMINSTER & PIMLICO

ASIAN

Jenny Lo's Tea House **£/££**
Started by the daughter of the late Kenneth Lo, whose **Memories of China** 67-69 Ebury St SW1 (5, H4) ☎ 7773 7734 raised Chinese food in London to a new level. Good soup, rice dishes and fried noodles.
✉ **14 Eccleston St SW1 (5, G5) ☎ 7259 0399 ⊖ Victoria 🕘 Mon-Sat 11.30am-3pm & 6-10pm [V]**

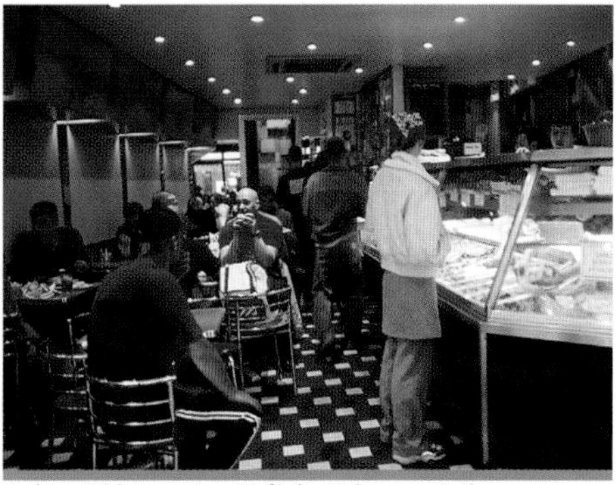
Simon Bracken
Soho's Old Compton Café (p. 97) opens 24hrs

ITALIAN

Uno 1 **£/££**
Pastas are particularly good value at this cheery dining room decorated in reds and yellows.
✉ **1 Denbigh St SW1 (5, G6) ☎ 7834 1001 ⊖ Victoria 🕘 Mon-Sat 12-3pm & 6.30-11.30pm 🚸 yes [V]**

MODERN BRITISH

Grumbles **££/£££**
This pleasant wine bar serves, among other things, stuffed aubergine, fish pie and sirloin steak. Grumbles is a popular place so it's advisable to book.
✉ **35 Churton St SW1 (5, G6) ☎ 7834 0149 ⊖ Victoria 🕘 12-2.30pm & 6-11pm**

INTERNET CAFES

easyEverything
A division of the no-frills airline easyJet, the first of what it says will be many 'Internet shops' across London.
✉ **12-14 Wilton Rd SW1, off Warwick St (5, G5) ☎ 7233 8456 [e] easyeverything.com ⊖ Victoria 🕘 24hrs $ £1/hr**

Buzz Bar
Upstairs from the Portobello Gold Hotel, Buzz Bar has a half-dozen terminals for hire.
✉ **95 Portobello Rd W11 (6, E1) ☎ 7460 4906 [e] buzzbar@hotmail.com, wwwbuzzbar.co.uk ⊖ Notting Hill Gate 🕘 Mon-Sat 10am-7pm $ £6/hr**

Cyberia
The first Internet cafe in London, Cyberia has full Internet access with a total of 27 terminals and also offers training.
✉ **39 Whitfield St W1 (6, C5) ☎ 7681 4224 [e] cyberia@easynet.co.uk, www.cyberiacafe. net ⊖ Goodge Street 🕘 Mon-Fri 10am-8pm, Sat 11am-7pm, Sun 11am-6pm $ £3/30mns; weekday training £30/2hrs**

Webshack
This is the most central cafe with 20 terminals available to use while you sip your coffee.
✉ **15 Dean St W1 (6, E5) ☎ 7439 8000 [e] webmaster@webshack-cafe.com, www.webshack-cafe.com ⊖ Tottenham Court Road 🕘 Mon-Sat 10.30am-midnight, Sun 1-8pm $ £3/5 ½/1hr**

Eating Reading

For hundreds of up-to-the minute reviews of London's eateries, check out Lonely Planet's *Out to Eat – London*, which provides comprehensive coverage of the best restaurants, cafes and gastropubs.

HIGH TEA

Given the important role that tea has always played in English culture and society, it should be no surprise that going out for 'afternoon tea', also known as 'high tea', is something dear to the hearts of Londoners.

Brown's Hotel   ££
Brown's dispenses tea in the Drawing Room every day, with a pianist to soothe away any lingering stress from the bustling streets outside. It's advisable to book.
✉ **30 Albemarle St W1 (6, F4)** ☎ **7493 6020** ⊖ **Green Park** ⊘ 3-6pm ♿ yes

Claridges Hotel (6, E3)   ££/£££
Claridges serves tea (and champagne 'tea') in its grand 18th century foyer. The opulent surrounds, elegant staff and fine cakes make this one of the best teas in town so booking is essential and men must wear jacket and tie.
✉ **Brook St W1** ☎ **7629 8860** ⊖ **Bond Street** ⊘ 3-5.30pm ♿ yes **V**

Fortnum & Mason (6, G4)   ££
The department store Fortnum & Mason serves tea at the Fortnum Fountain. It's a slightly less expensive tea than the hotels and booking ahead is advised.
✉ **181 Piccadilly W1** ☎ **7734 8040** ⊖ **Piccadilly Circus** ⊘ Mon-Sat 3-5pm ♿ yes

Meridien Waldorf Hotel (6, E8)   ££/£££
High tea is served week-days at the Waldorf in the splendidly restored Palm Court. At the weekend there's a chance to take part in the old-fashioned ritual of tea dancing, when booking is essential and prices rise.
✉ **Aldwych WC2** ☎ **7836 2400** ⊖ **Charing Cross** ⊘ Mon-Fri 3-5.30pm, Sat 2.30-5.30pm, Sun 4-6.30pm♿ yes **V**

Newens Maids of Honour   £
This old-fashioned tearoom wouldn't seem out of place in a Cotswold village. It owes its fame to the 'maid of honour', a special dessert made from puff pastry, lemon, almonds and curd cheese which was supposedly concocted by Henry VIII's 2nd wife, the ill-fated Anne Boleyn.
✉ **288 Kew Rd (2, C2)** ☎ **8940 2752** ⊖ **Kew Gardens** ⊘ Tues-Sat 2.30-5.30pm ♿ yes

Orangery   £/££
The graceful Orangery in Kensington Gardens is a superb place to have a relatively affordable all-day set tea; choose from one with cucumber sandwiches and scones or the more expensive champagne tea.
✉ **Kensington Gardens W8 (5, F3)** ☎ **7376 0239** ⊖ **High Street Kensington** ⊘ 10am-6pm Apr-Sept (till 4pm Oct-Mar) ♿ yes **V**

Ritz Hotel (6, G4)   £££
The Ritz is probably the best known place to take tea, although these days it's become something of a production-line process – the splendour of the florid pink and gold surroundings notwithstanding. You need to book a month ahead for weekdays and a ridiculous 3 months ahead for week-ends. Men must wear jacket and tie.
✉ **150 Piccadilly W1** ☎ **7493 8181** ⊖ **Green Park** ⊘ 2-6pm ♿ yes **V**

Savoy Hotel (6, F7)   ££/£££
Tea is served in the Savoy's enormous and opulent Thames Foyer accompanied by a pianist and a harpist. Bookings are essential and champagne tea is available. It's a strictly jacket and tie affair.
✉ **Strand WC2** ☎ **7836 4343** ⊖ **Charing Cross** ⊘ 3-5.30pm ♿ yes

Scrummy scones, sumptuous surrounds, super service

Simon Bracken

entertainment

It can be seriously difficult to entertain oneself in London – making the choice of what to do can be just too daunting. Whether you like your culture high or low; your dance in point shoes from afar or raving up close; your music symphony or indie; being sporty or watching the professionals at the cricket, football or tennis; drinking cocktails in a an elegant club or a bitter down the nearest pub; then London is your city.

London is the world's greatest centre for English-language theatre. Home to 5 symphony orchestras and major dance companies, along with many smaller more experimental outfits, it is also a major centre for classical music and ballet. Some remarkable venues such as the Royal Albert Hall (p. 87), hosting everything from rock concerts to classical performance, are worth the visit no matter what's on the program. Day or night all year around, there shouldn't ever be a problem finding something enjoyable to do in London and somewhere to do it.

Listings

To find out what's on, buy the comprehensive entertainment listings magazine *Time Out* (£1.80), which is published every Wednesday (though available Tuesday) and covers the week's events. *Hot Tickets*, free with the *Evening Standard* newspaper on Thursday, is another great source.

London Tourist Board's bimonthly *Events in London* or its *Annual Events* pamphlet provides information on the countless festivals and events held in and around London. The Board's Visitorcall service (☎ 09064-123 then dial 3 further digits; see p. 115 for further options) has listing for what's on this week (400), this month (410) and this quarter (401).

Bookings

Most theatre and concert hall box offices are open Monday to Saturday from 10am to 8 or 9pm. If a production is sold out you may be able to buy a returned ticket on the day of the performance, although for hit productions you might need to start queuing before returns actually go on sale.

Student stand-by tickets are sometimes available an hour before the commencement of a performance. Phone Student Theatre Line on ☎ 7379 8900 for further details on participating venues.

On the day of a performance you can buy half-price tickets for West End productions from the Leicester Square Half-Price Ticket Booth (7, D6; ⊖ Leicester Square). It's open 12 to 6.30pm, accepts cash only and charges £2 commission. Be wary of commercial ticket agencies near Leicester Square that advertise half-price tickets without mentioning the commission price.

Your best bet for concerts, musicals and other shows is Ticketmaster, which has a 24hr credit-card booking line (☎ 7413 1442 or 0990-344444; www.ticketmaster.co.uk). Also try Firstcall on ☎ 7420 1000. Many tickets can purchased from HMV or Tower Records, the Camden Ticket Shop attached to the Jazz Café at 3 Parkway NW1 (4, K4; ☎ 7344 0044 ⊖ Camden Town) or from the London Tourist Board centres at Victoria and Liverpool Street stations and at Heathrow.

What's On

January *London Parade* – on New Year's Day the Lord Mayor of Westminster leads a parade from Parliament Square to Berkeley Square

January/February *Chinese New Year* – lion dances in Soho (late Jan/early Feb)

March *Oxford vs Cambridge University Boat Race* – the traditional rowing race on the Thames from Putney to Mortlake

May *London Marathon* – a 42km (26 mile) run from Greenwich Park to the Mall via the Isle of Dogs and Victoria Embankment
Royal Windsor Horse Show – a showjumping event
Chelsea Flower Show – at Royal Hospital, Chelsea

June *Spitalfields Festival* – a 3 week celebration at Spitalfields Market with music, theatre, talks and walks
Beating Retreat – military bands and marching in Horse Guards Parade, Whitehall
Trooping the Colour – celebrates the Queen's official birthday with parades and pageantry in Horse Guards Parade
Wimbledon Lawn Tennis Championships – runs for 2 weeks in late June (p. 100)
City of London Festival – performances of music, dance, street theatre etc

July *Hampton Court Palace International Flower Show* – flowers galore in one of London's finest gardens
London Mardi Gras – features a gay & lesbian march and festival, Finsbury Park
Royal Tournament – world's biggest military tattoo, Earl's Court Exhibition Centre

July-September *Promenade Concerts* – classical music festival (p. 87)

August *Notting Hill Carnival* – a vast Caribbean carnival in Notting Hill on the last Sunday and Monday of the month

September *Open House* – general admission, on the third weekend of the month, to some 500 buildings and other sites normally closed to the public

October *Punch & Judy Festival* – a gathering of puppet fanatics in Covent Garden Piazza
Pearly Harvest Festival Service – brings over 100 Pearly Kings and Queens to a service at St Martin-in-the-Fields church
Trafalgar Day Parade – marching bands descend on Trafalgar Square to lay wreaths commemorating Nelson's victory over Napoleon in 1805

October-November *Dance Umbrella* – British and international companies performing at venues across London over a 5 week period

November *Guy Fawkes Day* – the 5th is the anniversary of an attempted coup with bonfires and fireworks – especially in Battersea Park (5, J4), Primrose Hill (4, J2), Blackheath (3, K5), Clapham Common (5, K5) and Crystal Palace Park (2, D3)
State Opening of Parliament – the Queen visits Parliament by state coach amid gun salutes
London Film Festival – at the National Film Theatre, South Bank
Lord Mayor's Show – on the 2nd Saturday the Lord Mayor travels by state coach from Guildhall to Royal Courts of Justice, amid floats, bands and fireworks
Remembrance Sunday – on the 2nd Sunday of the month, the Queen and government members lay wreaths at the Cenotaph to honour the dead of world wars

December *Lighting of the Christmas Tree* – at Trafalgar Square

THEATRE

There are some 50 West End theatres that stage a new crop of plays every summer – there's a lot more here than just *Cats, Rent* and *Phantom of the Opera.* If that isn't enough, at any time of the year London's many off-West End and fringe-theatres offer a selection of productions. With tickets so plentiful and reasonably priced, it would be a shame not to take in at least 1 or 2 of the best productions. Here's a selection of more established theatres and some lesser known ones and don't forget to check the program at the reconstructed Globe Theatre (p. 29).

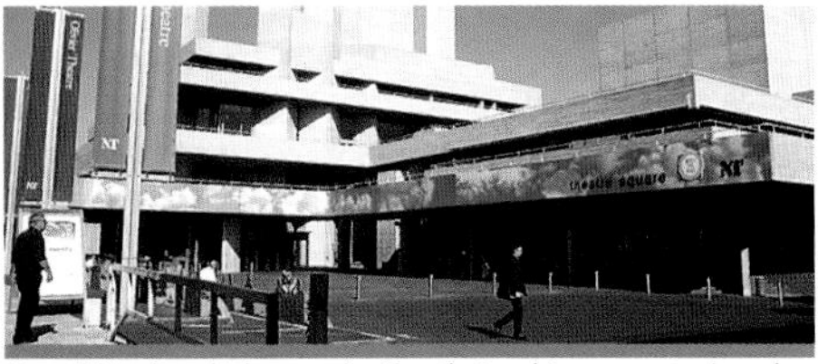

Juliet Coombe

Royal National Theatre in South Bank's concrete jungle

Almeida
In just a decade the Almeida has established itself as one of London's foremost and literate theatres and many of its ever-popular productions float at theatres in the West End.
✉ Almeida St N1 (5, B8) ☎ 7359 4404 ⊖ Angel or Highbury & Islington $ £6.50-19.50

Barbican (6, C12)
The London home of the Royal Shakespeare Company when it is not at Stratford-upon-Avon. There are 2 auditoriums – the Barbican Theatre and the smaller Pit. It has been criticised in the past for being less than cutting-edge.
✉ Silk St EC2 ☎ 7638 4141 (info), 7638 8891 (box office) ⊖ Barbican $ Barbican: £5-28; the Pit: £12-£20

Donmar Warehouse
This fine theatre near Covent Garden continues to stage some of the most sought-after productions in town, most recently *Oedipus* with Zoe Wanamaker and *The Blue Room* with Nicole Kidman.
✉ Earlham St WC2 (7, B6) ☎ 7369 1732 ⊖ Covent Garden $ £6.50-22

Royal Court
The Royal Court has returned home following a 4 year, £25 million refurbishment. It tends to favour the new and the anti-establishment – various *enfants terribles* from John Osborne to Caryl Churchill started here.
✉ Sloane Square SW1 (5, G5) ☎ 7565 5000 ⊖ Sloane Square $ cut-price tickets Mon

Royal National Theatre (6, G8)
The nation's flagship theatre has 3 auditoriums: the Olivier, the Lyttleton and the Cottesloe. It showcases classics and contemporary plays, and hosts guest appearances by the world's best young companies.
✉ South Bank SE1 ☎ 7452 3400 (info), 7452 3000 (box office) ⊖ Waterloo $ less for same-day purchase, standby, student and matinee tickets

Children's Theatre
Here's several theatres that play to a younger crowd:

Little Angel Theatre 14 Dagmar Passage N1 (5, C8) ☎ 7226 1787 ⊖ Angel
Polka Theatre for Children 240 The Broadway SW19 (2, D3) ☎ 8543 4888 ⊖ Wimbledon South
Unicorn Theatre for Children Pleasance Theatre, Carpenter's Mews, North Rd N7 (5, A7) ☎ 7609 1800 ⊖ Caledonian Rd

For other entertainment options for children see p. 42.

CLASSICAL MUSIC & OPERA

On any night of the year your classical music choice will range from traditional crowd-pleasers to new music and 'difficult' composers – most to a high standard, in brilliant venues and at reasonable prices. Opera can be more problematic because it's costly to produce and so costly to attend.

Barbican (6, C12)
The Barbican, not the most delightful of venues, is nevertheless home to the prestigious London Symphony Orchestra.
✉ Silk St EC2 ☎ 7638 4141 (info), 7638 8891 (box office) ⊖ Barbican Ⓢ student & over 60s stand-by £6.50/£9; normal price to £32

London Coliseum
(6, F6) The home of the English National Opera is a lot more reasonably priced than the Royal Opera House and presents opera in English. Reduced visibility tickets are available from 10am on the day of performance; expect a long queue.
✉ St Martin's Lane WC1 ☎ 7632 8300 ⊖ Leicester Square Ⓢ reduced-visibility £2.50; tickets normally £5-55

Royal Albert Hall
(5, F3) This splendid-looking (the acoustics are terrible) Victorian concert hall hosts all kinds of performances, including classical music. In summer, it stages the Proms – one of the world's biggest and most democratic classical music festivals.
✉ Kensington Gore SW7 ☎ 7589 8212 ⊖ South Kensington Ⓢ £5-£32; Proms standing room £3

Royal Opera House
(7, B8) Following a £213 million redevelopment, it has welcomed home the peripatetic Royal Opera and Royal Ballet. More proletarian post-makeover, the renovated Floral Hall is now open to the public during the day, with free lunchtime concerts, exhibitions and tours. The best opera seats will have you considering a second mortgage (less so for ballet).
✉ Covent Garden WC2 ☎ 7304 4000 ⊖ Covent Garden Ⓢ reduced-visibility seats from £6

South Bank Complex
(6, G8) The Royal Festival Hall, Queen Elizabeth Hall and the Purcell Room are 3 of London's premier venues for classical concerts – though the last 2 may yet be sacrificed to redevelopment.
✉ South Bank SE1 ☎ 7921 0600 (info), 7960 4242 (box office) ⊖ Waterloo Ⓢ £5-50

Wigmore Hall
This intimate Art Nouveau concert hall is arguably the finest place in London to hear classical music (chamber orchestras, pianists, classical guitarists etc). It offers a great variety of concerts and recitals; best are the Sunday recitals (11.30am) and Monday lunchtime concerts (1pm).
✉ 35 Wigmore St W1 (6, E2) ☎ 7935 2141 ⊖ Bond Street Ⓢ from £7; call for details

Elliot Daniel

The pit, Royal Albert Hall

The Proms
The real 'Prom' experience at the Royal Albert Hall is queuing for one of the 1000-odd standing (or 'promenading') tickets that go on sale an hour before the start of each concert staged from mid-July to mid-September. You can choose to stand in the gallery or the arena; queue separately for each. The Last Night of the Proms is one of those quintessential English affairs, all waving Union Jacks, drunken chanting of Elgar's *Land of Hope and Glory* and argument over whether the program was too modern. In recent years the action has also been relayed onto screens in nearby Hyde Park.

BALLET & DANCE

The Royal Ballet, the UK's best classical ballet company, has returned to the Royal Opera House (p. 87). Dance Umbrella sees British and international companies perform at venues across London in October and November. See London Dance Network (www.londondance.net) for more dance information.

Oodles of opera options

Charlotte Hindle

The Place

The Place, home to the Richard Alston Dance Company, is one of London's most important addresses for contemporary and experimental dance.
✉ **17 Duke's Rd WC1 (6, B6)** ☎ **7387 0031**
⊖ **Euston** Ⓢ **vary**

Riverside Studios

Riverside Studios is a mixed-media arts centre in west London with 2 good-sized auditoriums. It is particularly well known for staging small productions by small experimental and avant-garde dance companies.
✉ **Crisp Rd W6 (5, H1)** ☎ **7420 0100 (info), 8237 1111 (box office)**
⊖ **Hammersmith** Ⓢ **vary**

Sadler's Wells

(6, A10) Sadler's Wells, which reopened in 1998 after a total refurbishment, has been associated with dance ever since Thomas Sadler set up a 'musick house' next to his medicinal spa in 1683. This ultra-modern theatre attracts contemporary and classical dance troupes from around the world. Its second venue, the West End's **Peacock Theatre** at Portugal St WC2 (6, E8) ☎ 7863 8222 ⊖ Holborn, will now host the London Contemporary Dance Theatre and the London City Ballet.
✉ **Rosebery Ave EC1**
☎ **7863 8000**
⊖ **Angel** Ⓢ **vary**

COMEDY

London plays host to a number of clubs whose raison d'être is comedy; there are even more venues – especially pubs – that set aside specific nights for stand-up routine comedy acts.

Comedy Store

Mostly big acts appear at London's most established comedy club, now in its 3rd decade. The show starts Tuesday-Sunday at 8pm with a midnight show on Friday and Saturday.
✉ **1A Oxendon St SW1 (7, D5)** ☎ **7344 4444**
⊖ **Piccadilly Circus** Ⓢ **half-price concessions**

Improv Comedy Club

The Embassy Rooms, which recently hosted the Cockney Cabaret, is now a franchise of the American comedy chain. Saturday 10pm is the Rat Pack Club, with 'Frank Sinatra', 'Sammy Davis Jr' and 'Dean Martin'.
✉ **161 Tottenham Court Road W1 (6, D5)**
☎ **7387 2414** ⊖
Warren Street Ⓢ **£15**

Jongleurs Battersea

This is a branch of a comedy chain that plays it safe but keeps on packing them in. Other branches of the 'jugglers' chain include **Jongleurs Bow Wharf** at 221 Grove Rd E3 (2, C4 ⊖ Mile End) and **Jongleurs Camden Lock** at Dingwalls, Middle Yard NW1 (4, J4 ⊖ Camden Town).
✉ **49 Lavender Gardens SW11 (5, K4)**
☎ **7564 2500**
🚉 **Clapham Junction**
Ⓢ **usually £12**

ROCK & POP

London also boasts a wide range of rock and pop venues, and you can hear everything from megastars at Wembley (p. 101), Earl's Court and similar hangar-sized arenas, to hot new bands at numerous venues around town.

Smaller places with a more club-like atmosphere are worth checking out for local and visiting bands. The times given here are when you can expect to hear music; each venue may be open longer hours as a pub, club etc.

MEGA-VENUES
Brixton Academy
This enormous venue with a great atmosphere is popular with up-and-coming indie and rock groups.
⊠ **211 Stockwell Rd SW9 (5, K7)** ☎ **7924 9999** ⊖ **Brixton**

Earl's Court Exhibition Centre (5, H2)
This is one of a handful of venues in London for blockbuster concerts – the type that sell out well in advance.
⊠ **Warwick Rd SW5** ☎ **7373 8141** ⊖ **Earl's Court**

The Forum (4, H5)
Formerly the Town & Country club, this is still a great roomy venue despite some recent complaints about surly staff and the ageing sound system.
⊠ **9-17 Highgate Rd NW5** ☎ **8963 0940, 7344 0044** ⊖ **Kentish Town**

Hackney Empire
This superb Edwardian music hall hosts concerts as well as theatre, pantomime and comedy.
⊠ **291 Mare St E8 (2, B4)** ☎ **8985 2424** 🚉 **Hackney Central**

Shepherd's Bush Empire
Once part of BBC TV; now one of London's best venues for top rock, country, soul and indie bands.
⊠ **Shepherd's Bush**

Green W12 (2, C2) ☎ **8740 7474** ⊖ **Shepherd's Bush**

SMALL BUT LOUD
The Borderline
This small, relaxed basement venue has a reputation for big-name bands (REM, Blur, Oasis), many of whom have played under pseudonyms.
⊠ **Orange Yard, off Manette St W1 (7, B5)** ☎ **7734 2095** ⊖ **Tottenham Court Road** ◷ Mon-Fri 8-11pm

Camden Falcon
Oasis played their first London gig here (then known as Splash). It still attracts indie bands and their followers.
⊠ **234 Royal College St NW1 (4, K5)** ☎ **7485 3834** ⊖ **Camden Town** ◷ Mon-Sat 8-11pm, Sun 8-10.30pm

Dingwalls
Hosting indie acts Sunday to Thursday, it's comedy at the weekend (see Jongleurs Camden Lock, p. 88). There's a terrace bar overlooking Camden lock and market.
⊠ **Middle Yard, Camden Lock NW1 (4, J4)** ☎ **7428 5929 (info), 7267 3142 (box office)** ⊖ **Camden Town** ◷ Mon-Thurs 7.30pm-midnight, Sun 7.30-11pm

The Garage
Good venue for rock, industrial and punk.
⊠ **20-22 Highbury Cnr**

N5 (5, B8) ☎ **7607 1818** ⊖ **Highbury & Islington** ◷ Mon-Thurs 8pm-midnight, Fri-Sat 8pm-3am

Rock Garden
This small basement venue, often packed with tourists, hosts good bands.
⊠ **James St & The Piazza WC2 (7, C8)** ☎ **7240 3961** ⊖ **Covent Garden** ◷ Mon-Thurs 5pm-3am, Fri-Sat 5pm-5am, Sun 7pm-midnight

Subterania
An atmospheric place showcasing up-and-coming hip-hop and reggae acts.
⊠ **36 Acklam Rd, under Westway W10 (5, E1)** ☎ **8960 4590** ⊖ **Ladbroke Grove** ◷ Mon-Thurs 8pm-2am, Fri-Sat 10pm-3am, Sun 7pm-midnight

The Underworld
New bands play this small, crowded venue under the huge World's End pub.
⊠ **174 Camden High St NW1 (4, J4)** ☎ **7482 1932** ⊖ **Camden Town** ◷ 7.30-11pm

WKD
The smallish club downstairs has varied live music – jazz-rock the last time we visited. Upstairs is reserved for the glitterati.
⊠ **18 Kentish Town Rd NW1 (4, J4)** ☎ **7267 1869** ⊖ **Camden Town** ◷ Mon-Sat noon-2am, Sun noon-midnight

JAZZ

London has always had a thriving jazz scene and, with its recent resurgence thanks to acid-jazz, hip-hop, funk and swing, it's stronger than ever.

Jazz Café
Best book a table for this very hip restaurant venue.
✉ 5-7 Parkway NW1 (4, K4) ☎ 7916 6060
⊖ Camden Town
🕑 7pm-1am (till 2am Fri-Sat, midnight Sun)
Ⓢ £8-£15, cheaper in advance

100 Club
This legendary London venue, once showcasing the Stones and at the centre of the punk revolution, now concentrates on jazz. Once a month it

hosts a Northern Soul all-nighter that is said to be the dancing-est venue in London.
✉ 100 Oxford St W1 (6, E4) ☎ 7636 0933
⊖ Oxford Circus
🕑 Mon-Thurs 7.45pm-midnight, Fri 8.30pm-2am, Sat 7.30pm-1am, Sun 7.30-11.30pm

Pizza Express Jazz Club
Small basement venue beneath the main restaurant that goes for the big-name and the mainstream.

✉ 10 Dean St W1 (6, E5) ☎ 7439 8722
⊖ Tottenham Court Road 🕑 Mon-Thurs & Sun 9pm-11.30pm, Fri-Sat 9pm-midnight

Ronnie Scott's
Operating since 1959, this seedy and enjoyable venue attracts big-name talent, but is expensive if you're not a member.
✉ 47 Frith St W1 (6, E5) ☎ 7439 0747
⊖ Leicester Square
🕑 Mon-Sat 8.30pm-3am, Sun 7.30-10.30pm

FOLK, TRADITIONAL & WORLD MUSIC

Africa Centre
Has African music concerts on Friday and other one-offs on Saturday and during the week.
✉ 38 King St WC2 (7, C7) ☎ 7836 1973
⊖ Covent Garden
🕑 Fri-Sat 10pm-3am

Cecil Sharp House
The HQ of the English Folk Song & Dance Society, this is *the* venue for English folk music (an acquired taste, it must be said). On Tuesday at 8pm, as well as

esoterica such as barn and clog dancing, there's Cajun fiddling, Irish set dancing and Balkan circle dancing.
✉ 2 Regent's Park Rd NW1 (4, J2) ☎ 7485 2206 ⊖ Camden Town
🕑 variable

Mean Fiddler
This legendary venue excels in top-quality acoustic folk, Irish and country music.
✉ 24-28 High St NW10 (2, C2) ☎ 8961 5490 (info), 8961 5490 (box

office) ⊖ Willesden Junction 🕑 Mon-Thurs & Sun 8pm-2am, Fri-Sat 8pm-3am

Swan
Traditional Irish bands play every night in this large pub directly opposite the Stockwell tube station.
✉ 215 Clapham Rd SW9 (5, J7) ☎ 7978 9778 ⊖ Stockwell 🕑 Mon-Wed 5-11.30pm, Thurs 5pm-2am, Fri 5pm-3am, Sat 7pm-3am, Sun 7pm-2am

Not always the habitat of the lager lout; pubs can be perfect places to enjoy a quiet pint.

Simon Bracken

CINEMAS

During the 1950s and 60s many of London's great Art Deco cinema houses shut down. The first multiplex cinemas appeared in the late 80s and the revival continues. Offering more choice of films at one site and more comfortable seating, they can also be expensive and show mostly mainstream American fare. Full-price tickets can cost £8 to £10 for a first-run film; an afternoon weekday session and anytime on Monday is usually cheaper.

An ambitious refurbishment of the Edwardian Electric Cinema, 191 Portobello Rd W11 (5, E2 ⊖ Notting Hill), the oldest purpose-built movie theatre in the UK, may now be complete with a new 3 storey annexe, 200 comfy seats, a bar and a bookshop.

London Imax Cinema
Part of the British Film Institute, the new £20 million London IMAX Cinema is the largest in Europe, with a screen some 10 storeys tall and 26m wide. The 485-seat cinema screens the usual 2D and IMAX 3D films – documentaries about travel, space and wildlife. The building itself is impressive: shaped like a drum, it sits on 'springs' to reduce vibrations and traffic noise from outside, and the exterior changes colour at night.
✉ Waterloo Bullring SE1 (6, G9) ☎ 7902 1234 ⊖ Waterloo 🕘 Multiple screenings daily $ £6.50/5.50/ 4.50 a/s,st/c

National Film Theatre
The modern National Film Theatre, built in 1958, screens some 2000 films a year; for details check *Time Out*. It also hosts the **London Film Festival** (☎ 7420 1122): a cinematic cornucopia of less regularly screened gems.
✉ South Bank SE1 (6, H8) ☎ 7633 0274 (info), 7928 3232 (box office) ⊖ Waterloo

Prince Charles Cinema (7, C6)
Far and away central London's cheapest cinema, it shows several films each day and usually has a range of new releases, foreign and old films on the program.
✉ cnr Lisle St & Leicester Place WC2 ☎ 7437 8181, 0800-192 192 [e] www .cyborg.org/pcc ⊖ Leicester Square $ £2-£2.50

Fresh Air Culture
London can't boast the world's best weather but that doesn't mean you're limited to cinema outings or other indoor pursuits. When the sun shines, take in a Shakespearean play or a musical at the **Open Air Theatre** in Regent's Park (6, B1; ☎ 7486 2431), although you may find some of the dialogue drowned out by planes overhead. Another summer's day highlight is to see a classical concert in the grounds of **Kenwood House** (p. 34).

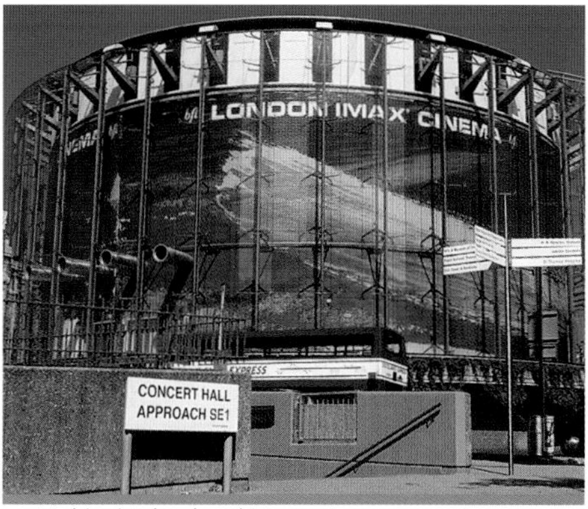

Elliot Daniel

It's big, it's loud and it's coming to a movie near you.

DANCE CLUBS

Though the majority of London's pubs still close at 11pm, there are clubs where you can carry on partying, although you'll have to pay to get in and the drinks are always expensive. Late-night venues often have a 'club' licence, which means you have to be a member to enter. In practice, they usually include the membership fee in the admission price.

Dress can be smart (ie no suits) or casual; the more outrageous you look the better chance you have of getting in. But in the end that all depends, of course, on the gorilla at the door.

It Costs to Club

Entry prices can be hefty, varying from £10 to £15. Drinks are likely to cost at least £3 a pop, and you'll have to leave a spare £10 in your pocket for the end of the night cab fare.

The Aquarium

The Aquarium is a converted gym with its own cool pool, spa and restaurant. It opens on Sunday too.
⊠ 255-260 Old St EC1 (6, B13) ☎ 7251 6136 ⊖ Old St ⏱ Fri 10pm-4am; Sat 10am-6pm, Sun 7pm-midnight

Browns

This is the stars' after-party, piss-elegant hang-out – dress way, way up.
⊠ 4 Great Queen St WC2 (6, E7) ☎ 7831 0802 ⊖ Holborn ⏱ Tue-Thurs 11pm-3.30am, Sat-Sun till 4am

Bug Bar

In the crypt of St Matthew's Church, with vaulted ceilings, pews and frescoes, Bug Bar is not for the superstitious. Bands play Tuesday, DJs at the weekend and it's techno night on Thursday.

⊠ cnr Brixton Hill & St Matthew's Rd SW2 (5, K7) ☎ 7738 3184 ⊖ Brixton ⏱ Mon-Sat 7pm-2am, Sun 5pm-10.30pm

The Complex

What was the Blue Note in Hoxton Square has moved to Islington and now has 4 floors of diverse sounds with the top one – the Love Lounge – reserved for chilling out (or whatever).
⊠ 1-5 Parkfield St N1 (5, C8) ☎ 7288 1986 ⊖ Angel ⏱ Fri 10pm-7am, Sat 10pm-5am

The Cross

One of London's leading venues, it's hidden under the arches. Brilliant DJs. Friday night's Liquid is aimed at 'the more sophisticated and educated clubbers'. Oh-oh.
⊠ King's Cross Goods Yard, off York Way N1 (5, C7) ☎ 7837 0828 ⊖ King's Cross ⏱ Fri-Sat 10pm-6am

Dogstar

Dogstar is as casual as you'd expect from a converted pub. Great Sunday tea dance from 2pm to midnight but the scrum is overwhelming.
⊠ 389 Coldharbour Lane, cnr Atlantic Rd SW9 (5, K8) ☎ 7733 7515

⊖ Brixton ⏱ Mon-Thurs noon-midnight, Fri-Sat noon-4am

Dust

A mixed bag club-bar with everything from techno and house to Latin and French funk. Free entry all week.
⊠ 27 Clerkenwell Rd EC1 (6, C10) ☎ 7490 0537 ⊖ Farringdon ⏱ Thurs noon-1am, Fri-Sat noon-2am

The Emporium

Popular with the beautiful set, Emporium is one of the trendiest clubs in town.
⊠ 62 Kingly St W1 (7, C3) ☎ 7734 3190 ⊖ Oxford Circus ⏱ Wed 9pm-4am, Fri-Sat 9pm-6am

The End

This club, with its postmodern industrial decor and free water fountain, is for serious clubbers who like their music underground.
⊠ 18 West Central St WC1 (7, A7) ☎ 7419 9199 ⊖ Holborn ⏱ Tue-Thurs 10pm-3am, Fri 11pm-5am, Sat 11pm-6am, Sun 8pm-4am

The Fridge

An excellent venue – not too big, not too small – has a variety of club nights. Saturday is gay night.

✉ 1 Town Hall Parade, Brixton Hill SW2 (5, K7) ☎ 7326 5100 ⊖ Brixton ⏱ Mon-Wed 9.30pm-2am, Thurs 9.30pm-4am, Fri-Sat 10pm-6am, Sun 6-11am & 8.30pm-12.30am

Hanover Grand
This split-level venue, voted 'Best Club in London' 2 years running, is worth queuing for. Saturday night is Future Perfect, with house, big beats and a strict dress code.
✉ 6 Hanover St W1 (7, B2) ☎ 7499 7977 ⊖ Oxford Circus ⏱ Wed-Fri 10.30pm-3.30am, Sat 10.30pm-5.30am

HQ
HQ is predominantly a garage and house club that tends to attract a mixed crowd due to its location.
✉ West Yard, Camden Lock NW1 (4, J4) ☎ 7485 6044 ⊖ Camden Town ⏱ Mon-Thurs 9pm-2am, Fri-Sat 8pm-2am, Sun 7pm-midnight

Iceni
Three floors of contrasting music, 6 bars and a friendly atmosphere make Iceni one of the more accessible clubs in town.
✉ 11 White Horse St, off Curzon St W1 (6, G3) ☎ 7499 5333 ⊖ Green Park ⏱ Fri 11pm-3am, Sat 10pm-3am

Leopard Lounge
LL is a large safari-theme club that attracts the more feral Londoner.
✉ The Broadway, Fulham Rd SW6 (5, H2) ☎ 7385 0834 ⊖ Fulham Broadway ⏱ Thurs-Sat 10pm-3am

Club is in the Air
Clubs can change from night to night, depending on the DJ and the targeted crowd – techno heads, gays, salsa fans etc. General opening times are given here, but for specific theme and time information, see *Time Out* or flyers at pubs and record shops around Soho.

Ministry of Sound
One of the most famous clubs (though well past its finest hour), this cavernous place attracts hard-core clubbers as well as people who just want to chill out.
✉ 103 Gaunt St SE1 (6, J11) ☎ 7378 6528 ⊖ Elephant & Castle ⏱ Fri 10.30pm-6am, Sat midnight-9am

Notting Hill Arts Club
The jewel in the crown of this cosy, groovy club is Thursday's Future World Funk.
✉ 21 Notting Hill Gate W11 (5, F2) ☎ 7460 4459 ⊖ Notting Hill Gate ⏱ Mon-Wed 7pm-1am, Thurs-Sat 7pm-2am, Sun 4-11pm

Smithfields
Smithfields is a 4 room club with a different beat in each. Thursday night is Soirée, with French hip-hop and DJs fresh in from Paris.
✉ 341-343 Farringdon St EC4 (6, C10) ☎ 7236 4266 ⊖ Farringdon ⏱ Mon-Wed 11am-11pm, Thurs-Sat 11am-3am

Velvet Room
The Room is an intimate, friendly club swathed in – wait for it – red velvet.
✉ 143 Charing Cross Rd WC2 (6, E6) ☎ 7439 4655 ⊖ Tottenham Court Road ⏱ 9pm till 2.30am Wed, 3am Thurs, 4am Fri-Sat

Vibe Bar
A watering hole in a former brewery in trendy Brick Lane with one-off club nights that attract students from the nearby Guildhall University. Friday is Bangla Town with Asian funk.
✉ Truman Brewery, 91 Brick Lane E1 (6, C5) ☎ 7247 1231 ⊖ Shoreditch or Aldgate ⏱ 11am-1am

Another London DJ scratching a living

Simon Bracken

PUBS & BARS

Pubs are perhaps the most distinctive contribution the English have made to urban social life and nothing really compares to a good one. What that constitutes – beyond a wide range of beer and real ales – is very subjective and almost indefinable. This can include a warm welcome, a sense of bonhomie, the feel of a 'local' (ie patronised by people from the neighbourhood and not just a bunch of faceless transients and tourists). The following includes some of our favourites, but there's no substitute for your own research. For more suggestions look for the *Evening Standard Pub Guide* (£9.99) or the *Time Out Pubs & Bars Guide* (£5.99).

The Anchor
This 18th century place just east of the Globe Theatre has superb views across the Thames from its terrace and is the nicest (and most popular) riverside pub in London.
✉ **34 Park St, Bankside SE1 (6, G12)**
☎ **7407 1577**
⊖ **London Bridge**
♿ **restaurant only**

The Angel
This riverside pub, off Jamaica Rd, dates back to the 15th century. Captain Cook supposedly prepared for his trip to Australia from here and Samuel Pepys quenched his thirst after he gorged on cherries in Cherry Gardens to the south-west. Just opposite in Cathay St are the remains of the Edward III's Moated Manor House built in 1361.
✉ **101 Bermondsey Wall East SE16 (6, H15)**

☎ **7237 3608**
⊖ **Rotherhithe** ♿ **dining area only**

Beach Blanket Babylon
This is one of our favourite 'crazies'; find it next to the Well Hung Gallery. It boasts extraordinary Gothic decor and is a great place for observing Notting Hill trendies at play and rest ('Oh, hi Hugh, hi Julia').
✉ **45 Ledbury Rd W11 (5, E2)** ☎ **7229 2907**
⊖ **Notting Hill Gate**
♿ **yes**

Bierodrome
The latest effort by the Belgo group (the people who introduced London to mussels, chips and mayonnaise) pays homage to the suds: over 200 types of beer are available.
✉ **173-174 Upper St N1 (5, B8)** ☎ **7226 5835** ⊖ **Highbury & Islington or Angel**

Cantaloupe
This was the first kid on the block when Hoxton and Shoreditch started to get trendy, and it still manages to feel arty enough without being overwhelming. There's a decent restaurant here.
✉ **35-43 Charlotte Rd EC2 (6, B14)** ☎ **7613 4411** ⊖ **Old St**
🕐 **Mon-Sat 11am-midnight, Sun 12-4pm**

The Captain Kidd
The Kidd, with its large windows, fine beer garden and mock scaffold recalling the hanging of the eponymous pirate in 1701, is our favourite north bank Thames-side pub.
✉ **108 Wapping High St E1 (5, F10)** ☎ **7480 5759** ⊖ **Wapping**

The Churchill Arms
This traditional English pub is renowned for its Winston

It's Beer o'clock – Pub Opening Hours
Pubs can have complex opening hours. In general, they're open Monday to Saturday 11am to 11pm and on Sunday noon to 10.30pm. In this chapter, we've only provided those opening hours that vary from the norm. Some neighbourhood and suburban pubs still close in the afternoon (which used to be the law) from 3pm to between 5.30 and 7.30pm.

Ahoy, it's the Cap'n

memorabilia, chamber pots suspended from a great height (go figure) and decent Thai food served in a lovely conservatory.

✉ **119 Kensington Church St W8 (5, F2)**
☎ **7727 4242**
⊖ **Notting Hill**

The Coach & Horses
The Coach is a small, busy pub that has a regular clientele but is nonetheless hospitable to visitors. It was made famous by the much missed alcoholic *Spectator* columnist Jeffrey Bernard.

✉ **29 Greek St W1 (6, E5)** ☎ **7437 5920**
⊖ **Leicester Square**

Denim
Denim is an ultra-trendy bar (and restaurant) for the glitterati, with hugely expensive drinks, a wall of blank TV screens and a restaurant on the mezzanine level. Clearly a place to be seen entering.

✉ **4A Upper St Martin's Lane WC2 (6, F6)** ☎ **7497 0376**
⊖ **Leicester Square** ⊘ **Mon-Sat noon-1.30am, Sun 12-10.30pm**

The Engineer
A pretty Victorian place converted into a highly successful pub and gastropub restaurant (upstairs, the Engineer attracts a groovy north London set).

✉ **65 Gloucester Ave NW1 (4, J3)** ☎ **7722 0950** ⊖ **Chalk Farm**
⚹ **yes**

The Fire Station
This immensely popular pub and gastropub is in a part of town that was once a culinary desert. There's jazz on Sunday afternoon.

Good for What Ales You
In public houses (or 'pubs') you can order wine or a cocktail, but the *raison d'être* of these establishments is to serve beer – be it lager, ale or stout in a pint (570ml) or half-pint (285ml) glass. The term lager refers to the amber-coloured bottom-fermented beverage found the world over. In general lagers are highly carbonated, of medium hop flavour and drunk cool or cold. Ale is a top-fermented beer whose flavours can run the gamut from subtle to robust. They can be very slightly gassy or completely still, have a strong hop flavour and are drunk at slightly above room temperature. There are dozens of varieties but when in doubt just ask for 'a bitter' and you'll be served the house ale.

✉ **150 Waterloo Rd SE1 (6, H9)** ☎ **7620 2226**
⊖ **Waterloo** ⊘ **Mon-Sat 11am-11pm, Sun 12-5pm** ⚹ dining room only

The Flask
The Hampstead Flask is a friendly local that's handy for the tube, with high ceilings, real ale and good Asian-inspired food. Not to be confused with its older sister pub across the heath also called **The Flask** (77 Highgate West Hill N6; 4, D5; ⊖ Highgate) which is a maze of snugs.

✉ **14 Flask Walk NW3 (4, E2)** ☎ **7435 4580**
⊖ **Hampstead**

The George Inn
The George is a rare bird indeed – a National Trust pub. It's London's last surviving galleried coaching inn dating from 1676 and is mentioned in Charles Dickens' *Little Dorrit*. Here too is the site of the Tabard Inn (thus Talbot Yard), where the pilgrims gathered that Chaucer's *Canterbury Tales* before setting out.

✉ **Talbot Yard, 77**

570ml of tepid liquid amber

Simon Bracken

Borough High St SE1 (6, G13) ☎ **7407 2056**
⊖ **London Bridge**
⚹ lunchtime only

Gordon's
This atmospheric wine bar (no beer) in ancient vaults beneath the street is as close as you'll get to drinking in the London Dungeon. The cold buffets are marvellous, but you'll need to nip in quickly after work to get a table.

✉ **47 Villiers St WC2 (7, E7)** ☎ **7930 1408**
⊖ **Charing Cross**
⚹ daytime only

Jamaica Wine House
The 'Jam Pot' is an authentic Victorian pub (yes, everything's real) on the site of London's first coffee house ('houses' were often just fronts for brothels). But the only whores (of both sexes) here nowadays are

Fancy a pint in the Rat & Codpiece?

These days traditional pubs can be thin on the ground in London; in many areas spruced-up chain pubs – look for the words 'slug', 'lettuce', 'rat', 'firkin', 'moon' and 'parrot' in their names – have taken over the role of 'local'. American-style bars and Irish pubs are also very popular.

the ones who sell their souls between 9am and 5pm Monday to Friday.
✉ **St Michael's Alley off Cornhill EC3 (6, E13)** ☎ 7626 9496 ⊖ **Bank** ⏱ **Mon-Fri 11am-11pm**

The King's Head & Eight Bells

This attractive corner pub pleasantly hung with flower baskets in summer has a wide range of beers and was a favourite of the painter Whistler and the writer Carlyle, who lived at 24 Cheyne Row.
✉ **50 Cheyne Walk SW3 (5, H4)** ☎ 7352 1820 ⊖ **Sloane Square** ⏱ **Mon-Sat 12-11pm, Sun 12-10.30pm**

The Lamb & Flag

Everyone's 'find' and thus always jammed. This

Conservatory, Churchill Arms

Simon Bracken

pleasantly unchanged pub was once known as the Bucket of Blood – either because of the fighters who favoured it as a local or because the poet John Dryden was attacked outside in 1679 for having written vicious verses about King Charles II's mistress.
✉ **33 Rose St WC2 (7, C7)** ☎ 7497 9504 ⊖ **Covent Garden** ♿ **lunchtime only**

Mash

Mash is a thoroughly groovy in-house brewery decorated to look like what the current decade would have appeared to some imaginative designer 30 years ago (a kind of arse-end-backward *Back in Time* concept).
✉ **19-21 Great Portland St W1 (6, D4)** ☎ 7637 5555 ⊖ **Oxford Circus** ⏱ **Mon-Sat 8am-2am, Sun 10am-10.30pm**

The Museum Tavern

After a hard day's work in the British Museum Reading Room, Karl Marx used to repair to this capacious pub, where you too can sup your pint and reflect on dialectical materialism in silence (no canned music or jukebox).
✉ **49 Great Russell St WC1 (6, D6)** ☎ 7242 8987 ⊖ **Holborn**

Princess Louise

This is a delightful and eternally popular example of Victorian pub decor with fine tiles, etched mirrors, columns, plasterwork and an open fire in winter.
✉ **208 High Holborn WC1 (6, D8)** ☎ 7405 8816 ⊖ **Holborn** ⏱ **Mon-Sat 11am-11pm**

The Queen's Larder

Located in a beautiful square off Russell Square, the Queen offers a handy retreat from the crowds, with outside tables and pub grub.
✉ **1 Queen's Square WC1 (6, C7)** ☎ 7837 5627 ⊖ **Russell Square**

The Salisbury

Brave the crowds here just to see the beautifully etched and engraved windows and other Victorian features that were miraculously brought back to life in the 1960s – a time when places like this were being torn down.
✉ **90 St Martin's Lane WC2 (6, F6)** ☎ 7836 5863 ⊖ **Leicester Square** ♿ **yes**

Three Kings of Clerkenwell

A friendly, family-run pub a stone's throw from the green, it's festooned with papier-mâché models, including a giant rhino head above the fireplace.
✉ **7 Clerkenwell Close EC1 (6, B10)** ☎ 7253 0483 ⊖ **Farringdon** ⏱ **Mon-Tues 12-3pm, 5.30-11.30pm, Wed-Fri 12-11pm, Sat 6.30-11pm**

Trafalgar Tavern

(3, G3) This cavernous pub with big windows

looking onto the Thames and the Millennium Dome is steeped in history. It stands above the site of the old Placentia Palace where Henry VIII was born. Dickens knocked back a few here and prime ministers Gladstone and Disraeli used to dine on the pub's celebrated whitebait.
✉ **Park Row SE10** ☎ **8858 2437** 🚃 **DLR Cutty Sark** ♿ **dining room only**

Waxy O'Connors
Waxy O'Connors is a large, multi-level Irish pub with a quirky, Gothic interior.
✉ **14-16 Rupert St W1 (7, C5)** ☎ **7287 0255** ♦ **Leicester Square**

Ye Olde Mitre
One of our absolute favourites, the Mitre is in a small alleyway linking Hatton Garden and Ely Place and is one of London's oldest and most historic pubs. But the 18th century-sized snugs can be a bit tight for us 21st-century punters.
✉ **1 Ely Court EC1 (6, D10)** ☎ **7405 4751** ♦ **Chancery Lane**

The Warrington
A former hotel and brothel is it's now an ornate Art Nouveau pub with character aplenty and a very laid-back atmosphere. There's courtyard seating and – inevitably – a Thai restaurant upstairs.
✉ **93 Warrington Crescent W9 (5, D3)** ☎ **7286 2929** ♦ **Warwick Ave**

OPEN ALL HOURS

London might party long, hard and late in the city's dance clubs (p. 92) but elsewhere it can be an early-to-bed kind of town. Still, there are options – if you know where to look.

CAFES & RESTAURANTS

Bar Italia
This great favourite has wonderful 1950s decor. It's always packed and buzzing (from the caffeine, no doubt).
✉ **22 Frith St W1 (7, B5)** ☎ **7437 4520** ♦ **Leicester Square** ⏰ **Mon-Sat 24hrs, Sun 7am-4am**

Mezzo
Another Conran venture that attracts a late-night media crowd and wannabes, the basement Mezzo (£££) is massive. Serving Modern European cuisine, it's a popular and fun place to eat, so book ahead. More casual and cheaper is the ground floor **Mezzonine**, an Asian fusion place (££).
✉ **100 Wardour St W1 (6, E5)** ☎ **7314 4000** ♦ **Piccadilly Circus** ⏰ **Mezzo: Mon-Thurs 6pm-12am (till 1am Fri-Sat, 11pm Sun); Mezzonine: Mon-Thurs 5.30pm-1am, till 3am Fri-Sat** ♿ **yes**

1997 Special Zone
For that 4am Peking duck craving or for comforting soup noodles anytime.
✉ **19 Wardour St W1 (6, F5)** ☎ **7734 2868** ♦ **Piccadilly Circus** ⏰ **24hrs**

Old Compton Café
A friendly, sometimes frantic cafe in the middle of Soho. It's mostly gay but welcomes everyone.
✉ **34 Old Compton St W1 (6, E5)** ☎ **7439 3309** ♦ **Piccadilly Circus** ⏰ **24hrs**

Vingt-Quatre
The place to go if you're looking for a late-night meal. '80' is an extremely popular place that has a proper menu at lunch and dinner but serves more basic stuff after midnight (when the bar closes). We only wonder why there aren't more places like this.
✉ **325 Fulham Rd SW10 (5, H3)** ☎ **7376 7224** ♦ **South Kensington then bus No 14 or 211** ⏰ **24hrs** Ⓥ

La dolce vita, Soho style

Simon Bracken

PUBS & BARS
Bar Rumba
This small cocktail/dancing bar, next to the Trocadero in the heart of Soho, has a loyal following not just because of its generous opening hours. Tuesday is Rumba Pa'ti, Saturday is Garage City and Asian fusion one Friday a month. ✉ **36 Shaftesbury Ave W1 (6, F5)** ☎ **7287 2715** ↔ **Piccadilly Circus** ⊙ **Mon-Fri 5pm-3.30am, Sat 7pm-6am, Sun 8pm-2am**

Duck into 1997 for early morning or late-night nosh-up

Charlie Wright's International Bar
This is a useful address if you want to carry on after usual pub hours in the Hoxton/Shoreditch area. Clientele is a mixed bag (as far as we can remember). ✉ **45 Pitfield St N1 (6, A14)** ☎ **7490 8345** ↔ **Old Street** ⊙ **Mon-Wed noon-1am, Thurs-Sun noon-2am**

Cuba
A downstairs bar with live band or DJ nightly. Does great mojito cocktails and there's salsa lessons too. ✉ **11-13 Kensington High St W14 (5, G2)**

☎ **7938 4137** ↔ **High Street Kensington** ⊙ **Mon-Sat 11am-2am, Sun 2-10.30pm**

Cuba Libre
A lively bar at the back of a fairly ordinary restaurant has great cocktails. ✉ **72 Upper St N1 (5, B8)** ☎ **7354 9998** ↔ **Angel** ⊙ **noon till 1am Mon-Wed, 2am Thurs-Sat, 10.30pm Sun**

Havana
You could hardly miss this place even if you did blink: it's a neon-lit blue and ochre tiled cocktail bar/restaurant with zebra-striped and

leopard-spotted seating. ✉ **490 Fulham Rd SW6 (5, H3)** ☎ **7381 5005** ↔ **Fulham Broadway** ⊙ **Mon-Sat noon-2am, Sun noon-midnight**

The O Bar
This bar masquerading as a club has 2 main drinking floors with a DJ downstairs at the weekend. Go for half-price pitchers of cocktails before 8pm weeknights. Has a branch at 111 Camden High St NW1 (4, K4). ✉ **83-85 Wardour St W1 (6, E5)** ☎ **7381 5005** ↔ **Piccadilly Circus** ⊙ **Mon-Sat noon-2am, noon-midnight**

GAY & LESBIAN LONDON

London's bars and clubs cater for every predilection, but there's a growing trend towards mixed gay and straight clubs. Check the press for men or women-only nights. Much of the activity is centred in Soho but you'll find pubs, cafes and clubs in every direction.

CAFES
Balans Café
Balan's is a moderately priced and popular, continental-style cafe. A branch called **Balans West** (☎ 7244 8838) is at 239 Old Brompton Rd SW5 (5, H2;

↔ Earl's Court). ✉ **60 Old Compton St W1 (6, E5)** ☎ **7437 5212** ↔ **Tottenham Court Road** ⊙ **8am-1am**

First Out
This long-established,

friendly lesbian-gay cafe serves vegetarian food and hosts exhibitions from time to time. ✉ **52 St Giles High St WC2 (6, D6)** ☎ **7240 8042** ↔ **Tottenham Court Road**

🕐 Mon-Sat 10am-11pm, Sun 11am-10.30pm

Freedom Café
A large hyper-trendy cafe and bar serving food and drink to a mixed clientele.
✉ 60-66 Wardour St W1 (6, E5) ☎ 7734 0071 ⊖ Piccadilly
🕐 11pm-3am

PUBS, BARS & CLUBS

The Astoria (6, E6)
In the basement of this dark, sweaty and atmospheric club are cheap gay nights on Monday and Thursday. The Astoria is the place to head on Friday when Camp Attack lets loose 1970s disco and retro funk.
✉ 157-165 Charing Cross Rd WC2 ☎ 7434 6963 ⊖ Tottenham Court Road 🕐 Mon, Thurs-Fri 11pm-4am

Candy Bar
The UK's first and only lesbian bar open 7 nights a week, the Candy Bar is the venue of choice among the clitorati of London and is always packed.
✉ 4 Carlisle St W1 (7, B4) ☎ 7494 4041 ⊖ Tottenham Court Road
🕐 Mon-Thurs 5pm-12am, Fri 5pm-2am, Sat 12pm-2am, Sun 5-11pm

Central Station
The ever-popular Central Station has a bar with special one-nighters, and the UK's only gay sports bar. It gets very cruisy later on.
✉ 37 Wharfdale Rd N1 (5, C7) ☎ 7278 3294 ⊖ King's Cross 🕐 Mon-Wed 5pm-2am, Thurs 5pm-3am, Fri-Sat 12-4am, Sun noon-midnight

Balan's is bang in the middle of 'gay village' Soho.

Heaven
London's most popular gay club has 3 floors, a new look and the full range of theme nights – from bubble gum pop on Tuesday to hard house on Thursday and Friday.
✉ Under the Arches, Villiers St WC2 (6, F7) ☎ 7930 2020 ⊖ Charing Cross or Embankment 🕐 Mon & Wed 10pm-3am, Fri-Sat 10.30pm-6am

Rupert St
Piss-elegant Rupert St, London's trendiest gay bar, is handily located on a street corner. It has large glass windows for looking, being looked at, looking at being looked at etc. Lots of looking, little cruising.
✉ 50 Rupert St W1 (7, C5) ☎ 7734 5164 ⊖ Piccadilly 🕐 Mon-Sat 11am-11pm, Sun 12-10.30pm

Turnmills
This large club has 3 gay nights. From 4am Saturday it's Trade, London's first all-nighter and arguably *the* gay superclub. Melt has techno and trance music on Sunday. Monday brings in Club Epsilon till dawn.
✉ 63b Clerkenwell Rd EC1 (6, C9) ☎ 7250 3409 ⊖ Farringdon 🕐 Sat 4am-1pm, Sun 10pm-6am, Mon 10pm-6am

The White Swan
If your tastes run towards barrow boys (some real, lots *faux*) with No 1 buzz cuts, check out the talent at the friendliest, cruisiest pub/club in the East End. Saturday night is BJ's.
✉ 556 Commercial Rd E14 (5, E10) ☎ 7780 9870 ⊖ Aldgate East 🚆 DLR Limehouse 🕐 9pm till 1am Mon, 2am Tues-Thurs, 3am Fri-Sat; Sun 5.30pm-12am

Gay & Lesbian News
The best starting point is to pick up the free *Pink Paper*, very serious and political, or *Boyz*, more geared toward entertainment, available from most gay cafes, bars and clubs. Magazines like *Gay Times* (£2.50) and the lesbian *Diva* (£2) also have listings. The gay section of *Time Out* is another excellent source of information.

SPECTATOR SPORTS

Athletics

Athletics meetings attracting major international and domestic stars take place regularly throughout the summer at the Crystal Palace National Sports Centre.

Cricket

Despite the average performance of the England team, the game is still popular. Test matches take place at Lord's and the **Oval** (5, H7). Tickets are pricey (£15-45), but tend to go fast. You might have more luck with a country fixture such as Middlesex at Lord's or Surrey at the Oval.

Football

There are a dozen league teams in London; around 6 enjoy the big time of the Premier League. So any weekend of the season, from August to mid-May, quality football is just a tube ride away. Phone for match details/credit card bookings: **Arsenal** ☎ 7704 4040, 7413 3366; **Chelsea** ☎ 7385 5545, 7386 7799; **Tottenham Hotspur** ☎ 8365 5000, 0870-840 2468; **Watford** ☎ 01923-496000, 01923 496010; **West Ham United** ☎ 8548 2748, 8548 2700; and **Wimbledon** ☎ 8771 2233, 8771 8841.

Rugby Union & League

South-west London is the focus for rugby union, with teams such as the Harlequins, Wasps and Richmond. Each year, starting in January, the 4 nations of the British Isles, France and Italy compete in the Six Nations Rugby Union Championship. The **London Broncos,** based at Stoop Memorial Ground, Craneford Way, Twickenham (2, D2; ☎ 8410 5000 🚇 Twickenham), is the only rugby league side in southern England.

Tennis

Tennis and **Wimbledon** are synonymous, but the queues, exorbitant prices, limited ticket availability and cramped conditions may have you

Strawberries and Wimbledon – two London summer delights.

Doug McKinlay

thinking that Wimbledon is just, well, a racket. Some seats for the Centre Court and Court Nos 1 & 2 are sold on the day of play but queues are painfully long (for tours of the Wimbledon Lawn Tennis Museum, see p 35).

The nearer to the finals it is, the higher the prices. Prices for the outside courts are cheaper and reduced again after 5pm. There's a public ballot (1 September to 31 December) for the best seats for the next year. To try your luck, send a stamped self-addressed envelope to: All England Lawn Tennis & Croquet Club, PO Box 98, Church Rd, Wimbledon SW19 5AE.

Racing

In June, **Ascot** (☎ 01344-622211) in Buckinghamshire can be nice, if rather posh. On Derby Day in June, **Epsom** (☎ 01372-470047) in Surrey can be a crushing experience in more ways than one. **Sandown Park** (☎ 01372-463072), also in Surrey, is another top racecourse. **Windsor** (☎ 01753-865234), by the castle, is an idyllic spot for an afternoon of racing.

Looking for a cheap and thrilling night out? Consider sampling greyhound racing. Going to 'the dogs' at **Catford Stadium**, (2, C4; Adenmore Rd SE6 ☎ 8690 8000 🚉 Catford Bridge ⏱ Thurs & Sat 7.30pm) is cheap and you'll rub shoulders with a subculture that's gregarious and more than a little shady.

MAJOR VENUES

Crystal Palace National Sports Centre
This is the No 1 stadium in London for a host of events and tournaments – from athletics and weightlifting to basketball and hockey.
✉ **Ledrington Rd SE19 (2, D3)** ☎ 8778 0131 (info), 8778 9876 (bookings) 🚉 Crystal Palace

Lord's (5, C4)
This is the true home of cricket and the base for the Marylebone Cricket Club, which governs the game. Daily tours, taking in the famous Long Room and Cricket Museum, are at 12 & 2pm Oct-Mar (additional tour at 10am Apr-Sept).
✉ **St John's Wood NW8** ☎ 7289 1300 (info), 7289 1611 (bookings) ⊖ St John's Wood

Twickenham
Is the shrine of English rugby union football. The Museum of Rugby here (☎ 8892 2000) is open Tues-Sat 10.30am-5pm, Sun 2-5pm and stadium tours are available.
✉ **Rugby Rd, Twickenham, Middlesex (2, D2)** ☎ 8892 8161 (info), 8744 3111 (bookings) ⊖ Hounslow East and then bus No 281 🚉 Twickenham

Wembley (2, B2)
The home of English football, where the national side has tradition-ally played matches and the FA Cup final took place, will be demolished in August 2000. Tours of the stadium continue to take place daily between 10am and 4pm. It will be replaced by a state-of-the-art 80,000 seat national stadium to be used for football, rugby league, athletics and the occasional mega-rock concert.
✉ **Empire Way, Wembley, Middlesex** ☎ 8902 8833 ⊖ Wembley Park

East End hoop art; for more on sport, see p. 46

Juliet Coombe

places to stay

Where you choose to stay in London is going to affect the kind of time you have in the city. You want ethnic London? Stay in Notting Hill. If your idea of the British capital is one of stately Georgian houses, crescents and leafy squares, book a place in Chelsea or South Kensington. Culture vultures should choose to stay in Kensington or Bloomsbury. You want workaday London with barrow boys, girls in white-heeled shoes and accents straight out of Central Casting? Go for the East End. And if you want to hang out with your Aussie 'mites', Earl's Court ('Kangaroo Valley') or Shepherd's Bush is for you.

Dennis Johnson

Room Rates
These categories indicate the cost per night of a standard double room.

Deluxe	from £220
Top End	£120-219
Mid-Range	£70-119
Budget	under £69

Sad to say, but wherever it is or whichever way you do it, staying in London is going to take a great wad out of your wallet. However, some of central London's deluxe hotels are so luxurious and historic that they're tourist attractions in their own right and might be considered worth every pound you pay. At the top end of the market you can always count on a private bath/shower and toilet, but these are only sometimes available in the mid-range establishments such as B&Bs, guesthouses and small hotels. Before you travel, it's worth checking whether transport and accommodation packages for mid-range rooms are cheaper than making arrangements on arrival.

B&Bs and guesthouses can be the cheapest option in London, although the latter, often just large converted houses with a few rooms, can be less personal than B&Bs. Demand can outstrip supply – especially at the bottom end of the market – so it's worth booking at least a night or 2 before arriving, particularly in summer (when rates can rise by up to 25%). Single rooms are in short supply in London, and places are reluctant to let a double room to one person without charging a hefty supplement. If staying out of season, for more than a couple of nights or if you don't mind missing out on a cooked breakfast, don't be afraid to ask for the 'best' price so that you can at least try to get some value for money.

Bookings

Free same-day accommodation bookings can be made at most tourist information centres. Telephone bookings (☎ 7932 2020) cost £5. Also worth a try:

British Hotel Reservation Centre – Victoria Station (☎ 0800-282888; 6am-11.30pm; £3)

Thomas Cook – charges £5 per booking. There are kiosks at the Britain Visitor Centre (p. 115), most major train stations, Earl's Court (☎ 7723 0184) and South Kensington (☎ 7581 9766) tube stations and Gatwick airport train station (☎ 01293-529372)

B&B bookings (usually for a minimum of 3 nights) – Bed & Breakfast (GB) (☎ 01491-578803), Accommodation Line (☎ 7409 1343; fax 7409 2606) and London Homestead Services (☎ 8949 4455; fax 8549 5492)

Host & Guest Service – (☎ 7385 9922; fax 7386 7575) books B&Bs and student digs

DELUXE

Brown's

This stunner of a 5 star, 118-room hotel was originally created from 11 houses joined together and was the first in London to have a lift, telephone and electric lighting.

✉ **30 Albemarle St W1 (7, E3) ☎ 7493 6020; fax 7493 9381 ✆ brownshotel@ukbusiness.com ✈ Green Park ✗ 1837 restaurant, Drawing Room tearoom**

Claridges (6, E3)

Claridges, a leftover from a bygone era, is one of London's greatest 5 star hotels. Many of the Art Deco features of the public areas and suites date from the late 1920s and some of the 1930s furniture once graced the staterooms of the decommissioned *SS Normandie*.

✉ **Brook St W1 ☎ 7629 8860; fax 7499 2210 ✆ info@claridges.co.uk ✈ Bond Street ✗ restaurant**

Covent Garden

As 'now' as the new millennium but in a reserved, British sort of way, this 50 room hotel prefers to use antiques, beautiful fabrics and something of a 'theatreland' theme to stake out its individuality.

✉ **10 Monmouth St WC2 (6, E6) ☎ 7806 1000; fax 7806 1100 ✆ covent@firmdale.com ✈ Covent Garden ✗ Brasserie Max**

Hempel

We've visited, inspected and stayed in many a hotel in our day, but we've never – ever – seen anything quite like the Hempel. It's a minimalist symphony in white and natural tones where Kyoto meets *2001: A Space Odyssey*. We can only say 'Wow!' at the design, the service and the room rates. The I-Thai, serving Italian and Thai cuisine, is one of London's more unusual fusion restaurants.

✉ **31-35 Craven Hill Gardens W2 (5, E3) ☎ 7298 9000; fax 7402 4666 ✆ the-hempel@easynet.co.uk ✈ Lancaster Gate or Queensway ✗ I-Thai restaurant**

Ritz (6, G4)

What can we say about a hotel that has lent its name to the English lexicon? Arguably London's most celebrated hotel, the ritzy Ritz has a spectacular view over Green Park and is the royal family's 'home away from home'. Its restaurants are decked out like rococo boudoirs, though the food is said to be uninspired.

✉ **150 Piccadilly W1 ☎ 7493 8181; fax 7493 2687 ✆ enquire@theritzhotel.co.uk ✈ Green Park ✗ The Long Gallery, The Restaurant**

Savoy (6, F7)

The landmark hotel is built on the site of the Savoy Palace, which was burned down during the Peasants' Revolt of 1381. Its rooms are so comfortable and have such great views that some people have been known to take up permanent residence.

✉ **Strand WC2 ☎ 7836 4343; fax 7240 6040 ✆ info@the-savoy.co.uk ✈ Charing Cross ✗ Savoy Grill, Thames Foyer tearoom**

The Savoy represents the pinnacle of luxury accommodation in London.

Charlotte Hindle

TOP END

Basil St
An antiques-stuffed hide-away in the heart of Knightsbridge, it's perfectly located for shopping raids on Harrods, Harvey Nichols or Sloane St.
✉ Basil St SW3 (5, G4) ☎ 7581 3311; fax 7581 3693 @ TheBasil@aol.com ⊖ Knightsbridge ✗ Parrot Club (women-only bar)

Blakes
For classic style, one of your first choices in London should be Blakes: 5 Victorian houses knocked into one and decked out with 4-poster beds, rich fabrics and antiques on stripped floorboards.
✉ 33 Roland Gardens SW7 (5, H2) ☎ 7370 6701; fax 7373 0442 @ blakes@easynet.co.uk ⊖ Gloucester Road ✗ Blakes

Durrants Hotel (6, D2)
The luxurious, sprawl-ing Durrants, just behind the Wallace Collection (p. 36), is excellently placed for shopping. Once a country inn, it retains that gentleman's club feel.
✉ 26 George St W1 ☎ 7935 8131; fax 7487 3510 ⊖ Marble Arch

Gore
This splendid hotel is a veritable palace of polished mahogany, Turkish carpets, antique-style bathrooms and has some 4500 artworks on the walls.
✉ 189 Queen's Gate SW7 (5, G3) ☎ 7584 6601; fax 7589 8127 @ reservations@gorehotel.co.uk ⊖ High Street

Kensington or Gloucester Road
✗ Bistrot 190

Hazlitt's
Built in 1718 from 3 Georgian houses, this is one of central London's finest hotels, with efficient personal service. All 23 rooms bear the names of former residents or visitors to the house and are individually decorated with antique furniture and prints.
✉ 6 Frith St, Soho Square W1 (7, B5) ☎ 7434 1771; fax 7439 1524 ⊖ Tottenham Court Road

Number Sixteen
Well situated on leafy Sumner Place, just off Brompton Road, Number Sixteen is a smart well-equipped hotel with a cosy lounge and library.
✉ 6 Sumner Place SW7 (5, G3) ☎ 7589 5232; fax 7584 8615 @ reservations@numbersixteenhotel.co.uk ⊖ South Kensington

Portobello
The beautifully appointed Portobello is in a great location and one of the most attractive hotels in London. Though it's pricey, most people think the money is well spent.
✉ 22 Stanley Gardens W11 (5, E1) ☎ 7727 2777; fax 7792 9641 ⊖ Notting Hill Gate

Rookery
This 33 room hotel has been built within a row of once derelict 18th century Georgian houses. The Rookery is fitted out with period furniture (with a museum-worthy collection of Victorian bathroom pieces), original Irish wood panelling and open fires.
✉ Peter's Lane, Cowcross St EC1 (6, C10) ☎ 7336 0931; fax 7336 0932 @ reservations@rookery.co.uk ⊖ Farringdon

Sandringham
The Sandringham Hotel is a delightful and warm 17 room place close to Hampstead Heath. It is welcoming and very well run and top-floor rooms overlook the city.
✉ 3 Holford Rd NW3 (4, D2) ☎ 7435 1569; fax 7431 5932 ⊖ Hampstead

Holy cow! It's the Rookery Hotel with its bouncing bovine mural featuring owner Peter McKay.

MID-RANGE

Abbey House
Just west of Kensington Palace, Abbey House is a particularly good-value small hotel, with pretty Laura Ashley-ish decor and very high standards.
✉ **11 Vicarage Gate W8 (5, F2)** ☎ **7727 2594** ⊖ **High Street Kensington**

Annandale House
At the bend of a quiet, tree-lined street, this discreet and traditional hotel is a good choice for the noise-sensitive. All rooms have *en suite* facilities, phone and TV.
✉ **39 Sloane Gardens SW1 (5, G5)** ☎ **7730 5051; fax 7730 2727** ⊖ **Sloane Square**

Crescent
The Crescent Hotel is a friendly, family-owned operation maintained at a very high standard in the heart of Bloomsbury.
✉ **49-50 Cartwright Gardens WC1 (6, B6)** ☎ **7387 1515; fax 7383 2054** ⊖ **Russell Square**

Edward Lear
Once the home of the eponymous Victorian painter and poet, the rooms in this small, comfortable place have great facilities.
✉ **28-30 Seymour St**

W1 (6, E1) ☎ **7402 5401; fax 7706 3766** ⊖ **Marble Arch**

Fielding
In a pedestrian walk a block away from the Royal Opera House, this hotel is remarkably good value, clean and well run. All rooms have private bathroom, a TV and telephone.
✉ **4 Broad Court, Bow St WC2 (7, B8)** ☎ **7836 8305; fax 7497 0064** ⊖ **Covent Garden**

Gate
The rooms in the Gate Hotel, an old converted town house with classic frilly English decor and lovely floral window boxes, all have private facilities.
✉ **6 Portobello Rd W11 (5, E2)** ☎ **7221 2403; fax 7221 9128** @ **gatehotel@aol.com** ⊖ **Notting Hill Gate**

Hotel 167
Hotel 167 is a small, stylish place and has an unusually uncluttered and attractive decor. All 19 rooms have private bathrooms.
✉ **167 Old Brompton Rd SW5 (5, H3)** ☎ **7373 0672; fax 7373 3360** ⊖ **Gloucester Road**

Inverness Court
This impressive pile was commissioned by Edward

VII for his 'confidante', actress Lillie Langtry, complete with a private theatre, now the cocktail bar. The panelled walls, stained glass and huge open fires of the public areas give it a Gothic feel but most of the 183 guestrooms – some overlooking Hyde Park – are modern.
✉ **Inverness Terrace W2 (5, E3)** ☎ **7229 1444; fax 7706 4240** ⊖ **Queensway** ✕ **bar**

Wilbraham
Just north of Sloane Square, this hotel boasts many original Victorian features in its public areas and 50 guestrooms, but Sloane Street can be a little noisy at night.
✉ **1 Wilbraham Place, Sloane St SW1 (5, G5)** ☎ **7730 8296; fax 7730 6815** ⊖ **Sloane Square**

Windermere
These 22 small, but individually designed rooms are in a sparkling white Victorian town house with its own restaurant.
✉ **142-144 Warwick Way SW1 (5, H5)** ☎ **7834 5163; fax 7630 8831** @ **windermere@ compuserve.com** ⊖ **Victoria** ✕ **Pimlico room**

BUDGET

Alhambra
A great find in this area and handy for the station, this hotel is a simple but spotlessly clean place and run by a charming French owner.
✉ **17-19 Argyle St WC1**

(6, A7) ☎ **7837 9575; fax 7916 2476** ⊖ **King's Cross**

Boka
Kitchen use is available in this relaxed, inexpensive

hotel located opposite the Earl's Court Exhibition Centre. Dorm beds: £10-16.
✉ **33 Eardley Crescent SW5 (5, H2)** ☎ **7370 1388; fax 7912 0515** ⊖ **Earl's Court**

Cavendish

The Hotel Cavendish and its sister-hotel at No 63 **Jesmond Hotel** (☎ 7636 3199; fax 7323 4373) are clean and pleasant family-run places.
✉ **75 Gower St WC1 (6, C5)** ☎ **7636 9079; fax 7580 3609**
⊖ **Goodge Street**

Europa House

Another excellent choice, where you're always assured a warm welcome (something not as common as you'd think at small London hotels).
✉ **151 Sussex Gardens W2 (5, E3)** ☎ **7723 7343; fax 7224 9331**
✆ **europahouse@ enterprise.net**
⊖ **Paddington**

Luna-Simone

If all London's budget hotels were like the central, spotlessly clean and comfortable Luna-Simone, we would all be happy

Accommodation Guides

London Tourist Board's *Where to Stay & What to Do in London* (£4.99), is a list of approved hotels, guesthouses, apartments and B&Bs. It also has the free *Accommodation for Budget Travellers*.

campers. A full English breakfast and free bag storage facilities included.
✉ **47 Belgrave Rd SW1 (5, G6)** ☎ **7834 5897; fax 7828 2474** ⊖ **Victoria**

Manzi's

Manzi's, a 'cheapie' above a seafood restaurant just north of Leicester Square, is no great shakes but as central as you'll get for a budget hotel in Soho.
✉ **1-2 Leicester St WC2 (7, C5)** ☎ **7734 0224; fax 7437 4864** ⊖ **Leicester Square**

Norfolk Court & St David's

Right in the centre of the action, the Norfolk Court & St David's Hotel is clean, comfortable and friendly with the usual out-of-control decor. All rooms have wash facilities of some description and also TV and telephone.
✉ **16-20 Norfolk Square W2 (5, E3)** ☎ **7723 4963; fax 7402 9061** ⊖ **Paddington**

Regent Palace

Ripe for a makeover, but pretty cheap for its position right beside Piccadilly Circus, the Palace has hundreds of rooms – all of them with shared bath.
✉ **Piccadilly Circus, cnr of Glasshouse St W1**

(6, F5) ☎ **7734 7000; fax 7734 6435**
⊖ **Piccadilly**

Romany House

Part of the Romany House Hotel is built into a 15th century cottage that has tales – real or imagined – of highwaymen. You'll share a bathroom, but breakfasts are good.
✉ **35 Longmoore St SW1 (5, H5)** ☎ **7834 5553; fax 7834 0495**
⊖ **Victoria**

Travel Inn Capital

In the former London County Hall, this is one of those one price, one room deals (£59.95 for up to 2 adults and 2 children). It's fairly spartan, and there are more rules here than in a Victorian grammar school, but the rooms are large and reasonable (for London standards).
✉ **London County Hall, Belvedere Rd SE1 (6, H8)** ☎ **7902 1600; fax 7902 1619** ⊖ **Westminster**

York House

The York House Hotel is good value for what and where it is – on a quiet crescent – and the welcome is warm. Rooms are basic; only some have showers.
✉ **27-28 Philbeach Gardens SW5 (5, H2)** ☎ **7373 7519; fax 7370 4641** ⊖ **Earl's Court**

SPECIALIST HOTELS

Philbeach

This fine budget to mid-range hotel is popular with gays and lesbians. It has a great garden restaurant and fab new basement bar.
✉ **30 Philbeach Gardens SW5 (5, G2)** ☎ **7373 1244; fax 7244 0149** ⊖

Earl's Court ✗ Wilde About Oscar restaurant

Pippa's Pop-Ins

This unique hotel for kids gives parents a break. It costs £60/70 for a week-day/weekend night or £100 for a 24hr period.

Children aged 2-12 are cared for by trained nannies; overnighters get midnight snacks as well as dinner, bed and breakfast.
✉ **430 Fulham Rd SW6 (5, H3)** ☎ **7385 2458; fax 7385 5706** ⊖ **Fulham Broadway**

facts for the visitor

PRE-DEPARTURE 108

Travel Requirements 108
Tourist Information Abroad 108
Climate & When to Go 108

ARRIVAL & DEPARTURE 109

Air 109
Bus 111
Train 111
Customs 112
Departure Tax 112

GETTING AROUND 112

Travel Passes 112
London Underground 113
Bus 113
DLR & Train 113
Taxi 114
Car & Motorcycle 114

PRACTICAL INFORMATION 115

Tourist Information 115
Embassies 115
Time 115
Money 115
Tipping 116
Discounts & Discount Cards 116
Opening Hours 116
Public Holidays 116
Electricity 117
Weights & Measures 117
Post 117
Telephone 117
Email/www 117
Doing Business 118
Newspapers & Magazines 118
Radio 118
TV 118
Photography & Video 118
Health 118
Emergency Numbers 119
Toilets 119
Safety Concerns 119
Women Travellers 120
Gay & Lesbian Travellers 120
Disabled Travellers 120
Language 120
Conversion Table 121

Punch and Judy at the Museum of London.

Simon Bracken

PRE-DEPARTURE
Travel Requirements
Passport
Must be valid for 6 months from date of entry. EU citizens can use their identity cards.

Visa
Not required by EU citizens and nationals of Australia, Canada, New Zealand, South Africa and the USA. Others should check with their local British embassy, high commission or consulate before leaving home.

Return/Onward Ticket
A return ticket may be required.

Immunisations
Immunisations not required.

Travel Insurance
A policy covering theft, loss, medical expenses and compensation for cancellation or delays in your travel arrangements is highly recommended.

Driving Licence & Permit
Your normal driving licence is legal for 1 year from the date you enter the UK. If you carry an International Driving Permit (IDP), it must be accompanied by a local licence.

Keeping Copies
Keep photocopies of important documents with you, separate from the originals, and leave a copy at home. You can also store details of documents in Lonely Planet's free online Travel Vault, password-protected and accessible worldwide. Check out www.ekno .lonelyplanet.com for details.

Tourist Information Abroad

The British Tourist Authority (BTA; www.visitbritain.com) stocks masses of information and has offices in the following countries:

Australia
Level 16, The Gateway, 1 Macquarie Place, Circular Quay, Sydney, NSW 2000 (☎ 02-9377 4400; fax 9377 4499)

Canada
Suite 120, 5915 Airport Rd, Mississauga, ONT L4V 1T1 (☎ 905-405 1840; fax 405 1835; toll-free ☎ 1 888 VISIT UK)

New Zealand
3rd Floor, Dilworth Building, cnr Queen & Customs Sts, Auckland 1 (☎ 09-303 1446; fax 377 6965)

South Africa
Lancaster Gate, Hyde Park Lane, Hyde Park, Sandton 2196 (☎ 011-325 0343; 325 0344)

USA
Suite 1510, 625 North Michigan Avenue, Chicago IL 60611 (toll-free ☎ 1-800 GO 2 BRITAIN); Suite 701, 551 Fifth Avenue, New York NY 10176-0799 (☎ 212-986 2200)

Climate & When to Go

London is a year-round destination. High season is June to August, with a better chance of good weather, but also huge crowds and booked-out venues. In April to May or September-October the weather can still be good and queues are shorter. November to March are the quietest months. Expect cloudy, cool weather and rain even in high summer.

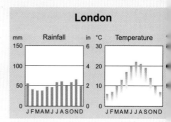

ARRIVAL & DEPARTURE

London can be reached by air from virtually everywhere in the world and by bus, train and boat from continental Europe and Ireland. There are nonstop connections from the USA, Asia and most European cities. Good bargains are available outside peak seasons; contact airlines or selected travel agents.

Air

London has 5 main airports: Heathrow is the largest, followed by Gatwick, Stansted, Luton and London City. Most major airlines have ticket offices in London – consult the business telephone directory for addresses and phone numbers.

Airports Direct (☎ 7602 8080) and Airport Transfer International (☎ 7603 5000) are 2 of many shuttle bus firms that service the airports.

Heathrow

Some 24km west of central London, Heathrow (LHR; ☎ 8759 4321) is the world's busiest commercial airport; it has 4 terminals, with another planned. Each terminal has competitive currency-exchange facilities, information counters and desks for booking accommodation.

The Heathrow Hotel Hoppa bus (£2) runs to hotels near the airport (6am-11pm). There are left-luggage facilities (£3/3.50 for 12/24hrs) at: Terminal 1 (☎ 8745 5301, 6am-11pm), Terminal 2 (☎ 8745 4599; 6am-10.30pm); Terminal 3 (☎ 8759 3344; 5.30am-10.30pm), and also at Terminal 4 (☎ 8745 7460; 5.30am-11pm). All can forward baggage.

Useful Numbers

British Airways ☎ 0990-444000, 8759 4321 (general inquiries & flight info)
Car Park Information ☎ 0800-844844
Hotel Reservation Service ☎ 8759 2719

Airport Access

Heathrow Express The fastest way to central London is via the Heathrow Express (☎ 0845-600 1515; £12/20 one-way/return; 5am-11:45pm; 15mn) linking Heathrow Central station (serving Terminals 1 to 3) and Terminal 4 station with Paddington train station (5, E3).

Underground The cheapest way to get to Heathrow is via the Underground (Piccadilly Line; 1hr; £3.40; 5.30am-11.30pm). There are 2 tube stations, one servicing Terminals 1, 2 and 3, the other servicing Terminal 4. There are ticket machines in baggage reclaim areas of all terminals.

Airbus Heathrow Shuttle The shuttle (☎ 7222 1234, 0990-747777; £6/10 single/return; every 30mns; 1¼hr trip) goes along Notting Hill Gate and Bayswater Rd to Russell Square and King's Cross.

Taxi A minicab to central London costs around £25; a metered black cab £35.

Heathrow Terminals

The following terminals at Heathrow serve the airlines listed:

Terminal 1, 2 & 3
All British Airways domestic and European flights; all other flights (except those listed below)

Terminal 4
Air Lanka, Air Malta, Atlantic Island Air, British Airways intercontinental flights, British Airways flights to Amsterdam, Paris, Moscow and Athens, British Mediterranean, Canadian Airlines International, KLM (Cityhopper & Royal Dutch Airlines), Kenya Airways, TAT, Qantas

Gatwick

Some 48km south of central London, Gatwick (LGW; ☎ 01293-535353) is smaller and better organised than Heathrow. The North and South terminals are linked by an efficient, free monorail service. The left-luggage office at the North terminal (☎ 01293-502013) is open 6am-10pm; the South Terminal office (☎ 01293-502014) operates 24hrs.

Airport Access

Train The Gatwick Express (☎ 0990-301530; £9.50; 30mn trip) links the station near the South Terminal with Victoria station every 15mns from 5am-12am (then every 30-60mns).

The Connex South Central (☎ 0345-484959) from Victoria, runs every 15-30mns (1/hr in the wee hours); it's slower but cheaper at £8.20.

There's also a Thameslink service from King's Cross, Farringdon and London Bridge (£9.50).

Bus Flightline buses (☎ 0990 747777; www.speedlink.co.uk; cost £7.50/11 single/return) run from central London to Gatwick hourly 7.15am-11.35pm (to London: 5am-8.10pm).

Taxi A minicab to central London costs around £35, a black cab around £50.

Gatwick Terminals

The following terminals at Gatwick serve the airlines listed:

North Terminal
Air France, Air 2000, Britair, British Airways, Brymon Airways, Delta Airlines, Deutsche BA, Emirates, Finnair, GB Airways, Maersk Air, MALEV, Royal Nepal Airlines

South Terminal
All other airlines

Stansted

At 56km (35 miles) to the north-east, Stansted (STN; ☎ 01279-680500) is the most remote airport serving London. This 3rd international gateway plans to double the 7 million passengers it handles each year.

Airport Access

Stansted Skytrain The skytrain (☎ 0345-484950; £10.50; 40mn trip) goes direct to Liverpool Street station (6, C14) departing every 30mns (5am-11pm).

Bus Flightline buses (☎ 0990 7474777; www.speedlink.co.uk; £9/13 single/return) link central London with Stansted hourly from 6am-9.30pm (from airport to London 8am-10.15pm).

Taxi Minicabs to/from central London will cost about £35, a black cab around £75.

Luton

A small, remote airport some 56km to the north, Luton (LTN; ☎ 01582-405100) caters mainly to cheap charter flights though discount airlines. Debonair (☎ 01582-395277) and easyJet (☎ 01582-445354) operate scheduled services from here.

Airport Access

Green Line bus No 757 serves Luton (£7.20/11.80 single/return; 1hr 20mn trip). Buses leave hourly 6.25am-11pm from south of Victoria station (5, G5; ☎ 8668 7261, 0345-788788) in the Victoria Place shopping mall at Bulleid Way SW1.

There's also a shuttle bus outside the arrivals hall for the 8mn trip to Luton station, for Thameslink trains to central London (£10.20; every 20mns, runs 24hrs; 35-45mn trip).

London City

London City Airport (LCY; ☎ 7646 0088), 10km east of central London in the Docklands, has flights to 21 European destinations.

Airport Access

A shuttle bus connects the airport with Liverpool St station (£5; 25mn trip) and Canary Wharf (£2) every 10mns 6.50am-9.20pm. Alternatively use the North London/Silverlink line and get off at the Silvertown & London City Airport stop or take the Docklands Light Rail (DLR) to Prince Regent Lane and then bus No 473.

A taxi costs about £15 to/from central London.

Bus

Within the UK

Bus travellers to London arrive and depart from the Victoria Coach Station (5, G5; ☎ 7730 3466) 164 Buckingham Palace Rd SW1. Queues can be horrendous, so try to book over the phone (☎ 7730 3499; Mon-Sat 9am-7pm). National Express (☎ 0990-808080) runs the largest bus network and is a member company of Eurolines. There are smaller competitors on the main UK routes such as Greenlines buses (☎ 8668 7261, 0345-788788).

Europe

You can still get to Europe by bus without using the Channel Tunnel (via bus-ferry/hovercraft-bus). Book Eurolines tickets direct (☎ 0990-143219), 52 Grosvenor Gardens SW1 (5, G5; ⊖ Victoria), through National Express, at the Victoria Coach Station or via travel agents.

Train

Within the UK

The main national rail routes are served by InterCity trains. One-week advance purchase are the cheapest tickets for non-railpass holders taking longer trips. Ring the 24hr National Rail Enquiries line (☎ 0345-484950) for timetables, fares and booking details.

BritRail The most useful travel passes for visitors are BritRail passes, which are *not available in the UK* and must be bought from overseas travel agents. The local passes, BritRail Rovers, are available from main-line train stations; a 7/14 day All Line Rover is £275/450. There are also regional Rovers.

Railcards Available from major stations, they give a range of discounts and are valid for 1 year. If you're planning to stay in south-east London or travel extensively in southern England, a £20 Network discount card (valid for all main-line routes within London and the entire south-east) is worth considering.

Europe

Eurostar Travelling via the Channel Tunnel, the high-speed passenger rail service Eurostar (☎ 0990-186186, 01233-617575 from outside the UK) links London's Waterloo International Terminal (6, H8) with Paris' Gare du Nord (3hrs; up to 20/day) and with Brussels (2hrs 40mns; up to 12/day). Fares vary enormously but a cheap APEX return is £89/79 Paris/Brussels.

Le Shuttle Trains (☎ 0990-353535, 0891-555566) transport motor vehicles between Folkestone and Coquelles (5km south-west of Calais); they run 24hrs (up to every 15mns). Five-day excursion fares (£70-135 for car and passengers) can be booked or purchased at the tollgate.

For European train inquiries contact Rail Europe/Rail International (☎ 0990-848848). The *Thomas Cook European Timetable*, updated monthly, gives a complete listing of train and ferry schedules and supplement and reservation information.

Train & Ferry Eurostar has eclipsed many of the more long-established rail/ferry links, but they still provide the cheapest cross-channel travel. There are train-boat-train services with Hoverspeed (☎ 0990-240241) from Charing Cross station (6, G7) to the Gare du Nord (£44/59 one way/return; 7-8hr trip). Another train/ferry operator is P&O Stena (☎ 0990-980980).

Customs

Like all EU nations, the UK has a 2 tier customs system: 1 for goods bought duty-free and 1 for goods bought in an EU country where taxes and duties have already been paid.

For goods purchased duty-free *outside* the EU the limits are: 200 cigarettes or 250g of tobacco, 2L of still wine plus 1L of spirits over 22% or another 2L of wine (sparkling or otherwise), 50g of perfume, 250cc of toilet water, and other duty-free goods (including cider and beer) to the value of £136.

You can buy items in another EU county, where certain goods might be cheaper, and bring them into the UK as long as taxes have been paid on them. Allowances are: 800 cigarettes, 200 cigars and 1kg of tobacco, 10L of spirits, 20L of fortified wines, 90L of wine (sparkling limited to 60L) and 110L of beer.

Departure Tax

All domestic flights and those to destinations within the EU from London attract a £10 departure tax. For flights to other cities abroad you pay £20. This is usually built into the price of your ticket.

GETTING AROUND

Everybody complains about the London Underground – and with good reason – but it is still *the* way to travel in this enormous city. Buses can prove more pleasant, particularly for tourists, but traffic congestion has reduced their speed to a snail's crawl. Black taxis (ie officially registered ones) are comfortable, efficient and expensive.

For general information on the Underground, buses, the DLR or trains within London ring ☎ 7222 1234 or consult the London Regional Transport (LRT) Web site at www.londontransport.co.uk. Travelcheck (☎ 7222 1200) provides service running information.

Travel Passes

One-day Travelcards usually offer the cheapest method of travelling, and can be used after 9.30am weekdays (anytime at the weekend) on all forms of transport – tubes, main-line trains, the DLR and buses. Most visitors find that a Zone 1 & 2 Travelcard (£3.80/1.90 a/c) is sufficient. If you plan to start moving before 9.30am on a weekday, you can buy a Zone 1 & 2 London Transport (LT) Card for £4.80/2.40.

Weekly Travelcards are available but require an ID card with a passport-sized photo. A Zones 1 & 2 card, allowing you to travel at any time of day and on night buses as well, costs £17.60. A Weekend Travelcard valid on Sat-Sun in Zones 1 & 2 costs £5.70/2.80. Family Travelcards, costing from £3/60p adult/child for Zones 1 & 2, allow 1 or 2 adults and up to 4 children to travel together.

London Underground

The London Underground, or 'tube', extends into the suburbs and as far afield as Buckinghamshire and Essex. It's a slow, unreliable, ageing and expensive system but normally the quickest and easiest way of getting around. LRT has information centres at all 4 Heathrow terminals and at larger train stations.

Fares & Passes

The Underground is divided into 6 concentric zones. The basic fare for Zone 1 is £1.40; to cross all 6 zones (eg to/from Heathrow) it's £3.40. A carnet of 10 Zone 1 tickets costs £10. If you're travelling through a couple of zones or several times in one day, consider a travel pass.

Bus

If you're not in a hurry, travelling around on London's famous double-decker buses can be more enjoyable than using the tube. The *All London Bus Guide Map* and a number of individual area maps are free from most LRT information centres (☎ 7371 0247). Most visitors find guide map No 1 (Central London) the most useful one.

Fares & Passes

Single-journey bus tickets sold on the bus cost 60p-£1.20, depending on whether you're travelling within one zone or crossing several of the 4 bus zones (a £1 all-in adult fare may be in effect by the time you read this). Children aged 5-15 pay a uniform 40p. A one-day bus pass valid on all 4 zones and before 9.30am weekdays is available for £2.80/1 adults/children.

Night Bus

Trafalgar Square is the focal point for all but 6 of LRT's network of 50 Night Buses (prefixed with the letter 'N'). They stop on request 12-7am but services can be infrequent. LRT publishes a free credit card-sized timetable that lists all the routes. Holders of weekly (or longer) Travelcards ride free.

Useful Bus Routes

No 19
> Upper St (Islington)-Clerkenwell-Holborn-New Oxford St-Charing Cross Rd-Shaftesbury Ave-Piccadilly-Sloane St-King's Rd

No 8
> Bethnal Green-Petticoat Lane-Liverpool St station-the City (Guildhall & Old Bailey)-Holborn-Oxford St-Marble Arch-Edgware Rd

Nos 9 & 10
> Hammersmith-Kensington-Knightsbridge (Albert Memorial, Royal Albert Hall)-Hyde Park Corner-Piccadilly-Piccadilly Circus-Trafalgar Square-Strand-Aldwych-Marble Arch-Oxford St-Tottenham Court Rd-Euston-King's Cross-Archway

No 24
> Hampstead-Camden-Gower St-Tottenham Court Rd-Leicester Square-Trafalgar Square-Whitehall-Westminster-Victoria station-Pimlico

Accessible Bus Travel

Wheelchair-accessible Stationlink buses (☎ 7918 3305; service info 7918 3312) have driver-operated ramps. Following a similar route to that of the Circle line, they join up all the main-line stations. From Paddington there are hourly services clockwise (route SL1) 8.15am-7.15pm, and anticlockwise (SL2) 8.40am-6.40pm.

DLR & Train

The driverless Docklands Light Railway (DLR) links the City at Bank and Tower Gateway at Tower Hill with services to Stratford and the Isle of Dogs. A DLR extension under the Thames as far as Lewisham, with stations at Cutty Sark and the train station at Greenwich, opened at the end of 1999. The DLR runs weekdays 5.30am-12.30am (shorter hrs on weekends); fares are the same as those on the tube. General information: ☎ 7918 4000 (24hrs); service information: Travelcheck ☎ 7222 1200; DLR Customer Services: ☎ 7363 9700.

Several rail companies also operate passenger trains in London, including the Silverlink (or North London line), which links Richmond in the south-west and North Woolwich in the south-east, and the crowded Thameslink, which goes from Elephant & Castle and London Bridge in the south through the City to King's Cross and as far north as Luton. Most lines interchange with the tube and Travelcards can be used on both systems.

Taxi

The 'black' London taxi cab is as much a feature of the cityscape as the red double-decker bus. Cabs are available for hire when the yellow sign above the windscreen is lit. Fares are metered, with flag fall at £1.40 and increments of 20p. To order a cab by phone (an extra £1.20) try Radio Taxis on ☎ 7272 0272.

Minicabs are cheaper freelance competitors to the cabs, but they can only be hired by phone directly or from a minicab office (every neighbourhood and high street has one). Some drivers have a *very* limited idea of how to get around efficiently (and safely) – you the foreigner may find yourself being pressed to navigate. Minicabs can carry up to 4 people and don't have meters, so it's essential to get a quote before you start; bargain hard – most drivers will start at

about 25% higher than the fare they're prepared to accept.

Small companies are based in particular areas. Try one of the large 24hr operators: ☎ 7387 8888, 7272 2612, 7383 3333, 8340 2450 or 8567 1111 or Internet booking (www .proteus.demon.co.uk/taxi.html).

Car & Motorcycle

Avoid bringing a car into London. Traffic moves slowly and parking is expensive. Traffic wardens and wheel clampers operate with extreme efficiency and if your vehicle is towed away, you won't see much change from £100 to get it back.

Road Rules

Motorists drive on the left-hand side of the road. Wearing seat belts in the front seat is compulsory and if they are fitted in the back, passengers must wear them as well. Motorcyclists must wear helmets at all times. Give way to your right at roundabouts.

The current speed limits are 30mph (48km/h) in built-up areas, 60mph (97km/h) on single carriageways, and 70mph (113km/h) on dual or triple carriageways.

Rental

Car hire rates are very expensive; the big international rental companies charge £150 to £200 a week for their smallest cars (Ford Fiesta, Peugeot 106). The main companies include Avis (☎ 0990-900500), British Car Rental (☎ 7278 2802), Budget (☎ 0800-181181), Europcar (☎ 0345-222525), Eurodollar (☎ 0990-365365), Hertz (☎ 0345-555888) and Thrifty (☎ 7403 3458). Holiday Autos (☎ 0990-300400) operates through a number of rental companies and generally offers excellent deals, starting at around £135 a week.

Motoring Organisations
The two main motoring organisations in the UK are: Automobile Association (AA; ☎ 0800-919595) and Royal Automobile Club (RAC; ☎ 0990-722722).

PRACTICAL INFORMATION

Tourist Information

The Britain Visitor Centre at Regent St SW1 (6, F5; ⊖ Piccadilly Circus) has a map shop, hotel booking centre, tourist information, travel desk and theatre ticket agency (Mon-Fri 9am-6.30pm, Sat-Sun 10am-4pm; Sat 9am-5pm June-Sept). Also try the British Tourism Authority (☎ 8846 9000; www.visitbritain.com).

Tourist Information Centres
The main TIC, at Victoria station (5, G3), is open Apr-Oct: Mon-Sat 8am-8pm, Sun 8am-6pm; Nov-Mar: Mon-Sat 8am-6pm, Sun 9am-4pm. Other TICs: Arrivals Hall, Waterloo International Terminal (6, H8; 8.30am-10.30pm); Liverpool St station (6, C14; Mon-Fri 8am-6pm, Sat-Sun 8.45am-5.30pm); Heathrow arrivals hall and tube station; all other airports have branches.

Visitorcall is a 24hr recorded guide (49p/mn). Dial ☎ 09064-123 then a further 3 digits for:

What's on this Week	400
Current Exhibitions	403
What's on for Children	404
Popular West End Shows	416
Rock & Pop Concerts	422
Shopping News	486
General Accomodation Advice	435

Embassies

Australian High Commission
  Australia House, Strand WC2 (6, E9; ☎ 7379 4334; fax 240 5333; ⊖ Temple)

Canadian High Commission
  1 Grosvenor Square W1 (6, F2; ☎ 7258 6600; fax 7258 6506; ⊖ Bond St)

New Zealand High Commission
  New Zealand House, 80 Haymarket SW1 (6, F5; ☎ 7930 8422; fax 7839 4580; ⊖ Piccadilly Circus)

South Africa High Commission
  South Africa House, Trafalgar Square WC2 (6, G6; ☎ 7451 7299; fax 7451 7284; ⊖ Trafalgar Square)

USA Embassy
  5 Upper Grosvenor St W1 (6, F2; ☎ 7499 9000; fax 7495 5012; ⊖ Bond St)

Time

Wherever you are in the world, the time on your watch is measured in relation to Greenwich Mean Time (GMT). British Summer Time (March to October) confuses things so that even London is 1 hour ahead of GMT.

Money

Currency
The British currency, the pound sterling (£), is divided into 100 pence (p). Coins of 1p and 2p are copper; 5p, 10p, 20p and 50p coins are silver; and the bulky £1 coin is gold-coloured. The £2 coin introduced in 1998 has a gold-coloured edge with a silver centre. Notes (bills) come in £5, £10, £20 and £50 denominations and vary in colour and size.

Travellers Cheques
Thomas Cook (☎ 01733-318950) and American Express (☎ 01222-666111) are widely accepted, don't charge for cashing their own cheques (though their exchange rates are not always competitive) and can often

arrange replacements for lost or stolen cheques within 24hrs.

Credit Cards

The following cards are widely accepted in London. For card cancellations, call:

American Express	☎ 01273-689955
Diners Club	☎ 01252-516261
MasterCard	☎ 01702-362988
Visa	☎ 0800-895082

Changing Money

Changing money is never a problem in London, with banks, *bureaux de change* and travel agencies all competing for business. There are 24hr exchange bureaux at Heathrow Terminals 1, 3 and 4 (Terminal 2 bureau open 6am-11pm).

The main American Express office (☎ 7930 4411), 6 Haymarket (6, F5; ⊖ Piccadilly Circus) opens weekdays 9am-5.30pm (Sat till 6pm) and Sun 10am-5pm. Thomas Cook's main office (☎ 7499 4000) 30 St James St (6, G3; ⊖ Green Park) is open weekdays 9am-5.30pm (from 10am Wed) and Sat 10am-4pm.

Tipping

Restaurants	10-15%
Hairdressers	10%
Taxis	round up to nearest £
Guides	10%
Porters	£2 a bag

Discounts & Discount Cards

Most venues offer discounts to some of the following groups:

- Children (check each venue for age limits)
- People under 25 or 26 with youth cards
- Students with ISIC cards (age limits may apply)
- People over 60 or 65 (sometimes 55 for women)
- Disabled visitors
- Family groups

Student & Youth Cards

The International Student Identity Card (ISIC), the Federation of International Youth Travel Organisations (FIYTO) card or the Euro26 Card (all £5) can produce discounts on many forms of transport, admission to venues, and meals in some student restaurants.

Seniors' Cards

Many attractions offer reduced price admission for people over 60 or 65 (can be as low as 55 for women); ask even if you can't see a discount listed. The railways offer a Senior Citizen Railcard (£18) for over 60s.

Opening Hours

Banks
  Mon-Fri 9.30am-3.30pm; some open on Sat 9.30am-12pm

Post Offices
  Mon-Fri 8.30/9am-5/5.30pm; some main ones open on Sat 9am-12pm or 1pm

Offices
  Mon-Fri 9am-5/5.30pm

Shops
  Mon-Sat 9/10am-6pm (some on Sun 10am-4pm or 12-6pm)

Pharmacies
  Mon-Sat 9am-6pm

Late-Night Shopping
  Thurs 9/10am-8pm in West End

Public Holidays

New Year's Day	1 Jan
Good Friday	Late Mar/Apr
Easter Monday	Late Mar/Apr
May Day Bank Holiday	May (1st Mon)
Spring Bank Holiday	May (last Mon)
Summer Bank Holiday	Aug (last Mon)
Christmas Day	25 Dec
Boxing Day	26 Dec

Most banks and businesses are closed on public holidays. Museums and other attractions may close on Christmas and Boxing days. Venues normally closed on Sunday are likely to close on bank holidays.

Electricity

The standard voltage throughout Britain is 230/240V AC, 50 Hz. Plugs have 3 square pins, and adapters to fit European-style plugs are widely available.

Weights & Measures

In theory, the UK has now embraced the metric system although non-metric imperial equivalents are likely to be used by much of the population for some time to come. Distances continue to be given in miles, yards, feet and inches though most liquids – apart from milk and beer (which come in half-pints and pints) – are now sold in litres.

Post

Call ☎ 0345-223344 for general postal inquiries.

Sending Mail

Stamps are sold at post office counters, vending machines outside post offices and at some newsagents and corner shops.

Postal Rates

Domestic 1st/2nd class mail costs 19/26p; postcards to Europe/Australasia and the Americas cost 30/64p.

Opening Hours

Trafalgar Square Post Office (GPO/poste restante) is open Mon-Fri 8am-8pm, Sat 9am-8pm.

Telephone

The country code for the UK is 44. Phones are either coin-operated or accept phonecards or credit cards. There's a wide range of local and international phonecards available at newsagencies. Lonely Planet's eKno Communication Card, specifically aimed at travellers, provides competitive international calls (avoid using it for local calls), messaging services and free email. Visit www.ekno.lonelyplanet.com for joining and access information

Area Codes

On 22 April 2000, the area codes for all of London changed to 020, and subscribers gained an extra digit at the front of their number. For calls within the London area, what was previously 0171-123 4567 is now 7123 4567 while the former 0181-765 4321 is now 8765 4321. The changes are reflected in all telephone and fax numbers used in this book.

Useful Numbers

Directory Inquiries	☎ 192
International Dialling Code	☎ 00
International Directory Inquiries	☎ 153
Operator	☎ 100
Reverse-Charge (collect)	☎ 155
Telemessage	☎ 0800-190190

International Codes

Australia	00 61
Canada	00 1
Japan	00 81
New Zealand	00 64
South Africa	00 27
USA	00 1

Email/www

Internet Cafes

If you can't access the Internet from where you're staying, London is full of cybercafes (see p. 82).

Useful Sites

The Lonely Planet Web site (www.lonelyplanet.com) offers a speedy link to many of Britain's

Web sites. Others to try include:

Virtual Tourist
wings.buffalo.edu/world

UK Directory
www.ukdirectory.com/travel

UK Weather
www.meteo.gov.uk

Time Out
www.timeout.co.uk

London Calling
www.london-calling.co.uk

Doing Business

The main sources of information are the *Financial Times* (Mon-Sat) and the weekly *Economist*. For word processing or other secretarial services go to Typing Overload (☎ 7404 5464), 1st Floor, 67 Chancery Lane WC2 (6, D9; ⊖ Chancery Lane). For photocopying, computer services like scanning, computer rentals and video-conferencing, try Kinko's (☎ 7539 2900), 326-328 High Holborn WC1 (6, D8; ⊖ Chancery Lane).

Newspapers & Magazines

Most major newspapers in the UK are national; the only daily that is well and truly a Londoner is the *Evening Standard*, an afternoon tabloid. The bottom end of the newspaper market in terms of content – though tops in circulation – is occupied by the *Sun*, *Mirror*, *Daily Star* and *Sport* tabloids. The middle-level tabs, the *Daily Mail* and *Daily Express*, are Conservative bastions. The *Telegraph* far outsells its other broadsheet rivals. The *Times* is conservative and influential. Others are the duller-than-dull *Independent* and the mildly left-wing *Guardian*. Almost every daily has a Sunday stablemate. See p. 84 for listings magazines.

Radio

London's own radio stations include Capital FM (95.8kHz FM), the favoured pop station in the city, and Capital Gold (1548kHzam) which plays 60s-80s oldies. GLR (94.9kHz FM) is a talk-back station with a London bias. Xfm on 104.9kHz FM bills itself as an alternative radio station and plays indie music.

Among the national stations are:

BBC Radio 1 (98.8kHz FM) – pop/rock
BBC Radio 2 (89.1kHz FM) – 60s, 70s and 80s goldies
BBC Radio 3 (91.3kHz FM) – classical music and plays
BBC Radio 4 (93.5kHz FM) – news and drama
Radio 5 Live (693kHzam) – sport and current affairs
BBC World Service (648kHzam) – coverage from around the world
Jazzfm (102.2kHz FM) – jazz and blues
Classic FM (100.9kHz FM) – classical music with commercials

TV

Choose from BBC1 and BBC2 (publicly funded); ITV, Channel 4 and Channel 5 (commercial), plus satellite and assorted cable channels.

Photography & Video

Print film is widely available, but slide film can be harder to find; try any branch of the Jessop Photo centre including the one at 63-69 New Oxford St WC1 (6, D6; ☎ 7240 6077; ⊖ Tottenham Court Road).

The UK, like most of Europe and Australia, uses the PAL system, which is incompatible with the American and Japanese NTSC system.

Health

Tap water is always safe and no immunisations are needed to visit Britain. Whether you eat British beef after the bovine spongiform encephalopathy (BSE) scare and the Creuzfeldt-Jakob (or 'mad cow') disease found in humans is up to you.

Insurance & Medical Treatment

EU nationals and some other nationalities (including Australians and New Zealanders) can obtain free emergency medical treatment and subsidised dental care through the National Health Service (NHS). However, travel insurance is advisable to cover other expenses (eg ambulance and repatriation).

Medical Services

Hospitals with 24hr accident and emergency (A&E) units include:

Guy's Hospital
(☎ 7955 5000) St Thomas St SE1 (6, H13; ⊖ London Bridge)

Royal Free Hospital
(☎ 7794 0500) Pond St NW3 (4, F2; ⊖ Belsize Park)

University College Hospital
(☎ 7387 9300) Grafton Way WC1 (6, B5; ⊖ Euston Square)

Dental Services

To find an emergency dentist phone the Dental Emergency Care Service (☎ 7955 2186) weekdays 8.45am-3.30pm or call into Eastman Dental Hospital (☎ 7915 1000) at 256 Gray's Inn Rd WC1 (6, B5; ⊖ King's Cross).

Pharmacies & Drugs

Chemists can advise on minor ailments. There's always one local chemist that opens 24hrs (see local newspapers or notices in chemist windows for duty chemist). Boots (☎ 7229 9266), 75 Queensway W1 (6, F2; ⊖ Queensway or Bayswater) is open Mon-Sat 9am-10pm and Sun 5-10pm.

HIV/AIDS

Help, advice and support is available from the National AIDS Helpline (☎ 0800-567123).

Emergency Numbers

Ring the operator on ☎ 100 (free call) for the address of a local doctor or hospital. In an emergency phone ☎ 999 (free call) for the fire services, police or an ambulance.

Toilets

Toilets at main train stations, bus terminals and attractions are generally OK, usually with facilities for disabled people and those with young children. At the stations you usually have to pay 20p to use the facilities. Public facilities in central London can be few and far between as many have been closed due to security concerns.

Many disabled toilets require a special key. Ask at tourist offices or send a cheque or postal order for £2.50 to RADAR (see p. 120).

Safety Concerns

London is remarkably safe considering its size and the disparity in wealth. That said, be careful at night and take particular care in crowded places like the London Underground, where pickpockets and bag snatchers might operate. Some precautions to adopt include:

- When travelling by tube at night, choose a carriage with other people.

- Carry your passport, papers, tickets and money in a sturdy leather pouch on your belt or put them in your hotel safe (see Keeping Copies p. 108).

- Don't leave valuables lying around in your hotel room or in parked cars.

- Report thefts to the police and ask for a statement, or your travel insurance won't pay out.

Lost Property

Most items found on buses and the tube end up at London Regional Transport's Lost Property Office (fax 7918 1028), 200 Baker St NW1 5RZ (6, C1; ⊖ Baker St), open Mon-Fri 9.30am-2pm. Items left on main-line trains end up back at the main terminals. For items left in black taxis, phone ☎ 7833 0996.

Women Travellers

Aside from the very occasional wolf-whistle and grope on the Underground, women will find the city reasonably enlightened.

Information & Organisations

The Well Women Centre (☎ 7388 0662), Marie Stopes House, 108 Whitfield St W1 (6, C4; ⊖ Warren St), dispenses advice on contraception and pregnancy Mon-Sat 9am-5pm (to 8pm Tues & Wed). The London Rape Crisis Centre hotline (☎ 7837 1600) is open weekdays 6-10pm, weekends 10am-10pm.

Gay & Lesbian Travellers

In general, Britain is fairly tolerant of homosexuality and London has a flourishing gay scene. But there remain pockets of out-and-out hostility and overt displays of affection are not necessarily wise away from acknowledged gay venues and areas like Soho (and Old Compton St in particular). The age of homosexual consent, currently 18, will probably have been lowered to 16 by the time you read this.

Information & Organisations

The 24hr Lesbian & Gay Switchboard (☎ 7837 7324) and the London Lesbian Line (☎ 7251 6911; Mon & Fri 2-10pm; Tues & Thurs 7-10pm) can help with most inquiries. For listings magazines, see p. 99.

Disabled Travellers

Large, new hotels and modern tourist venues are often accessible, unlike most older buildings. Newer buses and trains sometimes have steps that lower for easier access; check with London Transport (☎ 7918 3312). For a list of stations that have ramps and lifts (all DLR stations do) read Access to the Underground by London Transport Unit for Disabled Passengers, 172 Buckingham Palace Rd SW1 9TN.

Information & Organisations

Information on wheelchair access to cultural venues in London is available from Artsline (☎ 7388 2227). The Royal Association for Disability & Rehabilitation (RADAR) stocks Access in London (£7.95), which is required reading for visitors. Contact RADAR (☎ 7250 3222) at Unit 12, City Forum, 250 City Rd, London EC1V 8AF.

Language

The English language is by far and away England's greatest contribution to the modern world. It is astonishingly rich, containing an estimated 600,000 uninflected words and particularly abundant in descriptive words like nouns and adjectives; any thesaurus will prove that quick (fast, swift, speedy, rapid, fleet etc) smart. These days, however, you'll encounter a veritable Babel of languages – an estimated 300, in fact – being spoken in London, and there are pockets of the capital where English is very much in the minority. It's possible to meet Londoners who can't understand English at all – though this is only likely to be among older members of minority communities and recent arrivals.

Conversion Table

Clothing Sizes

Measurements approximate only; try before you buy.

Women's Clothing

Aust/NZ	8	10	12	14	16	18
Europe	36	38	40	42	44	46
Japan	5	7	9	11	13	15
UK	8	10	12	14	16	18
USA	6	8	10	12	14	16

Women's Shoes

Aust/NZ	5	6	7	8	9	10
Europe	35	36	37	38	39	40
France only	35	36	38	39	40	42
Japan	22	23	24	25	26	27
UK	3½	4½	5½	6½	7½	8½
USA	5	6	7	8	9	10

Men's Clothing

Aust/NZ	92	96	100	104	108	112
Europe	46	48	50	52	54	56
Japan	S		M	M		L
UK	35	36	37	38	39	40
USA	35	36	37	38	39	40

Men's Shirts (Collar Sizes)

Aust/NZ	38	39	40	41	42	43
Europe	38	39	40	41	42	43
Japan	38	39	40	41	42	43
UK	15	15½	16	16½	17	17½
USA	15	15½	16	16½	17	17½

Men's Shoes

Aust/NZ	7	8	9	10	11	12
Europe	41	42	43	44½	46	47
Japan	26	27	27.5	28	29	30
UK	7	8	9	10	11	12
USA	7½	8½	9½	10½	11½	12½

Weights & Measures

Length & Distance

1 inch = 2.54cm
1cm = 0.39 inches
1m = 3.3ft
1ft = 0.3m
1km = 0.62 miles
1 mile = 1.6km

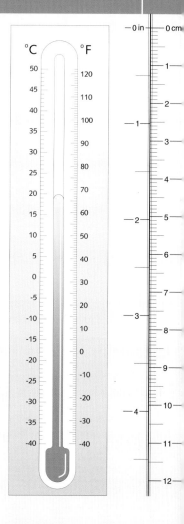

Weight

1kg = 2.2lb
1lb = 0.45kg
1g = 0.04oz
1oz = 28g

Volume

1 litre = 0.26 US gallons
1 US gallon = 3.8 litres
1 litre = 0.22 imperial gallons
1 imperial gallon = 4.55 litres

THE AUTHOR

Steve Fallon

Having fled from the overly fresh air, monotonous greenery and the deafening tranquillity of deepest rural Essex where he 'did time' for four years, Steve Fallon is now luxuriating in the pollution, concrete and general hubbub of London, one of the world's most vibrant and exciting cities. For this book, he did everything the hard way: walking the walks, seeing the sights, taking (some) advice from friends, colleagues and the odd taxi driver and digesting everything in sight – right down to that last pint. Says he: 'Thank God I'm a city boy (again).'

ABOUT LONELY PLANET GUIDEBOOKS

The story begins with a classic travel adventure: Tony and Maureen Wheeler's 1972 journey across Europe and Asia to Australia. Useful information about the overland trail did not exist at that time, so Tony and Maureen published the first Lonely Planet guidebook to meet a growing need.

From a kitchen table, then from a tiny office in Melbourne, Australia, Lonely Planet has become the largest independent travel publisher in the world, an international company with offices in Melbourne, Oakland (USA), London (UK) and Paris (France).

Today there are over 400 titles, including travel guides, city maps, cycling guides, first time travel guides, healthy travel guides, travel atlases, diving guides, pictorial books, phrasebooks, restaurant guides, travel literature, walking guides and world food guides.

At Lonely Planet we believe that travellers can make a positive contribution to the countries they visit – if they respect their host communities and spend their money wisely. Since 1986 a percentage of the income from books has been donated to aid projects and human rights campaigns.

ABOUT THE CONDENSED GUIDES

Other Lonely Planet pocket guides include: *Amsterdam* (due July 2000), *California*, *Crete*, *New York City*, *Paris* and *Sydney*.

ABOUT THIS BOOK

Series developed by Diana Saad • Edited by Gabrielle Green • Design by Andrew Weatherill • Layout by Csanád Csutoros • Publishing Manager Mary Neighbour • Cover design by Indra Kilfoyle • Maps by Charles Rawlings-Way • Software engineering by Dan Levin • Thanks to Adam McCrow, Andrew Tudor, Brett Pascoe, Charlotte Hindle, David Kemp, David O'Sullivan, Emma Miller, Fiona Cabassi, Fiona Croyden, Lara Morcombe, Paul Clifton, Penelope Richardson, Penny Calder, Scott McNeely, Tamsin Wilson, Tim Roufael, Tim Ryder and Tim Uden

LONELY PLANET ONLINE

www.lonelyplanet.com or AOL keyword: lp
Lonely Planet's award-winning Web site has insider info on hundreds of destinations from Amsterdam to Zimbabwe, complete with interactive maps and colour photographs. You'll also find the latest travel news, recent reports from travellers on the road, guidebook upgrades and a lively bulletin board where you can meet fellow travellers, swap recommendations and seek advice.

PLANET TALK

Our FREE quarterly printed newsletter is full of tips from travellers and anecdotes from Lonely Planet authors. Every issue is packed with up-to-date travel news and advice, and includes a postcard from Lonely Planet co-founder Tony Wheeler, mail from travellers, a look at life on the road through the eyes of a Lonely Planet author, topical health advice, prizes for the best travel yarn, news about forthcoming Lonely Planet events and a complete list of Lonely Planet books and products.

To join our mailing list, email us at: go@lonelyplanet.co.uk (UK, Europe and Africa residents); info@lonelyplanet.com (North and South America residents); talk2us@lonelyplanet.com.au (the rest of the world); or contact any Lonely Planet office.

COMET

Our FREE monthly email newsletter brings you all the latest travel news, features, interviews, competitions, destination ideas, travellers' tips & tales, Q&As, raging debates and related links. Find out what's new on the Lonely Planet Web site and which books are about to hit the shelves.

Subscribe from your desktop: www.lonelyplanet.com/comet

LONELY PLANET OFFICES

Australia
PO Box 617, Hawthorn, Victoria 3122
☎ 03 9819 1877 fax 03 9819 6459
email: talk2us@lonelyplanet.com.au

USA
150 Linden St, Oakland, CA 94607
☎ 510 893 8555 TOLL FREE: 800 275 8555
fax 510 893 8572
email: info@lonelyplanet.com

UK
10a Spring Place, London NW5 3BH
☎ 020 7428 4800 fax 020 7428 4828
email: go@lonelyplanet.co.uk

France
1 rue du Dahomey, 75011 Paris
☎ 01 55 25 33 00 fax 01 55 25 33 01
email: bip@lonelyplanet.fr
minitel: 3615 lonelyplanet

World Wide Web: www.lonelyplanet.com or AOL keyword: lp
Lonely Planet Images: lpi@lonelyplanet.com.au

index

for map references see also the Sights Index p.128

A

Abney Park Cemetery 44
accommodation, *see* places
    to stay
Africa Centre 90
AIDS, *see* HIV/AIDS
air travel 109-10, 112
airports 109-10
Al Casbah 75
Albert Memorial 37
All Souls Church 39
Almeida 86
ambulance 119
Anchor, The 94
Angel, The 94
antiques 61
Apsley House 38
Aquarium, The 92
arts 11
    see also antiques, galleries
Asakusa 71
Astoria, The 99
athletics 100
auction houses, *see* antiques

B

babysitting 106
Bah Humbug 70
Baker St Underground station 44
Balans Café 98
ballet 88
Balloon, The London 55
Bankside Gallery 36
Banqueting House 47
Bar Italia 97
Bar Rumba 98
Barbican 86, 87
bars, *see* pubs
Battersea Park 41
BBC Experience 42
Beach Blanket Babylon 94
Beckton Alps Ski Centre 45
Beefeaters 31
Belgo Centraal 74
Bellini's 76
Bermondsey Market 58
Bethnal Green Museum of
    Childhood 42
Bibendum 71
Bierodrome 94
Big Ben 18
black cabs, *see* taxis
Black Market 65
Blind Beggar 50
Bloomsbury artists 16
Blue Print Café 78
books 66-67
Borderline, The 89
Bramah Tea & Coffee
    Museum 34

Brick Lane Market 58
Brighton 51
British Library 37
British Museum 14
British Tourism Authority 115
Brixton Academy 89
Brixton Market 58
Browns 92
Buckingham Palace 15
Bug Bar 92
Burberry 63
bus travel 111, 113
business travellers 118
Buzz Bar 82

C

Cabinet War Rooms 34
cabs, *see* taxis
Café Base 75
Café in the Crypt 79
Café Spice Namaste 72
cafes, *see* places to eat
Cambridge 52
Camden Falcon 89
Camden Market 58
Camden Passage 59
Canary Wharf Tower 48
Candy Bar 99
Cantaloupe 94
Canterbury Cathedral 51
Cantina del Ponte 79
Captain Kidd, The 94
car travel, *see* driving
Carlyle's House 38
Casale Franco 76
Castle Climbing Centre 45
Cecil Sharp House 90
Central Station 99
changing of the guard 15
Chapter House 33
Charlie Wright's International
    Bar 98
Chaucer, Geoffrey 51, 67, 95
Chelsea 71
Chelsea Bun 75
Chelsea Physic Garden 44
chemists, *see* pharmacies
children
    places to stay 106
    shopping 68
    sights & activities 42-3, 86
Christie's 61
churches & cathedrals 27, 33,
    39
Churchill Arms, The 94
Churchill, Sir Winston 18
cinemas 28, 91
City Farms 43
classical music, *see* music
climate 108

Clore Gallery 30
clothing 62-3
Club 100, the 90
clubs, *see* dance clubs
Coach & Horses, The 95
Columbia Rd Flower Market 59
Comedy Store 88
comedy venues 88
Commons, the *see* Houses of
    Parliament
Complex, The 92
Constable, John 25, 30
Coram's Fields 43
coronation chair 33
Courtauld Gallery 16
Cranks 75
credit cards 115
cricket 100, 101
Cross, The 92
Crown Jewels 31
Crystal Palace National Sports
    Centre 101
Cuba 98
Cuba Libre 98
cuisine, *see* places to eat
currency, *see* money
customs regulations 58, 112
Cutty Sark 42
Cyberia 82

D

Da Vinci 72
dance 88
dance clubs 92-3, 99
Daquise 71
Denim 95
dental services 119
department stores 57-8
Design Museum 34
Diana, Princess of Wales 20,
    22, 33
Dickens' House 38
Dickens, Charles 24, 38
Dim Sum 72
Dingwalls 89
disabled travellers 119, 120
discos, *see* dance clubs
discounts 116
Docklands
    walking tour 48
Dogstar 92
Donmar Warehouse 86
driving 108, 114-15
drug stores, *see* pharmacies
Dulwich Picture Gallery 36
Dust 92

E

Earl's Court Exhibition Centre 89
East End walking tour 50

East One 73
EasyEverything 82
Eco Brixton 70
economy 9
Elizabeth II, Queen 15
email 82, 117-18
embassies 115
emergency 119
Emporium, The 92
End, The 92
Engineer, The 95
Enigma encrypting machine 19
entertainment 84-101
environment 8
Eton College 53
Eurostar 111
events, see festivals & special
    events
excursions 51-3

F
FA Premier League Hall of
    Fame 42
Fan Museum 34
fauna 40
ferry 111-12
festivals & special events 85
Fifth Floor 76
Fire Station, The 95
First Out 98
Fish! 79
Fitzwilliam Museum 52
Flask, The 95
Fleet St
    walking tour 49
flora 40
food, see places to eat
Food for Thought 74
food stores 64
football 100
    FA Premier League Hall of
        Fame 42
Fortnum & Mason 57, 83
Forum, The 89
Foucault's pendulum 28
Franx Snack Bar 80
free admission 13
Freedom Café 99
French House Dining Room 80
Freud Museum 38
Fridge, The 92

G
galleries 16, 21, 25, 30, 36
Garage, The 89
Gatwick airport 109-10
gay & lesbian travellers 120
    newspapers 99
    places to stay 106
    shops 66
    venues 98-9
Geffrye Museum 34
George Inn, The 95

Gibbons, Grinling 27
Gilbert Collection 16
Goddards Ye Olde Pie Shop 75
golf 46
Gordon's 95
Gourmet Pizza Company 79
government 9
Great Fire 7
Great Plague 7
Green Park 41
Greenwich
    Cutty Sark 42
    market 59
    Millennium Dome 23
    places to eat 75
Grumbles 82
Guildhall 37
gyms 46

H
Hackney City Farm 43
Hackney Empire 89
Ham House 44
Hampstead Heath 41
Hampton Court Palace 17
Hanover Grand 93
Harrods 57
Harvey Nichols 57
Havana 98
Hawksmoor, Nicholas 20, 33,
    48, 50
Hayward Gallery 36
health 118-119
Heathrow airport 109
Heaven 99
Henry VIII 17, 31, 53
history 6-7
HIV/AIDS 119
HMS Belfast 42
HMV Records 65
Hogarth, William 25, 30, 38
Hogarth's House 38
Horniman Museum 34
horse riding 46
hospitals 119
hotels, see places to stay
Houses of Parliament 18
HQ 93
Hyde Park 41

I
ICA Café 79
Iceni 93
IMAX cinema 28
immunisations 108
Imperial War Museum 19
Improv Comedy Club 88
insurance 119
Inter Mezzo 76
Internet 117-18
Internet cafes 82

J
Jamaica Wine House 95-6
James Smith & Sons 63
Jazz Café 90
Jenny Lo's Tea House 82
jewellery 63
Jewish Museum 34
Joe Allen 74
Dr Johnson's House 38
Jongleurs Battersea 88

K
Keats' House 38
Kensington Palace 20
Kenwood House 34
Kettners 81
Kew Gardens 21
King's Head & Eight Bells, The 96
Konditor & Cook 78

L
L'Accento 77
Lamb & Flag, The 96
language 120
Le Shuttle 111
Leadenhall Market 59
Leighton House 38
Lemon Grass 71
Liberty 57
Little Angel Theatre 86
London Aquarium 42
London Canal Museum 34
London City airport 110-11
London Coliseum 87
London Dungeon 45
London Eye 45
London Imax Cinema 91
London Planetarium 22
London Silver Vaults 61
London Transport
    Museum 34-5
London Underground 11, 113
London Zoo 42
Lord's Cricket Oval 101
lost property 120
Luton airport 110

M
Madame Tussaud's 22
magazines 84, 118
mail, see postal services
Mandola 77
Mangal 79
Mango Room 71
Manze's 78
Marianne North Gallery 21
markets 58-61
Marks & Spencer 57
Mash 96
Mean Fiddler 90
Mezzo 97
Mildred's 81

Millennium Dome 23
minicabs, *see* taxis
Ministry of Sound 93
Momo 81
money 115-16
Mongolian Barbecue 74
Monument, The 37
Moro 73
motorcycle travel, *see* driving
Mr Wu 80
Museum of... 45
Museum of Gardening
　　History 44
Museum of London 24
Museum Tavern, The 96
museums 14, 19, 24, 26, 28,
　　32-35, 38, 44, 45
music 11, 65, 87, 89-90

N
National Film Theatre 91
National Gallery 25
National Maritime Museum 35
National Portrait Gallery 36
Natural History Museum 26
Nelson's Column 47
New Culture Revolution 71
New Piccadilly 81
New Tayyabs 74
Newens Maids of Honour 83
newspapers 118
nightclubs, *see* dance clubs
No 10 Downing St 47
No 2 Willow Rd 38
North Pole 75
Notting Hill Arts Club 93
Novelli 73

O
O Bar, The 98
Old Compton Café 97
Old Friends 48
Old Naval College 37
Old Operating Theatre & Herb
　　Garret 35
Old Royal Observatory 37
Open Air Theatre 91
opening hours 13, 116
opera 87
Oxo Tower 78

P
palaces, *see* royal palaces
parks & gardens 40-41
　　City Farms 43
　　Hampstead Heath 41
　　Hyde Park 41
　　Kew Gardens 21
　　Orangery, The 20
　　Privy Gardens 17
　　Regent's Park 41
　　Richmond Park 41

St James's Park 41
　　Sunken Garden 20
passport 108
Pâtisserie Valerie 81
pay phones, *see* telephone
People's Palace 78
Pepsi Trocadero Segaworld 43
Petticoat Lane Market 60
pharmacies 119
photography 118
Pizza Express Jazz Club 90
Place Below 72
Place, The 88
places to eat 69-83
　　African 77
　　American 74
　　Asian 70-4, 80, 82, 97
　　Belgian 74
　　British 70-80, 82
　　cafes 75, 78, 81, 97-9
　　Eastern European 71
　　French 73
　　high tea 83
　　Indian 72, 74
　　International 71, 75, 76,
　　　　78, 79, 81, 97
　　Internet cafes 82
　　Italian 70, 72, 75, 76, 77,
　　　　79, 82
　　Kosher 78
　　late opening 97-8
　　Mediterranean 79
　　Middle Eastern 75, 76, 79, 81
　　Spanish 73
　　Vegetarian 70, 72, 74, 75,
　　　　76, 79, 81
　　West Indian 71
　　see also individual
　　　　restaurant names
places to stay 102-106
　　budget 105
　　deluxe 103
　　mid-range 105
　　specialist hotels 106
　　top end 104
Poet's Corner 33
police 119
politics 9
Polka Theatre for Children 86
Pollo 81
Pollock's Toy Museum 43
pools, spas & baths 46
Poons 80
Porters 74
Portobello Rd Market 60
postal services 117
Primrose Brasserie, *see* Trojka
　　Russian Tea Room
Prince Charles Cinema 91
Prince Henry's Room 37
Princess Louise 96
Privy Gardens 17
Proms, The 87
public holidays 116-17

pubs 94-7, 98, 99
Pyx Chamber 33

Q
Queen's Larder, The 96

R
racing 101
radio 118
Rasa 79
Ravi Shankar 76
Regent's Park 41
restaurants, *see* places to eat
Richmond Park 41
Ritz Hotel 83
River Café 75
Riverside Studios 88
Rock & Sole Plaice 74
Ronnie Scott's 90
Rough Trade 65
Royal Academy of Arts 36
Royal Albert Hall 87
Royal Court 86
Royal Courts of Justice 37
Royal Geographical Society 44
Royal National Theatre 86
Royal Opera House 87
royal palaces
　　Buckingham 15
　　Hampton Court 17
　　Kensington 20
　　Kew 21
royals, the 15, 22, 25, 53
rugby, *see* football
Rupert St 99

S
Saatchi Gallery 36
Sadler's Wells 88
St Bartholomew-the-Great
　　Church 39
St Bride's Church 39
St George's Chapel 53
St James's Park 41
St John 73
St John's Gate & Museum 35
St Katherine's Dock 48
St Martin-in-the-Fields 39
St Mary-le-Bow 39
St Paul's Cathedral 27
Salisbury, The 96
Satay Bar 70
Sauce barorganicdiner 71
Sausage & Mash Café 77
Savoy hotel 83
Science Museum 28
senior travellers 116
Serpentine Gallery 36
Shakespeare, William 29
Shakespeare's Globe 29
Shepherd's Bush Empire 89
Sherlock Holmes Museum 35

shopping
Algerian Coffee Stores 64
Antiquarius Antiques
    Centre 61
Benjamin Pollock's Toy
    Shop 68
Black Market 65
Books for Cooks 66
Borders 66
Chelsea Old Town Hall 61
Children's Book Centre 68
Compendia 68
Compendium 66
Fortnum & Mason 57, 83
Foyle's 66
Gay's the Word 66
Gerry's 68
Grant & Cutler 67
Hamleys 68
Harrods 57
Harvey Nichols 57, 76
HMV 65
Honest Jon's 65
Hype Designer Forum 62
Ian Allan 67
Into You 63
Jane Fitch 63
John Lewis 57
Kensington Market 62
Kite Store 68
Liberty 57
London Architectural
    Salvage & Supply Co. 61
London Silver Vaults 61
markets 58-61
Marks & Spencer 57
Mole Jazz 65
Murder One 67
Nicole Farhi 62
Oil & Spices Shop 64
On the Beat 65
Papier Marché 68
Paul Smith 62
Peter Jones 58
Ray's Jazz Shop 65
Reckless Records 65
Red or Dead 62
Rococo 64
Rough Trade 65
Sean Arnold Sporting
    Antiques 61
Selfridges 58
Silver Moon 67
Simply Sausages 64
Sportspages 67
Stanfords 67
Tea House, The 64
Tower Records 65
Travel Bookshop, The 67
Trax 65
Virgin Megastore 65
Vivienne Westwood 62
Waterstones 66
Zwemmer 67

Shri Swaminarayan Mandir 45
Smithfield Market 60
Smithfields 93
Sir John Soane's Museum 35
Soba 80
Sofra Bistro 76
Sotheby's 61
Soup 81
South Bank Complex 87
Southwark Cathedral 39
Speaker's Corner 41
Special Zone, 1997 the 97
Spiga 81
Spitalfields Farm 43
Spitalfields Market 60
sports
    keeping fit 46
    spectator sport 100-101
Stanfords 67
Stansted airport 110
Stockpot 81
student travellers 116
Subterania 89
Sugar Club 81
Sutton House 35
Swan, The 90

T
Tate Britain Gallery 30
taxis 114
telephone 117
television 118
Temple Church 39
tennis 46, 100-101
Thames Flood Barrier 43
theatre 29, 86
Theatre Museum 35
Three Kings of Clerkenwell 96
ticket agencies 84
time 115
tipping 71, 116
Tippoo's Tiger 32
toilets 119
Tokyo Diner 80
tourist information
    abroad 108
    within London 115
tours
    balloon 55
    bicycle 54
    bus 54
    canal & river cruises 54-5
    walking tours 54
Tower of London 31
Tower Records 65
Trafalgar Square 79
Trafalgar Tavern 96-97
train travel 111, 113-14
Traitors' Gate 31
transport
    arrival & departure 109-12
    travel passes 112- 13
    within London 113, 114-15

Travel Bookshop, The 67
travellers cheques 115
Trojka Russian Tea Room 71
Turner, JMW 25, 30
Turnmills 99
Twickenham 101

U
Undercroft Museum 33
Underworld, The 89
Unicorn Theatre for Children 86
Uno 1 restaurant 82
Upper St Fish Shop 76

V
value-added tax 58
Velvet Room 93
Veronica's 77
Vibe Bar 93
Victoria & Albert Museum 32
Victoria Memorial 15
video 118
Vingt-Quatre 97
Vinopolis 45
Virgin Megastore 65
visa 108

W
Wagamama 80
walks
    organised 54
    self-guided 47-50
Wallace Collection 36
Warrington, The 97
Waxy O'Connors 97
Webshack 82
weights & measures 117, 121
Wellington Museum, *see*
    Apsley House
Wembley 101
Westminster Abbey 33
Westminster Arms 47
Westminster Cathedral 39
Westminster Hall 18
White Swan, The 99
Whitechapel Art Gallery 50, 74
Wigmore Hall 87
Wimbledon 35, 46, 100-101
Windsor Castle 53
WKD 89
women travellers 67, 120
Wren, Sir Christopher 17, 27, 33

Y
Ye Olde Cheshire Cheese 72
Ye Olde Mitre 97
Yo! Sushi 80
Young's Ram Brewery 44

Z
Zoo, *see* London Zoo

sights index

Abney Park Cemetery p. 44 (5, A9)
Albert Memorial p. 37 (5, F3)
All Souls Church p. 39 (6, D3)
Bankside Gallery p. 36 (6, F10)
Battersea Park p. 41 (5, J5)
Beckton Alps Ski Centre p. 45 (2, C5)
Bethnal Green Mus. of Childhood p. 42 (6, B15)
Bramah Tea & Coffee Museum p. 34 (6, H15)
Brick Lane Market p. 58 (6, C15)
Brighton p. 51 (1, E2)
British Library p. 37 (6, A6)
British Museum p. 14 (6, C6)
Brixton Market p. 58 (5, K8)
Broadcast House p. 42 (6, D3)
Buckingham Palace p. 15 (6, H4)
Cabinet War Rooms p. 34 (6, H6)
Cambridge p. 52 (1, A3)
Camden Market p. 58 (4, J4)
Canterbury Cathedral p. 51 (1, C5)
Castle Climbing Centre p. 45 (2, B3)
Chelsea Physic Garden p. 44 (5, H4)
Chelsea Royal Hospital p. 37 (5, H4)
Courtauld Gallery p. 16 (6, F8)
Covent Garden p. 59 (6, F7)
Cutty Sark p. 42 (3, H2)
Denis Severs House p. 45 (6, C15)
Design Museum p. 34 (6, H15)
Dickens' House p. 38 (6, B8)
Dr Johnson's House p. 38 (6, E9)
Dulwich Picture Gallery p. 36 (2, C3)
FA Premier League Hall of Fame p. 42 (6, H8)
Fan Museum p. 34 (3, J3)
Freud Museum p. 38 (4, F1)
Geffrye Museum p. 34 (5, C10)
Green Park p. 41 (6, H3)
Greenwich Market p. 59 (3, H2)
Guildhall p. 37 (6, D12)
Ham House p. 44 (2, C2)
Hampstead Heath p. 41 (4)
Hampton Court Palace p. 17 (2, D2)
Harrods p. 57 (5, G4)
Harvey Nichols p. 57 (6, H1)
Hayward Gallery p. 36 (6, G8)
Highgate Ponds p. 46 (4, D4)
HMS Belfast p. 42 (6, G14)
Hogarth's House p. 38 (2, C2)
Horniman Museum p. 34 (2, C3)
Houses of Parliament p. 18 (6, J7)
Hyde Park p. 41 (5, F4)
Imperial War Museum p. 19 (6, K9)
Ironmonger Row Baths p. 46 (6, B12)
Jewish Museum p. 34 (4, K4)
Keats' House p. 38 (4, E2)
Kensington Palace p. 20 (5, F3)
Kenwood House p. 34 (4, C4)
Kew Gardens p. 21 (2, C2)
Leighton House p. 38 (5, G2)
Liberty p. 57 (6, E4)
London Aquarium p. 42 (6, H8)
London Canal Museum p. 34 (5, C7)
London Dungeon p. 45 (6, G13)
London Transport Museum p. 34 (7, C8)

London Zoo p. 42 (1, K2)
Madame Tussaud's p. 22 (6, C1)
Millennium Dome p. 23 (3, B5)
Monument, The p. 37 (6, F13)
Mudchute Park Farm p. 46 (3, E2)
Museum of Gardening History p. 44 (6, K8)
Museum of London p. 24 (6, D11)
Museum of... p. 45 (6, F10)
National Gallery p. 25 (6, F6)
National Maritime Museum p. 35 (3, J3)
National Portrait Gallery p. 36 (6, F6)
Natural History Museum p. 26 (5, G3)
No 2 Willow Rd p. 38 (4, E2)
Oasis Sports Centre p. 46 (6, E6)
Old Naval College p. 37 (3, H3)
Old Operating Theatre p. 37 (6, G13)
Old Royal Observatory p. 37 (3, K4)
Pepsi Trocadero & Segaworld p. 43 (6, F5)
Peter Jones p. 58 (5, G5)
Pollock's Toy Museum p. 43 (6, C5)
Portobello Rd Market p. 60 (5, E1)
Prince Henry's Room p. 37 (6, E10)
Regent's Park p. 41 (5, C5)
Richmond Park p. 41 (2, C2)
Ritz, The p. 103 (6, G4)
Royal Academy of Arts p. 36 (6, F4)
Royal Courts of Justice p. 37 (6, E9)
Saatchi Gallery p. 36 (5, C3)
St Bartholomew-the-Great p. 39 (6, D11)
St Bride's Church p. 39 (6, E10)
St James's Park p. 41 (6, H5)
St John's Gate & Museum p. 35 (6, C10)
St Martin-In-The-Fields p. 39 (7, E7)
St Paul's Cathedral p. 27 (6, E11)
Savoy, The p. 103 (6, F7)
Science Museum p. 28 (5, G3)
Selfridges p. 58 (6, E2)
Serpentine Gallery p. 36 (5, F3)
Shakespeare's Globe p. 29 (6, F12)
Sherlock Holmes Museum p. 35 (6, C1)
Shri Swaminarayan Mandir p. 45 (2, C2)
Sir John Soane's Museum p. 35 (6, D8)
Smithfield Market p. 60 (6, D10)
Southwark Cathedral p. 39 (6, G13)
Spitalfields Market p. 60 (6, C15)
Sutton House p. 35 (5, A10)
Tate Britain Gallery p. 30 (5, A10)
Temple Church p. 39 (6, E9)
Thames Flood Barrier p. 43 (2, C4)
Theatre Museum p. 35 (6, E7)
Tower of London p. 31 (6, F15)
Trafalgar Square p. 7, 47 (6, F6)
Victoria & Albert Museum p. 32 (5, G4)
Vinopolis p. 45 (6, G12)
Wallace Collection p. 36 (6, D2)
Wellington Museum p. 38 (6, H2)
Westminster Abbey p. 33 (6, J6)
Westminster Cathedral p. 39 (6, K4)
Wimbledon Lawn Tennis Museum p.35 (2, D3)
Windsor Castle p. 53 (2, D3)
Young's Ram Brewery p. 44 (5, K3)